Leo Strauss and the Conservative Movement in America

This book offers an original interpretation of the achievement of Leo Strauss, stressing how his ideas and followers reshaped the American conservative movement. According to this study, Strauss and his disciples came to influence the establishment Right almost by accident. The conservative movement that reached out to Strauss and his legacy was extremely fluid and lacked self-confident leadership. Conservative activists and journalists felt a desperate need for academic acceptability, which they thought Strauss and his disciples would furnish. They also became deeply concerned with the problem of "value relativism," which self-described conservatives thought Strauss had effectively addressed. Until recently, however, neither Strauss nor his disciples have considered themselves to be "conservatives." Strauss's followers continue to view themselves as stalwart Truman-Kennedy Democrats and liberal internationalists. Contrary to another misconception, Straussians have never wished to convert Americans to ancient political ideals and practices, except in a very selective rhetorical fashion. Strauss and his disciples have been avid champions of American modernity, and "timeless" values as interpreted by Strauss and his followers often look starkly contemporary.

Paul Edward Gottfried is Horace Raffensperger Professor of Humanities at Elizabethtown College. He is the author of numerous books, including *Conservatism in America: Making Sense of the American Right*, *The Strange Death of Marxism: The European Left in the New Millenium*, and *After Liberalism*.

Leo Strauss and the Conservative Movement in America

A Critical Appraisal

PAUL EDWARD GOTTFRIED
Elizabethtown College

CAMBRIDGE
UNIVERSITY PRESS

CAMBRIDGE UNIVERSITY PRESS
Cambridge, New York, Melbourne, Madrid, Cape Town,
Singapore, São Paulo, Delhi, Tokyo, Mexico City

Cambridge University Press
32 Avenue of the Americas, New York, NY 10013-2473, USA

www.cambridge.org
Information on this title: www.cambridge.org/9781107017245

First published 2012

Printed in the United States of America

A catalog record for this publication is available from the British Library.

Library of Congress Cataloging in Publication data
Gottfried, Paul.
    Leo Strauss and the conservative movement in America : a critical
appraisal / Paul Edward Gottfried.
        p.   cm.
    Includes index.
    ISBN 978-1-107-01724-5 (hardback)
    1. Strauss, Leo – Criticism and interpretation.   2. Strauss,
Leo – Influence.   3. Conservatism – United States – History – 20th
century.   I. Title.
    JC251.S8G67 2012
    320.52092–dc23   2011025633

ISBN 978-1-107-01724-5 Hardback

Contents

Acknowledgments

Professors David Gordon, Barry Shain, John Gunnell, Grant Havers, and Kenneth McIntyre all read parts of this text in earlier drafts and then sent me their well-considered judgments. Given that these readers were cited more than once, it seemed proper to let them see my handiwork before it went into print. Although the same courtesy was not extended to Peter Minowitz, who published a spirited defense of Strauss, I nonetheless received feedback when I sent him my critical observations. Peter acquitted himself so well in our vigorous exchanges that I suggest in my conclusion that he may be uniquely suited to overhaul what I criticize. Even more noteworthy from my perspective, Peter is the most affable and the least secretive professing Straussian whom I have met in fifty years.

Although only fragments of an early draft went to her, I did benefit from discussions with University of Pennsylvania professor Anne Norton. A graduate of seminars of Leo Strauss's students, Anne provided a central theme for my book, which came from her controversial study, *Leo Strauss and the Politics of American Empire*. According to this work, American (or Anglo-American) modernity was turned by Strauss and his disciples into the embodiment of all that is politically virtuous in the modern world. It became an actualized ideal that "political Straussians" view as a justification for an American conversionary mission. This book elaborates on those insights.

I also owe a debt of gratitude to Professor Ted McAllister, of Pepperdine, who read an earlier draft of my book for Cambridge.

In both his formal comments and later conversations with me, Ted offered helpful suggestions on how I might improve my manuscript. To his credit, he did not try to convert me to his interpretations, even as the author of a respected work on Strauss, Eric Voegelin, and the "revolt against modernity." Ted encouraged me to think more deeply about *my* arguments, for the purpose of clarifying and strengthening them. Grant Havers did the same as a reader. Although presently at work on a thematically related book with its own spin, Grant aided me in my efforts to construct my arguments independently of his.

Strangely enough, I did not encounter John Gunnell, who pioneered critical evaluations of Strauss's interpretive methods, until I had finished most of my first draft. I then discovered that Gunnell was already in the 1970s pointing explicitly toward my interpretation of the Straussian "Tradition." After exposure to his writings, thanks to well-preserved copies that I received from his former graduate student Professor W. Wesley McDonald, I began to think more deeply about Strauss and his understanding of political texts. I was above all delighted to learn that my critical judgments did not proceed from a solitary mind. This discovery was further confirmed by my contact with a young scholar, Kenneth McIntyre. Like Gunnell, McIntyre reached some of my conclusions before I did and stated them with deep conviction and copious evidence. He also graciously shared his sources, from which I greatly benefited.

I must also thank my wife Mary and Professor David Brown for keeping me focused while I was still agonizing over this book. The composing did not come easily. I was repeatedly bedevilled by the need to reduce elaborate arguments and ponderous expositions to summarizing paragraphs. Each time I became depressed over what one reader noticed in an earlier draft was the "Byzantine structure" of my project, my wife and David raised my spirits in a timely fashion. Cambridge editor Lew Bateman performed a similar kindness, with his notes sent at regular intervals. Each time I was at the point of laying down my manuscript in weariness or despair, Lew asked for more of my work, until it was done.

I should also acknowledge the aid of the Elizabethtown College library staff, which helped me track down obscure references and obtain books on loan. Without this time-consuming assistance, and the particularly heroic efforts of research librarian Peter de Puydt, my labors would have been even more painful. Cambridge University Press arranged for the index, and I am quite pleased with the results. I am also indebted to Jayashree Prabhu and her team at Newgen for managing the project; to the copyediting team at PETT Fox Inc in New York, who worked on the editing with noteworthy efficiency; to Anne Lovering Rounds at Cambridge University Press in New York, who arranged for the imaginative graphics for this attractively designed work; and to Barbara Degnan of BIM Indexing and Proofreading Services for creating an excellent index. The Earhart Foundation, which has financed my scholarship for many decades, furnished funds for the index and for other last-minute tidying up. Last but certainly not least, I should mention my son, Dr. Joseph D. Gottfried, along with Kathy Kelly and Kathy Hanna, whose computer skills enabled me to submit a relatively professional-looking manuscript. What I was technically incapable of doing, these helpers provided without complaint.

Elizabethtown, Pennsylvania

I

Introduction

In the last few years, numerous books and articles have appeared that seek to vindicate in the face of attack the German Jewish political thinker Leo Strauss (1889–1973) and his disciples. One such defender, Peter Minowitz, recently published a work aimed at Strauss's detractors, *Straussophobia*. In the first chapter, which sets the stage for later assaults or counterassaults, Minowitz lets it be known that "All hate Leo Strauss."[1] The rest of the book is commentary on this allegedly widespread, unjustified prejudice. What Minowitz cites in the text and endnotes would suggest in any case that neither Strauss nor his followers are winning academic popularity contests.

Straussophobia was published three years after the appearance of an earlier and denser apologetic work, *The Truth about Leo Strauss: Political Philosophy and American Democracy*, by Michael and Catherine H. Zuckert, two former students of Leo Strauss who are now professors of political theory at Notre Dame University.[2] The Zuckerts set out to demonstrate two key points, the first of which is also broached by Minowitz: (1) Leo Strauss and his followers are innocent of the charge that the political Left has leveled against them,

---

[1] Peter Minowitz, *Straussophobia: Defending Leo Strauss and Straussians against Shadia Drury and Other Defenders* (Lanham, MD: Lexington Books, 2009), 19–38.

[2] Catherine and Michael Zuckert, *The Truth about Leo Strauss: Political Philosophy and American Democracy* (Chicago: University of Chicago Press, 2006); and David Lewis Schaefer, "Shadia Drury's Critique of Leo Strauss, *Political Science Reviewer* 32 (1994): 80–127.

of being antidemocratic elitists; and (2) the Straussians and neoconservatives, contrary to the customary association, have separate identities. The Zuckerts insist that although the Straussians are tireless advocates of American democracy, they are not political activists in the same way as the neoconservatives. The Zuckerts portray the Straussians as true scholars who should not be equated with government advisors and certainly not with political journalists.

The impression conveyed by these and other thematically related tracts is that the Zuckerts' and Minowitz's subjects are a beleaguered band of thinkers. Their professional survival within the Academy depends on their ability to keep certain powerful enemies at bay. These foes are almost always seen as being on the political left. Although Straussians have incurred criticism from non-leftists, they usually dismiss such critics, particularly if they carry right-wing associations, and typically in footnotes, as eccentrics who are obsessively anti-Israeli and in some cases stridently anti-Semitic.

The only meaningful critics Straussians acknowledge are on the left. These are sometimes, but not always, depicted as hardened enemies of American democracy. In Allan Bloom's *The Closing of the American Mind*, the advocates of cultural disintegration are seen as connected to antidemocratic German thinkers and French postmodernists. Straussians write with undisguised bitterness about these leftist anti-Americans, who have declared war on them and what Straussians consider to be quintessentially American values. Only by remaining on guard against their foes can they pursue their mission of awakening interest in political theory while affirming the universal validity of American democracy.

This confrontation in which the Straussians have embroiled themselves is largely one of their own choosing. The enemy they wish to engage does not threaten them professionally or intellectually. Their most cogent critics are in no position to challenge them, and therefore the Straussians have elected not to grapple with them. Unlike their mostly ignored critics but like the ones they accuse of marginalizing them, the Straussians are heavily represented in elite universities, including the Ivies; and they write periodically even for that part of the press that they depict as their sworn enemy.

Critical commentators on the left, and perhaps most notably Shadia Drury, have often treated their subjects as giants bestriding the world of scholarship.[3] Such critics have reinforced the image that the Straussians have cultivated for themselves, as patriotic Americans with vast humanistic learning. And the Straussians have returned the favor by showering attention on their preferred critics. While Minowitz aims his shafts at Drury, he also explained in an interview with Scott Horton in *Harpers* that he admires his antagonist: "She is learned, creative, courageous, and very readable."[4] The Straussians have recognized two types of critics, both on the left: those who occupy the "unpatriotic" or "undemocratic" left, whom they never tire of denouncing; and those who, like Stephen Holmes of the University of Chicago, they consider worthier opponents.

This work will not focus primarily on these welcome encounters. Rather it will present the case of those whom Straussians prefer not to notice, that is, their critics on the intellectual right and a less classifiable but nonetheless pesky opposition made up of recognized scholars whom the Straussians hope to ignore. Of the two groups, the critics on the right may be the more persistent, if not the more decorated with academic honors. As my book (now out in paperback), *The Search for Historical Meaning*, intimated in 1987 and as the Italian scholar Germana Paraboschi asserts in *Leo Strauss e la Destra Americana* (1993), the battle between Strauss and his followers and the "anti-Straussian Right" is a battle that continues to be deferred.[5] Although not the only adversaries in the faces of the Straussians, they are the ones who refuse to go away.

These despised critics have also been more correct than their leftist counterparts when explaining why Straussians emphasize founders and the crafting of regimes, particularly with regard to the United States. This practice has less to do with antidemocratic elitism than it does with what Strauss and his followers seek to ignore, namely the ethnic and cultural preconditions for the creation of political orders. Straussians focus on those who invent regimes because they wish to present the construction of government as an open-ended, rationalist

[3] Shadia B. Drury, *Leo Strauss and the American Right* (New York: St. Martin's Press, 1997).
[4] See Scott Horton's interview with Minowitz on Harpers Online, http://www.harpers.org/archive/2009/09.90005789.
[5] Germana Paraboschi, *Leo Strauss e la Destra Americana* (Rome: Editori Riuniti, 1993).

process. All children of the Enlightenment, once properly instructed, should be able to carry out this constructivist task, given enough support from the American government or American military. The last thing Straussians would ever say (or care to have said) is that successful constitutional orders are the expressions of already formed nations and cultures. But here we are not speaking about anything that would bother those critics whom Straussians are engaged with. Although not as smitten with the indispensable role of founders as those they criticize, these critics would likely share the Straussians' constructivist view of governments and societies.

Although the historically minded right has argued strenuously against this and other aspects of the Straussian worldview, there are two qualifications that should be made at the outset. One, the American intellectual right has generally welcomed Strauss and his followers with open arms. This right, and particularly its Catholic and, more recently, neoconservative representatives, have treated Strauss's interpretations and political stands as a godsend, as a means of combating what are considered to be the all-pervasive dangers of relativism and nihilism. We are speaking therefore not about all "conservative" publicists, but only about traditionalist critics who have undertaken to dissect Straussian arguments.

Two, the counterarguments that have emanated from these critics are not consistently original. These refutations draw on a wide range of thinkers, going from Burke, Hegel, and Marx down to Heidegger, Hans Georg Gadamer, Quentin Skinner, and John Gunnell. Clearly some of the arguments devised by less well-known scholars can be found more fully developed in the work of more prominent ones; nonetheless, those on the American intellectual right who in recent decades have applied the ideas in question have not always been aware of these derivations and connections. To their credit, these scorned figures have the virtue of staying around to fight another day. They do not accept contemptuous silence as an answer from their opponents.

Because the following text is itself partially a polemic, it may be advisable to indicate certain guidelines about what follows. This work will investigate *representative* Straussian texts, as opposed to those that do not exemplify the distinctive methodology or worldview of the group being considered. Extraneous for our purposes are works by Straussians that could have been written by nonmembers, or works that incorporate some Straussian techniques but are not identifiably Straussian in their general orientation.

These qualifications seem justified when examining the representative texts of any school of thought. Although English classicist Francis Cornford sympathized with the Communist Party, it would be fruitless to examine his translation of Plato to understand Cornford's politics. Likewise, one could read Dashiel Hammett's *Maltese Falcon* or look at Picasso's art, obviously with the exception of something as ideologically loaded as "Guernica," without being able to guess that the artist was a Communist. Partisans in the past often produced works that told little or nothing about their partisanship. In a similar way, one could read Steven Smith on Hegel, usually Catherine Zuckert on Plato, and Eugene F. Miller on David Hume without being struck by the Straussian dimension of their exegesis.

There are also Catholic political theorists, like Daniel J. Mahoney, who have been affected by Strauss but who are not unreservedly of the Straussian persuasion. The same would apply to the French intellectual historian and Sorbonne professor Pierre Manent, although here the Straussian grid may be more apparent than in Mahoney's case. Straussian tendencies may be easily discerned in such writers but are less conspicuous in their work than they would be in nonhyphenated members of the school. At the same time, one finds particularly striking illustrations of Straussian hermeneutics among other Catholic scholars with Straussian leanings, for example, Father Ernest Fortin, a former Jesuit professor at Boston College, who suggests that Dante may have been a religious skeptic pretending to be an orthodox Christian. Discovering atheistic or skeptical subtexts in "political philosophers" conventionally deemed to be committed theists is characteristic of the Straussian exposition of texts.

It is certainly not being argued in this book that nothing that Strauss or his disciples produced has intrinsic value. Being critical of a school of thought is not the same as rejecting everything it has brought forth. It would be wrong to offer such a sweeping condemnation, and particularly as someone who has benefited from Strauss's early works and the insights of some of his students.

This work will approach its subject in a way that may upset hardcore anti- Straussians. Although there are intimations of the characteristic positions of his epigones in the works of the master, these are often more subdued in their original presentation than how these tendencies reveal themselves in succeeding generations. There is something to be said for Stanley Rosen's contention that his fellow Straussians read into their teacher ideological positions that may not have been consistently his.

Moreover, the genealogical connection becomes even vaguer the further one moves back in time. While the young Strauss in Germany previewed the intense Zionism of his later followers, one can find passages and indeed entire works by him that could not have come from them. This may be ascribed to the fact that Strauss had far greater erudition than most of his students. Equally important, his positions on politics and culture were less predictable than those of the next generation, and this was especially true of his early work. It was only after he fled Germany as a Jewish refugee that one can find in sharp profile the dominant worldview of his students.

This worldview became increasingly noticeable after Strauss came to the United States in 1937. But even afterward, he published commentaries that are hardly in line with his students' ideological priorities. One may note this difference without agreeing in every detail with the interpretation that Stanley Rosen advances in *Politics and Hermeneutics*. Here Rosen highlights Strauss's subtle defense of aristocracy while presenting him as "almost a Nietzschean," albeit one who hid his hand while defending traditional social mores.[6]

However, there are other interpretive possibilities beside Rosen's, or the even more unlikely idea that Strauss was a "fascist" who trained

---

[6] Stanley Rosen, *Hermeneutics as Politics* (New York; Oxford University Press, 1987), 124. A more systematic attempt to locate the core of Strauss's political teaching in Nietzsche can be found in Laurence Lampert, *Leo Strauss and Nietzsche* (Chicago: University of Chicago Press, 1996). The interpretation of Strauss that is being offered does not follow Lampert's argument. Rather, it takes Strauss and his followers at their word when they denounce Nietzsche as an antidemocratic thinker verging on nihilism. No attempt is made here to generalize from Strauss's early infatuation with Nietzsche to turn him and his school into surreptitious practitioners of Nietzschean elitism. The most that is conceded to the Lampert-Rosen thesis is what the Zuckerts assert in *The Truth about Leo Strauss*, 90, namely that Strauss "was not a hesitant Nietzschean so much as an admiring anti-Nietzschean." This contention should not be confused with what is argued in Chapter 4 of this volume, that Strauss and his school were "illiberal liberals" in the sense of being what postwar German reeducators called "streitbare Demokraten (aggressive democrats)" – that is, militant supporters of a particular concept of modern democracy.

like-minded followers. My explanation as to why Strauss sometimes differed from his students in his remarks about modern politics is less interesting but also less labored. Strauss was more intelligent and came out of a richer cultural world than his followers – indeed a Teutonic one that most of his prominent students detested.

It is possible to arrive at this judgment even without buying the complete Strauss portrait as found in Ted McAllister's *Revolt against Modernity*. In this study, McAllister defends Strauss as a protector of the Western intellectual "Tradition" against the threat of moral disintegration.[7] The reverence for Strauss in this work, however, is not extended to all of his students. McAllister has no compunctions about challenging the less-than-rigorous thinking that he uncovers in some of Strauss's disciples. He is particularly hard on those who turn Strauss's pronouncements into window dressing for partisan policy statements.

Although this book does not completely reject McAllister's distinction, it seems that there is more continuity between the master and his epigones than some would care to admit. One may begin this reassessment by questioning whether Strauss was as much an enemy of modernity as is sometimes contended. This book will be returning to this problem with some regularity in Chapters 2 and 3, which go through Strauss's life and hermeneutic. In these chapters, there will be a discussion of the neglected modernity of Strauss's thinking, an aspect of his thinking that reflected the crises of his life in Germany and the reaction to his success in the New World. My interpretation flies in the face of conventional wisdom by suggesting that Strauss became an American thinker, indeed an America booster, despite his German past.

Among the commonplace observations this study will dispute is that there is something unmistakably "conservative" or "traditionalist" about how Strauss read texts. An investigation of this belief requires us to look at the manner in which Strauss interpreted political theoretical texts, going back to his studies on Plato and Thucydides. A key question here is whether Strauss – if we might speak like his disciples – proposed a "classical alternative to the modern enterprise." Did his

---

[7] Ted V. McAllister, *The Revolt against Modernity: Leo Strauss, Eric Voegelin, and the Search for a Postliberal Order* (Lawrence: University Press of Kansas, 2007), 176–204, 271–80.

reading of the Ancients lead him away from his recognizable political persona of the 1950s and 1960s, as a Cold War liberal with strong Zionist sentiments? Did Strauss's attachment to the Ancients result in his embracing and advocating a more classical way of life from the one that existed in postwar America?

Or is there in fact a considerable overlap between Strauss's preferred, selective concept of antiquity and the ideals of modern democratic life? What may have helped Strauss become a celebrated *American* teacher of values is the fit between his interpretation of old political texts and how Americans view their political heritage. It was his Americanness and (dare one to say?) his affirmation of the political status quo that brought him worldly recognition in his adopted land. Contrary to the stereotype that he admired the ancient Greeks more than he did modern Americans, one would be hard-pressed to find such a teaching in Strauss. There is no evidence that he "wished to take us back to the ancients," beside the overblown attacks of some and the misguided praise of others.

One is tempted to ask for concrete evidence that "Strauss reinforced the parameters of the Old Right" and instructed us in "a mode of piety, the beginning of true wisdom, and the knowledge of the whole hierarchy of being."[8] Supposedly Strauss and his students could do all of this and more because of their "fundamental distinction between antiquity and modernity." One should ask such encomiasts whether they can prove this transformative effect. Certainly the conservative movement as manifested in the media does not show any indebtedness to the world of the polis. Equally noteworthy, Strauss not only moved out of a modern situation to look for his selective lessons from the ancient world. His view of ancient wisdom, as Chapter 4 will try to show, has a distinctly modern look.

Chapter 5 of this book will focus on an objection among prominent Straussians that they are being unfairly identified with neoconservatives. I try to counter this by providing evidence for this association. I also undertake to show that the nexus between neoconservatives and

---

[8] See J. David Hoeveler, *Watch on the Right: Conservative Intellectuals in the Reagan Era* (Madison: University of Wisconsin Press, 1991), 18. No attempt is made in this reference to single out Professor Hoeveler. What he expresses about Strauss and his school is a very conventional opinion.

Straussians is so tight that it may be impossible to dissociate the two groups in any significant way. This is not necessarily a condemnation of either movement, but recognition of a continuing symbiotic relation between them. Neoconservatives draw their rhetoric and heroic models from Straussian discourse. They also have never hidden their debt to Strauss and the Straussians, even when neoconservative journalists have garbled or vulgarized the message. The Straussians have benefited from the neoconservative ascendancy by gaining access to neoconservative-controlled government resources and foundation money and by obtaining positions as government advisors. It is also hard to think of any critical political issue that has divided the two groups. It is therefore worth considering why Straussians are determined to prove that they are fundamentally different from neoconservatives.

Chapter 6 will examine the now infectious Straussian practice of referring to political theory as "political philosophy." This practice has spread across departments of politics and has taken root even among those who know little about Straussian hermeneutics but who consider it chic to refer to the object of their work as philosophy. This habit is by no means inconsequential. It entails the upgrading of the examination of political opinions to ontological and metaphysical discourse. Underlying this elevation is a glorification of political life as the highest form of human moral and intellectual activity. It is this association that has enabled Straussians to misrepresent as philosophical inquiries what are often homilies about American liberal democracy.

When Strauss referred to the study of political tracts as an examination of "political philosophy," he clearly had two things in mind: the Platonic discussion of philosophical questions in the context of trying to define the best of all regimes; and engaging such questions within the framework of his interpretation of important political works. But this concept, once brought into vogue, became a slippery slope, eventually leading to the taking of ideological stands as an exercise in speculative philosophy. By now the term in question is so hopelessly tendentious that it may be best to drop it from our vocabulary.

At least some of the arguments presented in this book should be familiar from my earlier works, especially *The Search for Historical Meaning*. What is offered here, however, more than in this earlier study, is an extended critique of Strauss's interpretive methods.

Interpretive perspectives often attract users, or so it seems, because they confirm what people already believe about their time and culture. Strauss's approach to past thinkers, particularly as now applied, does not require historical imagination or any serious acceptance of the possibility that others, separated by time and circumstance, were not like themselves, namely religious skeptics who would have celebrated their good fortune in being able to live in a materialistic democracy.

One may note here a chief reservation expressed by some professional historians about Straussian readings of past thinkers. Too often Strauss and his followers have disregarded what makes the past different from the present, although not necessarily inferior. It is entirely possible and even likely that those in an earlier time, including its great minds, were religious Christians and often staunch monarchists. The late-sixteenth-century political theorist Jean Bodin was a stark political realist who talked the language of the scientific revolution then in progress. Equally significant, however, Bodin feared witches and seems to have remained a believing Catholic. Such characteristics may be less appealing to Straussians than the belief that Bodin was a religious skeptic who, given enough time, might have evolved into a political democrat.

In the hands of his disciples, Strauss's hermeneutic has become a means of demystifying the past, by turning "political philosophers" into forerunners of the present age. One encounters in this less an affirmation of a permanent human nature than a graphic example of Herbert Butterfield's "Whig theory of history."[9] We should admire in the past what foreshadows a later age and, more specifically, our late modern society. This celebration of the American present, as opposed to any march into the past, is a defining characteristic of the Straussians' hermeneutics. It is a trait that nonetheless goes mostly unnoticed among their journalistic critics – and precisely among those critics whom the Straussians see fit to highlight. And while this tendency cannot be entirely laid at the doorstep of the founder, it was not altogether absent from his writings or from what he transmitted to his followers.

---

[9] Herbert Butterfield, *The Whig Theory of History* (London: G. Bell and Sons Ltd., 1968), 64–71.

2

A Significant Life

A Jew in Exile

Among the defining aspects of Leo Strauss's early life, three seem to stand out: that he was born a Jew, in Germany, at the end of the nineteenth century.[1] Strauss's being born to Jewish parents in Germany in 1899 may tell more about the rest of his earthly existence than would other biographical details – for example, that he was born in the village of Kirchhain, in the Prussian administrative province of Hesse-Nassau, that his father, Hugo Strauss, operated a livestock and farm supply business with Leo's uncle, or that his mother Jennie's maiden name was David. Most biographical sketches of Strauss indicate that his family were conventionally but not zealously orthodox Jews.[2] In his youth he was sent to the local Volksschule and later to the Gymnasium Philippinum, which was a preparatory school for the University of Marburg, an institution that had been founded in 1527 by Philip of Hesse, one of the early champions of the Protestant Reformation and a protector of Martin Luther.

From 1912 until his graduation from the Philippsuniversität in 1917, Leo boarded at Marburg with the local cantor and, in this

---

[1] Anne Norton begins her polemical work about Strauss and the Straussians with this statement of fact in *Leo Strauss and the Politics of American Empire* (New Haven, CT: Yale University Press, 2004).

[2] The fullest account of the early Strauss and his family is Joachim Lüders and Ariane Wehner, *Mittelhessen – eine Heirat Für Juden? Das Schicksal der Familie Strauss aus Kirchhain* (Marburg: Gymnasium Philippinum, 1989).

setting, came into contact with the students of the Jewish neo-Kantian philosopher (1842–1918) Hermann Cohen. A celebrated professor at Marburg, Cohen was then defining Jewish religious practice in a way that fitted Kant's notion of a rationally based ethic. Harmonizing an inherited legal tradition with a rationalist ethical system was a task of some importance for Jewish neo-Kantians in the early twentieth century. But Cohen also engaged other projects. His extensive study of Maimonides was partly as an attempt to find a distinguished Jewish precursor for his ethically based religion. Perhaps even more relevant for Strauss, Cohen linked Maimonides to the Muslim scholar Averroes (1126–1198), who first enunciated the concept of the double truth in his commentaries on Aristotle. Cohen – and later Strauss – took from Averroes the notion that philosophy and religion teach seemingly incompatible truths that could only be reconciled in God's mind.[3] And although Strauss did not appropriate Cohen's Kantian theory of knowledge, he did espouse a "classical rationalist" approach to philosophy, a mode of thinking that was not alien to Cohen's work.

In the last years of his life, Cohen turned to another, perhaps more timely task. Once Imperial Germany had entered the Great War, Cohen tried to build a conceptual bridge between a rationalistic or Kantianized Judaism and the German cultural heritage. In his wartime apologetic writing, Cohen was at pains to present his country not only as tolerant of Jews (and reproducing Hebraic thinking through the Protestant Reformation) but also as nurturing the ethical rationalism that found its apogee in Moses Mendelssohn and Kant (whatever the differences may have been between these thinkers).[4] Strauss, who served in the German Imperial Army from July 1917 until December 1918, may well have shared Cohen's hope at that time for some kind of German-Jewish synthesis.

Those who were hopeful about this integrated identity for German Jews did not necessarily belong to the national right. Cohen was a social democrat, and the figure who guided Strauss's worked at the University of Hamburg, where he went as a graduate student after the

---

[3] See the English edition of Hermann Cohen, *Ethics of Maimonides* ed. A. S. Bruckstein (Madison: University of Wisconsin Press, 2004).

[4] See Cohen, *Jüdische Schriften* (New York: Ayer Publisher, 1980), 2:73–75; also Irene Abigail Piccini, *Una guida fedele. L'influenza di Hermann Cohen sul pensiero di Leo Strauss* (Turin: Trauben, 2007).

War, the Kantian Ernst Cassirer (1874–1945), was a man of the center-left. Like other German professors of philosophy, Cassirer supported the moderately leftist Demokraten during the Weimar Republic.[5] Strauss's dissertation topic, which was submitted to Cassirer, dealt with free will and ethical responsibility in the Enlightenment-critic, Friedrich Jacobi (1743–1819). This topic may have seemed a strange choice for the one who chose it, namely a young Jewish scholar from a traditional Jewish home focusing on a passionate opponent of the German *Aufklärung*. Jacobi had excoriated both Moses Mendelssohn and Kant for introducing "nihilism" into European culture. They had done this by shrinking religious beliefs into the narrow limits of rationalist discourse. (It was Jacobi who invented the term "nihilism" that was destined for an honored place in the Straussian lexicon.) Jacobi was a vigorous defender of traditional Christian faith against what he deemed the unjust claims of Reason: In the late eighteenth century, he became Germany's most widely recognized and perhaps most contentious advocate of this position.[6] One can easily imagine the problems Strauss faced doing his doctoral dissertation on Jacobi under a well-known rationalist.

The problem went beyond offending Cassirer. The intellectual illiberalism of Jacobi (although one would be hard-pressed to find any overt anti-Semitism in his work) would not have resonated among Strauss's fellow Jews. Most German Jews of the 1920s would not have linked their ascent in German society to what German conservatives considered the national heritage. German Jews had begun their emancipation in the early nineteenth century as the result of what were seen as liberal reforms, and most of the Jewish community associated their gradually improved status in German society with a cosmopolitan, rationalist

---

[5] See Toni Cassirer, *Aus Meinem Leben mit Ernst Cassirer* (New York: Leo Baeck Institute, 1951) for the moving account of her husband's life by Ernst Cassirer's widow. On the generally pro-Republican orientation of German philosophy departments at this time, see Christian Tilitzki, *Die deutsche Universitätsphilosophie in der Weimarer Republik und im Dritten Reich*, 2 volumes (Berlin: Akademie Verlag, 2002), 1–30, 241–43, and 348–50; and my German review essay on Tilitzki's research, "Philosophen im Dritten Reich," *Neue Ordnung* 1:10 (Winter, 2010), 15–18.

[6] See *Das Erkenntnisproblem in der Philosophischen Lehre Friedrich H. Jacobi* in Strauss's *Gesammelte Schriften*, ed. Heinrich Meier (Stuttgart: J. B. Metzler, 1977), 2: 235–92; and David Janssens, "The Problem of the Enlightenment: Strauss, Jacobi, and the Pantheism Controversy," *Review of Metaphysics* 56 (2003); 605–32.

tradition of thought. In the mid-nineteenth century, Jews had generally supported conservative parties in the Prussian diet (*Landtag*), and throughout the 1870s, the majority had backed the National Liberals, who were allied to the government of Otto von Bismarck. However, in the 1890s, German Jewry turned toward the parliamentary left, a trend that continued to manifest itself during the Weimar Republic.[7]

Although Strauss in his later correspondence with the German legal theorist Carl Schmitt raised questions about the character of liberalism, we may assume that, like most other Jews of his time, he generally supported the center left in German politics. This orientation and his intense Zionism must be taken into account in order not to read too much into a remark that he made in a letter to Karl Löwith in June, 1935: "I can only say that Nietzsche so dominated and bewitched me between my twenty-second and thirtieth years that I literally believed everything that I understood of him."[8] Strauss would spend the second half of his life exhorting others to abandon what had been *his* youthful obsession.

In any case, there is no reason to treat his enthusiasm for Nietzsche as an endorsement of the German nationalist Right, a connection that is sometimes made without sufficient evidence by Strauss's critics.[9] In *Leo Strauss and the Politics of Exile*, Eugene R. Sheppard presents the young Strauss as a "Weimar conservative Jew," who held the view that "Germany and the West were immersed in a fundamental crisis and modern rationalism and bourgeois culture were bereft of meaning."[10]

[7] See Donald L. Niewyk, *The Jews in Weimar Germany* (Baton Rouge: Louisiana State University Press, 1980); on the subject of the Frankfurt Lehrhaus, see Michael Brenner, *The Renaissance of Jewish Culture in Weimar Germany* (New Haven, CT: Yale University Press, 1998); and David Lipton, *Ernst Cassirer* (Toronto: University of Toronto Press, 1978). On the changes in German Jewish politics from the time that Jews achieved civil equality in Prussia in 1847, see Jacob Toury, *Soziale und politische Geschichte der Juden in Deutschland 1847–1971* (Düsseldorf: Droste Verlag, 1977), especially pages 110–30.

[8] Translated and printed in *The Independent Journal of Philosophy* 516 (1988): 183.

[9] For the most detailed attempt to link Strauss to the German and European far Right, see William H. F. Altman, *The German Stranger: Leo Strauss and National Socialism* (Lanham, MD: Lexington Books, 2010); my review, "Cryptic Fascist?' in *The American Conservative* 10.2 (February, 2011): 47–50; and Grant Havers's comments on "Voegelin View," http://www:voegelinview.com/final-volley-in-the-strauss-wars-review.html

[10] Eugene R. Sheppard, *Leo Strauss and the Politics of Exile: The Making of a Political Philosopher* (Waltham, MA: Brandeis University Press, 2006), 18.

However, Sheppard adds to this characterization that Strauss's stance "did not necessarily entail a political position on the right. There are countless examples of Weimar figures, and specifically Weimar Jewish figures, who held these principles and adopted positions on the left." Moreover, when Sheppard comes to the stand that Strauss took in response to his picture of the disintegration of liberalism, it has nothing to do with a German or European identity: "Strauss's writings reflect his critical stance toward *galut* [Jewish exile] consciousness as something that needs to be overcome because of its servile and unreflective qualities."[11] The question that needs to be asked is whether a Weimar-right location applies to someone who viewed himself and his coethnics as living in exile in the West. In what sense, if any, did Strauss see himself as belonging to a society that he was urging Jews to leave, as a foreign environment?

The German-Jewish world for Strauss was sharply bifurcated. And this was the case long before he left Germany in 1932, with a Rockefeller Fellowship, to take up residence in Paris. Strauss's Jewishness was more than a "theological problem," which he wrestled with while doing a book on Spinoza in the early 1930s. Interpreters such as Steven Smith, Michael Zank, and Daniel Tanguay have emphasized a "political-religious" turning point in Strauss's life. Those were the years when their subject was struggling toward a commitment to "classical" or Rabbinic Judaism. Strauss went through this ordeal without accepting a worldview that he was then exploring, which was the "neo-Orthodox" formulation of Judaism identified with Franz Rosenzweig (1887–1929).[12]

In the 1920s, Strauss was drawn to Rosenzweig, who was then formulating and teaching a neo-Orthodox form of Judaism. Between 1922 and 1924, Strauss participated in the activities of Rosenzweig's educational center in Frankfurt, the Freies Jüdisches Lehrhaus, and while there, developed an interest in Maimonides and began to read Spinoza. But it was Rosenzweig who provided the cynosure of attention

---

[11] Ibid., 18–19. For a study of a German Jew who was on the German right, see Frank-Lothar Kroll, *Hans Joachim Schoeps und Preussen* (Berlin: Duncker & Humblot, 2010) and the memoirs of Schoeps, a German Jewish monarchist, *Ja Nein Trotzdem. Erinnerungen, Begegnungen, Erfahrungen* (Mainz: Hase& Koehler, 1974).

[12] See Rosenzweig's most widely read work, *The Star of Redemption*, trans. William Hallo (New York: Holt, Reinhart and Winston, 1970).

for those who were studying at the Lehrhaus. This broadly educated teacher tried to blend Rabbinic religiosity with an existentially based theology that drew heavily on Protestant sources. Smith indicates that Rosenzweig's view, which regarded "the problems of Judaism as ultimately beyond history – and literally above time and impervious to political solutions," commanded Strauss's attention during his period of intense preoccupation with religious questions.[13]

Strauss "learned from Rosenzweig that the modern Jew is torn between two competing homelands, faith and reason, law and philosophy, *Deutschtum und Judentum.*" Even though a Zionist who worked for the Zionistic Academy for Jewish Research in Berlin, Strauss came to see the Jewish nationalist path as problematic and as a departure from Rabbinic Judaism. His first book, *Die Religionskritik Spinozas als Grundlage seiner Bibelwissenschft*, which was published in Berlin in 1930 and dedicated to Rosenzweig, was, according to Smith, a critical commentary not only on Spinoza's *Ethics*, but also on the belief "that human reason alone can give a theoretically and practically satisfying explanation of Nature, of everything that is."[14]

Although in the 1920s Strauss was pondering theological questions, what may have been more crucial for him was something he declared at age seventeen: It was then that he "converted to simple, straightforward political Zionism."[15] Overshadowing the range of possibilities within Strauss's Jewish identity was his commitment to *am yisrael*, the Jewish people. This commitment remained determinative for his life, although Strauss never took the road back to the Orthodox tradition that his parents upheld – however loosely. Despite his talk about the need for Jews to return to the "ancient faith," Strauss gives no evidence of having done this. And although he strongly defends some Hebraic theological assumptions against their detractors, particularly the doctrine of Creation, he does not seem to have shown interest in Rabbinic legal codes. Any return to normative Jewish religious life would have rested on the study and practice of such Talmudic texts.

[13] Steven B. Smith, *Reading Leo Strauss: Politics, Philosophy, Judaism* (Chicago: University of Chicago Press, 2006).
[14] Ibid.
[15] Found in Leo Strauss, *Jewish Philosophy and the Crisis of Modernity; Essays and Lectures in Modern Jewish Tought*, ed. K. H. Green (Albany: State University of New York Press, 1997), 3.

All the same, Strauss honored the "Jewish tradition" as an alternative to Greek rationality. According to Daniel Tanguay, "Judaism (for Strauss) is distinguished from other religions because it articulated this moral alternative in the most coherent manner: the personal, biblical God is a hidden God, whose face cannot be seen; he is absolutely free."[16] But would this theology differ in any significant way from the stress on the hidden face of God that one meets in Luther and Calvin or from the concept of God's total and absolute power and otherness expounded by European Nominalists in the fourteenth century? And does the Rabbinic legal culture in which Strauss was allegedly raised represent a "classical" theological alternative to Greek philosophy? Or was Strauss defending something closer to what he sometimes recognized as a collective witness to God, embodied by the Jewish nation?

In a preface to the English-language edition of his Spinoza work in 1965, Strauss is explicit in underlining the need for something other than political nationalism to ensure a future for the Jewish people. He proposes a return to the faith that had kept the Jews together for millennia. The same concerns were implicit in Strauss's dissertation, seeing that his subject, Jacobi, was the best-known critic of Spinoza in the eighteenth century. Jacobi had ascribed to Spinoza a critical role in discrediting a biblically based religious faith, a charge that had whetted Strauss's interest in Spinoza, as the theoretical source for a turning away from religious conviction, which was particularly apparent among educated German Jews.

This concern about the erosion of religious faith, and most critically for Strauss the loss of faith within the Jewish community, leads back to a question that has already been posed: Which Jewish religion does Strauss have in mind in his early writings? Did he wish to have contemporary Westernized Jews return to the lives of their ancestors – that is, lives structured around Talmudic studies and highly restrictive ritual practices? If not, what exactly is the religious tradition to which Strauss would have other Jews go back, as an act of collective survival?

A Straussian, Peter Berkowitz, asserts in the *Weekly Standard* (June 2, 2003) that although Strauss was "a religious doubter," he

---

[16] Daniel Tanguay, *Leo Strauss; An Intellectual Biography*, trans. Christopher Naden (New Haven, CT: Yale University Press, 2007), 212.

nonetheless thought religion "was rich in wisdom about the human condition."[17] Religion for Strauss, as something to be respected if not believed as divine revelation or as a series of historical happenings, was to be found, according to Berkowitz, in Hebrew Scripture. This brings us to Strauss's complex reaction to someone who questioned his Jewish preference for revealed truths. As is famously known, Spinoza in his *Theologico-Political Treatise* had presented the Gospels as being morally superior to the Mosaic code, because Jesus had taught universal charity. Partly because of this explicit preference, Strauss's mentor Cohen had accused the seventeenth-century Sephardic Dutch philosopher of a "humanly incomprehensible betrayal of the Jewish people." Although Strauss did not go as far in condemning Spinoza for his textual predilections, he did stress his "anti-theological ire."[18]

A strange bird that Strauss described "as the greatest man of Jewish origin who had openly denied the truth of Judaism without becoming a Christian," Strauss's Spinoza conceptualized a deity who "is simply beyond good and evil." The Spinozistic pantheistic deity brought forth "love and hatred, nobility and baseness, saintliness and depravity," in contrast to the Jewish deity "who forms light and darkness, makes peace and creates evil."[19]

Despite his critique (which was partly foreshadowed by Jacobi) of Spinoza's view of a divine being who acts out of necessity, without the power to alter His actions, Strauss, according to Smith, "does not reject the Spinozistic conception of God." Although Smith does not prove this contention, he does indicate something more pertinent for our argument. Strauss praised Spinoza because he preached the coming of a "secular liberal society," one that "holds out the possibility of reconstituting a Jewish state."[20] If there was a silver lining in Spinoza's religious-political speculations, it was that he viewed the Jews as an

---

[17] See Peter Berkowitz, "What Hath Strauss Wrought?" *Weekly Standard* 8.7 (June 2, 2003): 14–15.

[18] Leo Strauss, *Spinoza's Critique of Religion*, trans. E. M. Sinclair (New York: Shocken Books, 1965), 240–44; Daniel Tanguay, Strauss: *An Intellectual Biography*, 108–10; and Steven B. Smith, *Spinoza, Liberalism, and the Question of Jewish Identity* (New Haven, CT: Yale University Press, 1997), 27–54.

[19] See Leo Strauss, *Preface to Spinoza's Critique of Religion* in *Jewish Philosophy and the Crisis of Modernity*, 242–43.

[20] Ibid., 246.

intact nation and that he knew that the Torah, the Jewish written and/or Ritual laws, according to Strauss, were "not from heaven" but were national creations. Strauss admired Spinoza as a "Jewish philosopher" for the same reason that did David Ben Gurion, the leading political Zionist of the twentieth century and Israel's first premier. Ben Gurion sent wreaths with the inscription "min amechah [from your people]" to adorn the gravesite of Spinoza in The Hague: Both he and Strauss viewed the seventeenth-century Jewish philosopher as a Zionist precursor.

Noting this Jewish concern does not cast doubts on Strauss's accomplishments. It simply indicates an immutable reference point in his intellectual odyssey and political teachings. For example, it would be unacceptable in discussing Ernst Renan as a religious-political commentator to ignore his strong French patriotism. Ethnic or national loyalties were a shaping influence on a multitude of thinkers, and in Strauss's case such a factor is particularly relevant. A profound preoccupation with his Jewishness runs through Strauss's life, and it is evident well before Strauss was forced to flee from Nazi tyranny. This situation would not have been the same for more assimilated German Jews of Strauss's generation, whether Herbert Marcuse on the Marxist Left or such distinctly German nationalist Jews of the interwar years as the medievalist Ernst Kantorowicz, the literary scholar Friedrich Gundolf, or the historian Hans Joachim Schoeps. Strauss's concerns were more Jewish-centered than were the politics of other German Jewish thinkers.

Documenting such a focus is rather easy. Indeed the problem may be providing more illustrations than are needed to prove one's point. Strauss grew up in the life world of what Germans called the *Halbassimilanten*, of those Jews who spoke German, attended German schools and whose families may have lived in Germany for centuries but whose interests and associations were almost entirely Jewish. Whether at home in Kirchhain, at school in Marburg, or working for the Academy of Jewish Research in Berlin, Strauss inhabited a Jewish, but not necessarily Orthodox, *Lebenswelt*. The associations he formed at Marburg took place in Jewish circles, whether with Cohen's disciples, the Latvian Jewish classicist and mathematician, who migrated to Germany, Jacob Klein (1899–1978), or the fervent Zionist and later Israeli nationalist and scholar of medieval Jewish mysticism, Gershom

Scholem. Exposure to this Jewish social world would continue to be the case with Strauss's experience at Rosenzweig's Lehrhaus. His dissertation advisor at Hamburg, Cassirer, was Jewish; and after settling in Paris, Strauss married a German Jewish widow, Miriam Berensohn, and adopted his wife's daughter from an earlier marriage.

In Paris, where Strauss stayed until 1934, he expanded his ambience to establish a lifelong friendship with an uncharacteristically leftist Russian émigré, Alexandre Kojève (1902–1968). This relation became noteworthy because of the correspondence between the two friends, and because of a widely read dialogue on Xenophon's discussion of tyranny in the *Hiero* carried on between Strauss and Kojève. Strauss also received visits in Paris from his postwar correspondent, the hermeneutic scholar Hans-Georg Gadamer; and he met in France the writer on Renaissance neo-Platonism, Alexandre Koyré, and the historian of sociology Raymond Aron.[21]

By then, however, Strauss's ethnic-political attachments were already formed. In Marburg he became associated with the Zionist Right, led by the charismatic Russian Jew, Ze'ev Jabotinsky (1880–1940). However conflicted Strauss may have been about the Orthodox Jewish path to righteousness or Jewish neo-Orthodoxy, his Zionism, according to the commentator on his early work, Michael Zank, was a political given. Years later he described in *Jewish Philosophy and the Crisis of Modernity* the excitement of meeting Jabotinsky. As a "political Zionist in my youth," explains Strauss, "I occasionally met Jabotinsky, the leader of the Revisionists." Strauss revered this leader of a wing of the Zionist movement that wished to occupy both sides of the Jordan, even at the cost of subjugating or expelling the Arabs. From Strauss's account, it seems that Jabotinsky approved of his interest in "Jewish history and Zionist theory," but was disappointed that the Revisionist Zionists in Marburg failed to "take rifle practice." [22]

Steven Smith's study of Strauss as a Jewish thinker makes a critical observation about one of Strauss's early tours de force, his commentary

---

[21] A work about Strauss's exile in France, which highlights other topics from this biographical chapter, is Eugene R. Sheppard, *Leo Strauss and the Politics of Exile: The Making of a Political Philosopher* (Lebanon NH: Brandeis University Press, 2006), particularly 89–90.

[22] For the Strauss-Kojève correspondence, see the appendix to Strauss's *On Tyranny*, ed. Victor Gourevitch and Michael Roth (Chicago: Universrity of Chicago Press, 2000).

on Carl Schmitt's examination of friend-enemy relations, *The Concept of the Political*. Although Strauss was then an obscure recipient of the doctoral requirement for teaching at a German Gymnasium, who had not been accepted for a postdoctoral dissertation (*Habilitationsschrift*), a benefit that would have allowed him to teach at the university level, Schmitt approved his essay for inclusion in the 1932 edition of his work. Schmitt (1888–1985) was properly impressed by the critical comments that Strauss had submitted concerning his understanding of "the political" as "the most intense of all friend-enemy relations." Strauss praised Schmitt's attempt to divorce the "political" from cultural and aesthetic activities. He also agreed with Schmitt's linking of "political" struggle to the "critical situation," in which the individual is required to risk his life for others.[23]

Strauss objects, particularly toward the end of his *Anmerkungen*, that "Schmitt's polemic against liberalism bogs down in polemic and once diverted is forced to remain at the level of liberalism." Strauss argues that "going beyond the horizons of liberalism" requires moving beyond the liberal belief that "all political concepts, notions and principles have a polemical significance," and then embracing a more audacious position, which is already implicit in Schmitt's work. This is an "integral knowledge" that cannot be derived from concrete political existence, or the situation of the present age, but can only take place through a return to [what Schmitt himself designates as] an "unblemished, uncorrupt nature."[24]

It is common to read into such passages a foreshadowing of Strauss's later concern with relativism and historicism and his defense of Nature against appeals to changing historical situations. The German Straussian Heinrich Meier, who is severely critical of Schmitt, interprets this "dialogue between absent participants" as a wise teacher's response to someone who had already marked out European Jewry for destruction.[25] However, Smith suggests an interpretive possibility

---

[23] See Heinrich Meier's edition of the *Anmerkungen* in *Carl Schmitt, Leo Strauss and "Der Begriff des Politischen." Zu einem Dialog unter Abwesenden* (Stuttgart: J. B. Metzler), 99–102.

[24] Ibid., 125. For a detailed discussion of "Der Begriff des Politischen" and Strauss's commentary on this work, see my *Carl Schmitt: Politics and Theory* (Westport, CT: Greenwood Press, 1990), 41–55.

[25] Heinrich Meier, 81–96.

that requires less editorializing. He sees Schmitt for what he was at the time, someone whose view of the "dangerousness" of human nature and the inevitability of mortal struggle led him to "embrace a form of Catholic authoritarianism that drew inspiration from the counter-Enlightenment."[26]

Smith also understands where Strauss then stood, as someone who was aware "of the illusions of liberal cosmopolitanism and a belief that the fate of Jews could be entrusted to either benevolent government or the norms of international communities." Jews "must take affairs into their own hands, must use their own "hardware," so to speak. If the Jews are a people, they must start to act like a people and provide themselves with "more natural conditions of existence."[27] Although Smith downplays the reference at the end of the commentary to "integral knowledge," he nonetheless explains convincingly why Strauss was drawn to Schmitt's concept. It justified the belief that nationalism – and more specifically, Jewish nationalism – was the alternative to aesthetic and social pleasures. This "cultural sphere," which flourished in a bourgeois society, appealed to German-Jewish assimilationists, but, according to Strauss, aesthetic activities would not allow Jews to withstand the *Ernstfall*. "Nature" in this context meant what Jabotinsky and his German Jewish acolytes understood it to mean. It was the natural condition toward which world Jewry would have to move for its own good, by creating a powerful Jewish state.

It is possible to find evidence of Strauss's Zionist loyalties after his coming to America – and even after he had established himself as an academic celebrity in the 1950s as the Robert Maynard Hutchins Distinguished Professor at the University of Chicago. Many of Strauss's most intimate students, such as Allan Bloom, Harry V. Jaffa, Ralph Lerner, Stanley Rosen, Harry Clor, William Galston, Abram Shulsky, Werner Dannhauser, Seth Benardete, Steven Salkever, Hadley Arkes, and his frequent collaborator, Joseph Cropsey, have been Jewish – and strong supporters of Israel and usually of the Israeli Right.

The same judgment would apply to such non-Jewish students of Strauss as Harvey Mansfield, Jr., Thomas L. Pangle, Mark Lilla, and

---

[26] Steven B. Smith, *Reading Leo Strauss*, 61.
[27] Ibid., 62. Smith's study may be the only one that explains Strauss's remarks about Schmitt against the background of his Zionist nationalism.

Walter Berns. One of Strauss's non-Jewish students, George Anastaplo, noted the special favor that the master showered on those who expressed his "ahavat yisrael," love of Israel, but also the scorn that he sometimes reserved for those who were imprudent enough to show the opposite sentiment.[28] Although Strauss did not choose to move to Israel and remained a "Jew in exile," he nonetheless spent one memorable year at the Hebrew University, from 1954 to 1955, and recalled that year fondly afterward.

His oft-cited defense of political Zionism as "problematic" but also "a moral force in an era of complete dissolution" was printed as a letter to the conservative fortnightly *National Review* (January 5, 1956). In it, Strauss was responding to a charge that had previously appeared in the same publication, namely that Israel exhibited racist hostility against the Palestinians. Strauss challenged this charge and then went on to extol Israel and Jewish nationalism for their "conservative function." Zionists and Israelis were helping "to stem the tide of progressive leveling of ancestral differences."[29]

Strauss characterizes Israel as "the only country which as a country is an outpost of the West in the East and in which a single book absolutely predominates in elementary schools and in high schools, the Hebrew bible." Whether or not Scripture, rather than English or Hebrew grammar or mathematical textbooks, predominated in Israeli public education is secondary. Strauss was arguing not so much for Israel's Western character as insisting that it be considered "conservative" because it is authentically Jewish.

This becomes obvious in comments in the same letter about the "heroic austerity supported by the nearness of biblical antiquity" of

---

[28] See *Jewish Philosophy and the Crisis of Modernity*, 37: George Anastaplo, *The Artist as Thinker: From Shakespeare to Joyce* (Columbus: Ohio State University Press, Swallow Press, 1983), 64–67 and 255–70. Two devotional essays among many others on the intensity of Strauss's devotion to the Jewish people are Werner Dannhauser, "Leo Strauss as Jew and Citizen," *Interpretation* 173 (Spring 1991): 433–47; and Ralph Lerner, "Leo Strauss 1899–1973," *American Jewish Year Book* 76 (1976): 91–97. A work that clearly stresses the Jewish, existential focus of Strauss's early work is Michael Zank's long preface to *Leo Strauss: The Early Writings, 1921–1932*, ed. and trans. Michael Zank (Albany: State University of New York Press, 2002). Zank's work clarifies what is the specifically Jewish aspect of Strauss's ambivalent relation to liberal modernity.

[29] *National Review* (January 5, 1956), 23.

Israel's inhabitants, a phrase that we may assume did not pertain to apartment dwellers in Tel Aviv or Haifa or to tour guides in Jerusalem. Strauss then informs the reader that the "Jewish moral spine" was broken by emancipation. Even though this problem is related to the fact that the granting of equality was sometimes "merely formal," Strauss was alluding here to something beyond a promise of emancipation not fully kept.[30] He was echoing Jabotinsky, even if he had not become a gun-toting Israeli settler himself. Only by living in a Jewish land, and moreover in the ancient Jewish homeland, Strauss strongly suggests in his letter and elsewhere, could Jews be authentically Jewish.

This position was not inconsistent with Strauss's tributes to "liberal democracy." As a Jew, he wished to be in a society in which he felt safe, although the nationalist entity he desired for Jews would not necessarily be the kind of society that he would wish to reside in as a Jew in exile. While in Germany before the rise of the Nazis, he may have hoped for a time to see the land of his birth become such a haven, but when forced to emigrate, he transferred his hopes to Anglophone societies. In England, where he found temporary employment at Cambridge in 1935, Strauss came to idolize Churchill, the adversary of the Nazis and, perhaps even more significantly, the personification for him of Anglo-American democratic practice. [31]

This was the gist of a speech that Strauss delivered at Cambridge in 1937, contrasting a democratic England to an authoritarian Germany steeped in antidemocratic habits and thought patterns. This speech, and particularly the contrast drawn between Germans and Englishmen, became paradigmatic for Strauss's disciples. Indeed, contrasting the sinister "German connection" to Anglo-American democracy would become an overshadowing theme in *The Closing of the American Mind* (1987), which was the best-selling attack on relativism and

---

[30] Ibid., 24. Shadia Drury in *Leo Strauss and the American Right* (New York: St. Martin's Press, 1999) cites such passages to show that Strauss was full of "romantic nationalism" and therefore inimical to "liberalism and modernity" and "sympathetic to the American nationalist right." Drury's characterization attributes to those who preach a foreign nationalism a more or less thoroughgoing right-wing orientation. She never asks the obvious question: Why must a Zionist, Black Nationalist, or member of the IRA be a rightist in the context of American politics?

[31] Steven Smith, 196–97; and for a less favorable assessment of this passion, see Anne Norton, *Leo Strauss and the Politics of American Empire*, 127–30.

pop culture produced by Strauss's star student, Allen Bloom.[32] But whether *deutsche Kultur* was to be admired or demonized may have been less important for Strauss than a more practical concern. Given what he considered his Jewish marginality, it seemed best to promote a "liberal democratic" society in which he and others of his kind would feel secure.

Coming to America

Strauss was an American success story in a way that few intellectuals born in Europe have been. Referring to him as a German émigré would be misleading, given that almost all of his fame was achieved after he had settled in the United States. Strauss's writings illustrate this fact, although he certainly arrived in the New World with many accomplishments to his credit. Among these achievements were his commentary on Schmitt's *Concept of the Political*, a work on Spinoza, an abstruse study on the Jewish legal commentator and philosopher Maimonides, exhibiting an impressive knowledge of Arab and Aramaic sources, and, in 1936, *Hobbes' politische Wissenschaft in ihrer Genesis*.

While Strauss was immersed in Jewish theoretical questions in the early 1930s, he was already preparing a study on the ancient materialist and historical sources of the new "political science" of the English thinker Hobbes. In a published letter (March 13, 1932) to Schmitt, who had provided him with a glowing reference letter to the Rockefeller Foundation, Strauss thanked his benefactor for "the interest you've kindly bestowed on my study of Hobbes."[33] In a subsequent letter (July 10, 1933) that Strauss sent to Schmitt from Paris, he conveyed his desire to meet the French monarchist Charles Maurras, as someone "who reveals striking similarities with Hobbes."[34]

By then, Strauss was deeply immersed in his Hobbes project, which, he told Schmitt in the same letter, might cause him to visit Harvard, where Professor Carl Friedrich was bringing out a complete edition of

---

[32] Allen Bloom, *The Closing of the American Mind* (New York: Simon and Schuster, 1987), 141–56, 217–26.
[33] This correspondence is appended to Henrich Meier's work *Carl Schmitt, Leo Strauss und "Der Begriff des Politischen,"* 131.
[34] Ibid., 135.

Hobbes's work. Although Strauss was then trying to get as far away from the gathering Nazi storm as he could, it seems that his preoccupation with Hobbes continued throughout this period. This interest took shape while he was still immersed in Latin, Aramaic, and Arabic sources and dealing with Spinoza and Maimonides.

Despite his erudite German writings, Strauss became a celebrated figure writing in English for a predominantly American public. Starting with *On Tyranny: An Interpretation of Xenophon's "Hiero"* in 1947, *Persecution and the Art of Writing* (1952), his lectures in *Natural Right and History* (1953) and then continuing through *The City and Man* (1964) and such multilayered tomes as *Thoughts on Machiavelli* (1958), *What Is Political Philosophy?* (1959), *Liberalism: Ancient and Modern* (1968), *Xenophon's Socratic Discourse* (1970), *Xenophon's Socrates* (1972), and finally, in essays dealing with relativism, the rebirth of political rationalism, and Thucydides as a moral teacher, Strauss built up a reputation as the restorer of ancient political thought. By the 1950s, his English works were being translated into French and German, while his original German texts were being made available in English translation.

Moreover, the Walgreen Lectures that Strauss delivered at Chicago in 1949, and which were published in 1953 as *Natural Right and History*, did more than anything else to establish him as a premier "conservative" thinker on the postwar American scene. The influence of this publication on political theory was perhaps only rivaled by that of another landmark book, *History of Political Philosophy*. Strauss compiled this anthology of essays, which were written by handpicked contributors as well as Strauss himself, with his long-time collaborator, Joseph Cropsey, in 1963. By now this collection has gone through multiple editions and has spawned numerous imitations.[35]

If the anthology allowed Strauss and his devotees to determine those political thinkers who would be taught in political theory courses, *Natural Right and History* did even more for its author. It constructed

[35] Although *The History of Political Philosophy* was first published by the University of Chicago Press in 1963 and underwent its last major revision in 1987, the anthology continues to sell well on Amazon.com in both the hardcover and paperback editions. The same would hold true for the French and Spanish editions, which first appeared in the 1990s. The glowing reviews that are presently on Amazon.com pertain to an anthology that has changed only minimally since 1963.

a compelling narrative about the decline from the high ideals of ancient political theory and its Platonic quest for the Good and the best of all regimes into the materialist, atomistic, and morally cynical thought of the early modern period. This descent was illustrated by the amoralism and naturalism of Machiavelli and Hobbes; nonetheless, this was not the end of political thought or political practice. There was, as Strauss seems to imply, the historical equivalent of the Platonic re-ascent of the soul – or in this case, the "liberal democratic" second chance. Anne Norton correctly observes that Strauss wishes to convince his audience that Anglo-American democracy is offering "an escape from this historical epoch": In the United States, there was "the chance for modernity to be something more than merely modern."[36]

Despite its materialist, individualistic framework going back to John Locke, "liberal democracy," according to Strauss, is decent and worth preserving. This is only possible, however, by promoting the right kind of modernity and by immunizing ourselves against those subsequent "waves of modernity" that came after the American founding. These waves were due to the value-relativist British counter-revolutionary Edmund Burke and to various nineteenth-century German romantic worshippers of History, some of whom are mistaken for "conservatives." The destructive waves, once begun, rolled on with Friedrich Nietzsche and Martin Heidegger, both of whom combined nihilism with hatred for liberal societies.

The Lectures are particularly harsh when they come to the final, identifiably Teutonic wave of modernity. Strauss's warnings against Nietzsche, Heidegger, and Weber would provide the substance for moralizing tracts by his disciples for decades afterwards.[37] The Lectures, however, were an intellectual historical milestone for other reasons. Whether attacking "liberal relativism," "radical historicism," or historicism as a "particular form of positivism," Strauss anticipated what became popular themes by the 1950s. Like Walter Lippmann who was then proposing a return to Natural Law thinking, Strauss in the Walgreen Lectures attracted those who were searching for moral permanence in postwar America.

---

[36] See *Leo Strauss and the Politics of American Empire*, 118.
[37] See Leo Strauss, *National Right and History* (Chicago: University of Chicago Press, 1953), 5–8, 26–27, 320–21.

The introduction includes an apparent attempt to bridge the gulf between "two hostile camps": one occupied by the liberals of various description, the other by the Catholic and non-Catholic disciples of Thomas Aquinas.[38] These are the two opposing camps made up of those who, on the one hand, believe in natural rights as conceptualized by John Locke, and those who, on the other hand, cling to an older tradition of Natural Law. Strauss argues, however, that the differences between these groups can be reconciled, if not entirely overcome:

> [Both sides are] in the same boat. They are all modern men. We are all in the grips of the same difficulty. Natural right in its classical form is connected with a teleological view of the universe. All natural beings have a natural end, a natural destiny, which determines what kind of operation is good for them. In the case of man, reason is required for discerning these operations; reason determines what is by nature right with the ultimate regard to man's natural end. The teleological view of the universe, of which the teleological view of man forms a part, would seem to have been destroyed by modern natural science.

Strauss goes on to suggest that the problem at hand exists even for those who cling to Thomism. They too must live with a dualism "of a non-teleological natural science and a teleological science of man."[39]

The discussion of Locke in a later Walgreen Lecture, "The Crisis of Natural Right," links natural right to a worldview that is hedonistic, materialistic, and not really open to religious revelation. In fact, it is hard to find any dissection of Locke, even by a Thomist or Burkean, which is quite as ruthless and persuasive as the one found in the Lectures. In calling for reconciliation between Thomists and natural right liberals, Strauss attaches the term "classical" to the proponents of natural rights.[40] One may ask whether the reference to "classical natural rights" has any function except to designate ancient sources for medieval notions of a normative morality. Did "classical natural right" foreshadow the modern concept centering on a view of man based on self-preservation and the maximization of wealth? Note that this is the

---

[38] Ibid., 7.

[39] Ibid., 7–8.

[40] Ibid., 120–64; For an examination of Strauss's "classical natural right" and moral critique in a Catholic, Thomistic key, see James V. Schall, "A Latitude for Statesmanship: Strauss on St. Thomas" in *Leo Strauss: Political Philosopher and Jewish Thinker*, ed. Kenneth L. Deutsch and Walter Nicgorski (Lanham, MD: Rowman and Littlefield, 1994), 212–15.

position that Strauss ascribes to Locke. If the Lockean concept is the standard for defining "natural rights" in general, it is difficult to imagine how the "two hostile camps" could be harmonized.

Strauss returns to the theme of "classical natural right" in his fourth lecture, dealing with Cicero and Thomas Aquinas. What he presents here, however, does not seem to be a usable tradition, and certainly not in its Thomistic formulation. In that scholastic account of "classical natural right," also known as natural law, ethics is shown to be "practically inseparable not only from natural theology – i.e. from a natural theology which is, in fact, based on biblical revelation-but even from revealed theology." In the Thomistic recasting of Aristotle, "natural reason creates a presumption in favor of the divine law, which completes or perfects the natural law."[41]

The reconciliation of the two natural-rights traditions, according to Strauss, would come through the shared use of reason, but not necessarily in its metaphysical mode. Strauss prescribed what he understood as "political rationalism," and which he saw as already operative in ancient political thought. In contrast to Burke's view of the British constitution as an accumulation of particularities evolving over the centuries into a coherent regime, Strauss points to the "classical" ideal in which "the best constitution is a contrivance of reason, i.e., of conscious activity or of planning on the part of a group of individuals." It is natural because it aims at "the perfection of human nature," but it is also "a work of design, planning, conscious making; it does not come into being by a natural process or by an imitation of nature."[42]

There is another clear implication in Strauss's references to the two groups that appealed to "Nature." One of these camps was playing with an exceedingly poor hand. Advances in the natural sciences had shaken the cosmology that was attached to an earlier understanding of man's relation to the universe, and so there was no plausible way – or so one might read into Strauss without too much reaching – of returning to medieval metaphysical notions. Despite this setback for the metaphysicians, we are led to assume that all would turn out well for the United States. Unlike Burke's conception of the unwritten British constitution,

[41] *Natural Right and History*, 8; 163–64.
[42] Ibid., 314.

the American regime was built on a "design" or "contrivance of reason." This artifice of Reason was therefore in some sense a return to what Strauss presents as the "classical" model of natural right or even better, a project that could conceivably be traced back to Plato.

Such arcane investigations aside, it must be stressed that the Lectures appealed to what might be described as a value-conscious conservative public. Strauss had sounded the tocsin against the enemies of the hour, relativism, positivism, and historicism, and he urged a return to the study of the ancients. Not even his recurrent assaults on Burke, who in the 1950s was being revived as a natural-rights critic and Natural Law defender, served to dim his luster. Strauss's narrative resonated among those who idealized postwar America as well as among those who believed it had strayed. America would flourish as a liberal democratic society because it could be modern and moral at the same time. Finally, Strauss presented his lectures following a war that had been fought and won against the antidemocratic Axis. And this at a time when a global struggle against the Soviets, widely understood as pitting a capitalistic-democratic free world against antidemocratic socialists, had already begun.[43]

One should not forget when considering the smashing success of the Lectures Strauss's situation when he arrived in the United States. In 1931, his career seems to have dead-ended, when the Jewish institute that provided him with a post ran out of money. In the early 1920s, Strauss had gone to Freiburg for postdoctoral studies, where he heard the lectures of the phenomenologist Edmund Husserl and Husserl's prodigy Martin Heidegger. He also briefly attended lectures in Marburg and Berlin, where he audited the classes of the classicist Werner Jäger. In 1931, however, when he approached the radical Protestant theologian Paul Tillich at the University of Frankfurt, asking him to supervise his *Habilitationsschrift*, the applicant was summarily turned down.[44]

[43] For an excellent overview of this attempted "recovery of tradition and values," see George H. Nash, *The Conservative Intellectual Movement in America since 1945*, second edition (Wilmington, DE: Intercollegiate Studies Institute, 1996), 50–73. For an examination of the American reception of *Natural Right and History*, see James W. Ceaser, "The American Context of Leo Strauss's *Natural Right and History*," in *Democracy Reconsidered*, ed. Elizabeth Kaufer Bush and Peter A. Lawler (Lanham, MD: Rowman and Littlefield, 1999), 13–24.

[44] *Jewish Philosophy and the Crisis of Modernity*, 458–61.

Strauss held on at the Jewish institute while applying for grants to do research outside Germany. The resemblance of his situation then to that of American graduate students of a later period is too obvious to be missed. However unpalatable his opportunistic decision to join the Nazi party in May 1933 may seem, Schmitt treated Strauss in a courtly manner. He called attention to his commentary on *The Concept of the Political* and helped Strauss obtain a Rockefeller grant that allowed him to leave his now inhospitable homeland.

Neither in Paris nor afterward at Cambridge could Strauss find permanent employment, and it was not until he arrived in the United States that a path opened for him, at Columbia, the New School for Social Research, and finally at the University of Chicago. Only after he made his way in the United States did he become known in Europe. Contrary to a conventional report, most of Strauss's notable German connections were established only after he advanced in his adopted land. Unlike many of his later contacts, Klein, Löwith, Scholem, and Kojève were his long-time, trusted friends.[45] Gadamer visited Strauss once while they were both in Paris during Easter, 1933. Strauss's sputtering relationship with Gadamer was jump-started in the mid-1950s, after a push from the then-distinguished professor at Chicago. His admirers often stress the magnificent lectures and events that Strauss attended in Europe, such as a widely publicized debate between Cassirer and Heidegger, which took place in Davos, Switzerland, in 1929.[46] Such an experience may have been memorable, but it should not be confused with access to academic circles. It was precisely such access that Strauss lacked in Germany, as reflected in his stalled career.

A Conservative Star is Born

Strauss's American fame was at least partly owing to his association with the postwar intellectual Right. Even though Smith is correct to describe his mentor as "a cold war liberal of his generation,"[47]

---

[45] Ibid.; and *Reading Leo Strauss*, 43–64.
[46] On this debate between Weimar intellectual giants and its philosophical implications, see Peter E. Gordon, *Continental Divide: Heidegger, Cassirer, Davos* (Cambridge, MA: Harvard University Press, 2010).
[47] *Reading Leo Strauss*, 15.

Strauss's core themes played especially well among postwar conservatives and perhaps most successfully among Catholic conservatives.[48] His attacks on relativism and historicism, his assault on the German sociologist Max Weber for making what Strauss considered an untenable "fact-value distinction," his labored distinctions between medieval natural law and John Locke's conception of natural right, and his general disdain for the victory of "positivism" in the social sciences all appealed powerfully to Catholic conservatives. Given that the postwar conservative movement was full of refugees from Nazism and communism, Strauss was far from the only Central European in its pantheon who warned against the Zeitgeist or against the totalitarian threat posed by the Nazis and the Soviets.

Strauss's admonitions about the German intellectual legacy were more than a single man's opinion. His remarks about the cultural aberration leading to the German catastrophe resembled the judgments of others who were then present on the American intellectual Right. Among them were Hungarian Catholics Thomas Molnar and John Lukacs, the German philosopher of history Eric Voegelin, and Voegelin's follower Gerhart Niemeyer. In a study of Catholic intellectuals and the post–Second World War intellectual Right, Patrick Allitt stresses the concern with moral crisis that marked the Catholic intellectual awakening of the 1950s.[49] Among these Catholic intellectuals, the Lectures must have struck a particularly strong chord.

It would be wrong to assume that Strauss's popularity on the American Right originated with the rise of neoconservatism. His influence among conservatives was already firmly established decades earlier. The McCarthyite populist and one-time Yale professor Willmoore Kendall (who had been William F. Buckley's teacher) became familiar with Strauss in the course of countering arguments in favor of free speech for communists. Kendall found (or thought he found) in Strauss a politically usable defense of the moral foundations of popular government, and he converted to both Catholicism and Straussianism around the same time. Kendall went on to teach at the

---

[48] On the Catholic-Straussian synthesis, see James V. Schall, "A Latitude for Statesmanship? Strauss and St. Thomas," *Review of Politics* 53 (Winter 1991), 126–45.

[49] See Patrick Allitt, *Catholic Intellectuals and Conservative Politics in America* (Ithaca, NY: Cornell University Press, 1995), 6–10; and Walter Lippmann, *Essays in The Public Philosophy* (Boston: Little, Brown and Company, 1955), especially 97 and 113.

University of Dallas, an institution that added to its Catholic trad-itionalist reputation a secondary honor, as a seat of political philoso-phy faithful to the teachings of Leo Strauss.[50] Dallas has continued to blend these two traditions down to the present day.

A one-time teacher of mine, Anton-Hermann Chroust, who in the 1960s was a professor of law at Notre Dame, a guest professor at Yale, and a widely published Aristotle scholar, used to joke about Strauss's visits to South Bend: "The natural law Catholics came out in force, and as soon as St. Leo started talking, they were like Moses receiving the Law."[51] Chroust may have had a point, however sarcastically he chose to make it. Fifty years ago, it would have been hard to miss the honor accorded to Strauss and his ideas in the *Review of Politics* and the *New Scholasticism*, both of which were then Catholic publications published at Notre Dame. Another conservative and Catholic – or Anglo-Catholic – quarterly, *Modern Age*, has been equally favor-able to Strauss and has given considerable space to his critiques of relativism. To its credit, however, *Modern Age* has printed dissenting views as well.[52]

Two votaries of Strauss – Amherst professor Hadley Arkes and a former student of Allan Bloom's and a black conservative activist Allan Keyes – have been especially prominent in the right-to-life movement. Both have featured in their battle against the pro-choice movement a view of America as a modernist enterprise. Proceeding from their Straussian hermeneutic, Arkes and Keyes have subordinated argu-ments from medieval Natural Law to Lockean ideas about the "natural rights" of the unborn. Both of these advocates, devout Catholics, have also periodically tried to fit Locke's notion of right into a Thomistic framework, thereby bringing together their metaphysical assumptions with what Strauss deemed characteristically modern thought.[53]

---

[50] See Jeffrey Hart's biographical essay, "Willmoore Kendall: American," in *Willmoore Kendal Contra Mundum*, ed. Nellie D. Kendall (New Rochelle, NY: Arlington House, 1971), 9–26.

[51] Personal conversation with the author, November 12, 1967.

[52] See, for example Barry Shain, "Harry Jaffa and the Demise of the Old Republic", *Modern Age*, 49.4 (Fall 2007): 476–89; and Paul Gottfried, "On Straussian Teachings," *Modern Age*, 49.1 (Winter 2007): 77–81.

[53] See Hadley Arkes, *Natural Right and the Right to Choose* (Cambridge: Cambridge University Press, 2002); and Alan Keyes, *Our Character, Our Future* (Grand Rapids, MI: Zondervan, 1996). Keyes has famously spoken about how his life was turned

While among European interpreters, Strauss is associated with Catholic Natural Law or a return to Antiquity, in the United States, he has become identified with neoconservative politics. In some ways this second development goes back to older memories on the postwar American Right, as one learns from reading the now-neoconservative publication, *National Review*. An article there by Charles Kesler, the disciple of Strauss's disciple Harry Jaffa (December 19, 2005), extols Strauss and Lincoln as two indispensable teachers of democratic values. Kesler also manages to praise Strauss for another reason that *National Review* might have given in its earlier days, when it was still an emphatically pro-Catholic, anticommunist fortnightly. Strauss is seen as an infallible guide for waging a philosophical crusade "against relativism and nihilism." Now this crusade is being turned against new foes, namely the enemies of democratic equality and human rights. Strauss was urging us to fight against these antidemocratic forces, and fortunately for this generation, he left behind disciples who are "challenging the smug relativism of today's academy and endeavor[ing] to reconnect specialized inquiries with the permanent, unifying questions of human life."[54]

Some on the right attach to Strauss a less egalitarian merit than the one that Kesler and *National Review* stress: They see in him someone who defended aristocracy as the best of governments. Although this view has been ripped out of context (Strauss was careful to point out that rule by the morally and intellectually best is almost impossible to attain), self-styled elitists have read into his work something dramatically different. They locate in Strauss's writings their elitist proclivities, and they particularly relish the tendency ascribed to Strauss and his followers to hide what they really believe behind Plato's "noble lie." Supposedly this deception, which is practiced for the benefit of the many, betokens an aristocratic worldview going back to Strauss himself.[55]

---

around when he read Bloom's account of the black student who refused to participate in an antiwar demonstration in Bloom's *Closing of the American Mind*, 316.

[54] See Charles Kesler, "All against All," *National Review* (August 18, 1989): 39.

[55] For an ecstatically approving view of this interpretation, see Robert Locke, "Leo Strauss, Conservative Mastermind," on FrontPageMagazine.com, May 31, 2002. Another equally extreme but undocumented statement of this view of Strauss as an antidemocratic elitist is William Pfaff's "The Long Reach of Leo Strauss," *International Herald Tribune* (May 15, 2003): 2.

Those who make this connection also cite the cult of the democratic hero that has emerged among Straussians. This is a form of devotion Strauss himself initiated for Winston Churchill, who, as he explained to Karl Löwith in August 1946, exhibited "megalopsuxia [greatness of soul]."[56] Strauss came to idolize Churchill, from his stay at Cambridge in the 1930s until the end of his life. Equally indicative of Strauss's "conservative" renown is his place in George H. Nash's *The Conservative Intellectual Movement in America since 1945*, in which Strauss personifies the "revolt against the masses."[57] This may seem an unusual way to characterize a FDR-Truman Democrat – that is, someone who found even that uncertain Republican Dwight Eisenhower to be a bit too far to the right for his taste.[58]

Lest these critical comments generate the wrong impression, we should also stress that Strauss exhibited considerable strengths as a scholar. His knowledge of ancient and modern languages was truly breathtaking, and his production of multiple manuscripts revealing close textual readings and intensive philological training indicate far more than conventional scholarly skills. During a heated debate between Strauss and the free-market Austrian economist Ludwig von Mises after the Second World War, on whether the fact-value dichotomy could be defended (Strauss, unlike Mises, argued that it could not), Mises made the dismissive remark: "He's only a Gymnasiallehrer." The Austrian economist was intimating that Strauss debated like someone who had never qualified for university teaching but was only fit to instruct in a secondary school. Although Mises may have had the better of the argument, his slight was unfair. Strauss's work, and not least of all his German work, proves beyond doubt that he was worthy of multiple doctoral degrees.[59]

---

[56] Letter to Karl Löwith (August 20, 1946), *Independent Journal of Philosophy*, 516 (1988): 111.

[57] *The Conservative Intellectual Movement since 1945*, 44–46.

[58] Interview with Walter Berns conducted at the University of Toronto, July 28, 1973. According to Peter Minowitz, in *Straussophobia: Defending Leo Strauss and Straussians against Shadia Dury* (Lanham, MD: Lexington Books, 2009), 184–85, Strauss may have voted for Barry Goldwater in 1964. His decision was tied to his anxieties about the Cold War and does not indicate any veering toward the far Right. Most of Strauss's students at the time continued to regard themselves as liberal democrats.

[59] This remark came from Murray Rothbard, a renowned student of Mises who attended the symposium on morality and relativism held by the William Volker Fund in 1961.

Arguably his most impressive scholarship, however, may have been the least responsible for his later American fame. His perceptions about *The Concept of the Political*, his works on Spinoza and Maimonides, and his remarkably original interpretation of the "alternative ancient tradition" and its effects on Hobbes did less for his career than *Natural Right and History* and its previewing in a lecture series. It was Strauss, the liberal democratic moralist, and not a young German Jew pouring over ancient texts, who built a prominent school of thought.

That Americanized Strauss had immense appeal among Jewish students, who were drawn to his teachings and personality because of their Jewish concerns. At the same time Catholics also turned to Strauss to pull their moral-theological chestnuts out of the fire. Rarely did these Catholic admirers look very closely at Strauss's reading of medieval philosophy. If they had, they might have been better instructed but also less mesmerized. In any case, Strauss and his growing American following seemed made for each other. Although the American Strauss was implicit in the German one, it was the prominence achieved by the first that aroused interest in the second.[60] In this respect, Strauss's career paralleled that of Marx, whose early work became an object of intense study only after he had achieved celebrity for his later writings.

Finally, it was Straussian hermeneutics, as a hardened methodology, which held together his following. Although this methodology clearly had political implications, it was presented as something that stood above political and cultural fashions. Like Marxism, Strauss's interpretive method became for his afficionados science, dogma, and politics all rolled into one. Still, it is worth considering how much of this final product was intended by its putative creator when he arrived in the United States.

In a counterfactual reality, Strauss might now be remembered as one among other German refugee scholars who left behind worthwhile books. This honor list would have room for, among others, Ernst Cassirer, Paul Oskar Kristeller, Hannah Arendt, Kurt Riezler, Alfred

---

At that time, Strauss and Mises both presented papers that offered opposing views on the fact-value distinction. The proceedings were subsequently published in a single volume, *Relativism and the Study of Man* (Princeton, NJ: Nostrand, 1961).

[60] See the flattering but informative sketch of Leo Strauss at the University of Chicago by Edward Banfield, "Leo Strauss" in *Remembering Teachers, Scientists and Scholars*, ed. Edward Shils (Chicago: University of Chicago Press, 1991), 490–501.

Schütz, Erich Auerbach, and Ernst Kantorowicz. These were among the stellar figures who shared Strauss's interests and exile experience, and more than a few of them had been his colleagues in New York before he went off to Chicago in 1949. Instead, like another refugee, whom Strauss may not have liked, Herbert Marcuse, he became a cultic figure, surrounded by adulators. This fate of "being turned into an idol" was one that Nietzsche scorned when he expressed preference for being a clown to an object of worship. All the same, this fate was not peculiar to the author of *Natural Right and History*. It was the destiny of other movement founders, some of whom do not fare well in Strauss's work.

3

Constructing a Methodology

Relevant and Irrelevant Criticisms

A major legacy of Leo Strauss's life and scholarship was a distinctive way of reading texts. Despite Strauss's attempt to assure Hans-Georg Gadamer in 1954 that his "hermeneutic experience is very limited and excludes the possibility of a universal hermeneutic theory," his assertion is not to be taken uncritically.[1] Strauss pioneered a way of studying political classics that his students took over and disseminated. Once created, this method was carried from Strauss's redoubt at Chicago into departments of political science and political theory across the United States and Canada.

One can identify Strauss's hermeneutic by how its adherents examine texts and by the political thinkers they interpret. Plato, Averroes, Maimonides, Machiavelli, Hobbes, Spinoza, Locke, Montesquieu, Rousseau, and Tocqueville – and less often Aristotle, Burke, and Hegel – are thinkers whom Strauss and his disciples have considered worthy of scrutiny. By contrast, they care less (except for the Catholic Straussians) about any distinctly Christian political heritage. This disinclination may come from the belief that the best political thinkers are thought to have been religious skeptics. Some Straussians have also claimed to find concealed skepticism about religious or political

---

[1] Leo Strauss, "Correspondence Concerning 'Wahrheit und Methode'," The Independent Journal of Philosophy, 2 (1978): 5–6.

authority in medieval writers who are conventionally considered orthodox Catholics.

Ours may be an age of diminished Christian faith in the West, but Straussians believe that the American regime has tended in this direction from its theoretical beginnings. Strauss's students Thomas L. Pangle and Michael Zuckert have tried to demonstrate that the United States was founded explicitly on the ideas of John Locke. In their view, Locke, if properly read, can be seen to have harbored a skeptical attitude toward religious revelation. The "American regime" was a distinctly modernist and implicitly post-Christian project, one whose Lockean founders considered religious concerns to be less important than individual material ones.[2]

Straussians employ an interpretive approach that they find outlined in their teacher's work. It may profit us to look at this method's constituent elements and to locate their sources in Strauss's writings. Like the author of *Natural Right and History*, his disciples warn against relativism, historicism, and positivism (which may be called the triple scourge); furthermore, they deny the possibility of separating facts from values, a mistake they ascribe to modern positivists and, more distantly, to Max Weber and to Weber's quest for "freedom from value judgments [Werturteilfreiheit]." Although Straussians talk up philosophy, they identify it mostly with political theory, which in its truest form, as practiced by Strauss, is "political philosophy." Philosophy in this sense usually does not mean (although there are exceptions) metaphysics or epistemology. It is preeminently about political life and the ideals that inform it.[3]

The search for the Good as an exercise in Reason is contrasted to theology, which is grounded in faith. Political philosophers may pay homage to religious myth but their real concern is conceptualizing "the best of all regimes." Straussians insist there are esoteric meanings in the texts they expound. Strauss himself had "demonstrated" this in

[2] See the introduction to Thomas L. Pangle, *The Spirit of Modern Republicanism: The Moral Vision of the American Founders and the Philosophy of Locke* (Chicago: University of Chicago Press, 1988).

[3] A lucid presentation of this view is in Hilail Gildin's introduction to *What Is Political Philosophy: Six Essays by Leo Strauss* (Indianapolis and New York: Pegasus, 1975); and the reprint of Strauss's essay "What is Political Philosophy?" 3–58.

his work on "the art of secret writing." Premodern authors hid their questioning of religion and traditional political authority by inserting different layers of meaning into their tracts. But modern interpreters can understand what they really meant because of the hints these authors put into their work. Straussians believe this tradition of esotericism started in the ancient world. Thinkers even back then were engaged in the arduous quest of protecting "philosophy" from the prying eyes of priestly and ecclesiastical authorities. This quest was common to great minds across the ages, and this esoteric tradition is accessible to the properly trained modern reader looking for the interface between politics and religion in earlier thinkers.[4]

Political thought follows a trajectory extending from the ancient and medieval periods into the modern age, which begins with the Renaissance and the scientific revolution. The older political thought was more concerned than its successor with man's moral nature and with the possibility of glimpsing the "best of all possible regimes." From the sixteenth century on, however, political thought becomes increasingly fixated on material satisfaction and, inevitably after the rise of a capitalist economy, on bourgeois comfort. Even more disturbingly, later attempts to move beyond these goals by appealing to the traditional and heroic end up glorifying violence and nihilism. This is illustrated by certain contagious, destabilizing ideas that developed most fully in Germany and which resulted in what Allan Bloom has characterized as "the German connection."

The best modernity offers can be seen in Anglo-American "liberal democracy," a form of government that emphasizes equality and natural or human rights. We should treasure this legacy as a safeguard against destructive forms of modernity. We protect liberal democratic society by providing the appropriate civics and history lessons in our schools and by talking to the young about such "democratic heroes" as Lincoln and Churchill. We thereby recapture some of the civic virtue of the ancient Greek polis and transfer it to a modern setting. In our democratic epoch, however, we should never seek to go back to the identitarian politics of the ancient world. Rather we should stress what is universal about the American political

---

[4] A defense of this hermeneutic can be found in Strauss's essay "On a Forgotten Kind of Writing," *Chicago Review*, 8, 1 (Winter–Spring 1954): 64–75.

experiment. Our American democracy, its European counterparts, and Israel (as understood through the Straussian filter) epitomize all that is best in modernity, as products of constructive Reason and as embodiments of truths that are held to be universal and universally applicable.

It is hard for outsiders to know whether Straussians truly believe in the ontological status of American democratic values. It is assumed by critics, on the basis of Strauss's comments about myth and philosophy in Plato and his approving treatment of the double truth in Averroes, that he and his disciples are transmitting exoteric teachings for those who are incapable of facing a universal moral void. This involves a distinction between exoteric and esoteric truths, a relation that has special relevance for the Straussian approach to organized religion. It is widely believed by their critics that Straussians consider religion a kind of pabulum (if not quite opium) for the philosophically weak. Although religion rightly applied can teach civic virtue and render democratic citizens more willing to fight for their regime, it is not something that a thoughtful person would wish to imbibe in large doses.

Certain objections would likely come from the Straussians, if they chose to respond to these generalizations. They might cite as a counterargument to the one proposed Stanley Rosen's informative writing on Hegel's *Science of Logic*, Steven Smith's examination of Spinoza's theology, and works on Plato by Catherine Zuckert and Joseph Cropsey.[5] All such monographs prove that Straussians have dealt with specifically philosophical problems. They might also point to such spokesmen for traditional Catholicism as Pierre Manent, Daniel Mahoney, James V.Schall, Robert P. Kraynak, and Ernest Fortin, who find no contradiction between Straussian methodology and religious faith. These political thinkers, it may be argued, combine both.[6]

---

[5] See Stanley Rosen, *G.W.F. Hegel: An Introduction to the Science of Wisdom* (New Haven, CT: Yale University Press, 1971); Joseph Cropsey, *Plato's World: Man's Place in the Cosmos* (Chicago: University of Chicago Press, 1995); Steven Smith, *Hegel's Critique of Liberalism* (Chicago: University of Chicago Press, 1991); and Catherine Zuckert, *Plato's Philosophers: The Coherence of the Dialogues* (Chicago: University of Chicago Press, 2009). The last work explores at great length the pivotal role of the figure of Socrates in the progression of Plato's dialogues. .

[6] See the interview with James V. Schall in *Telos* 148 (Fall 2009): 16–27. Robert V. Kraynak, "Living with Liberalism" in *The New Criterion* (December 2005).

Finally Strauss's defenders might note that he and his disciples have written reams of pages on the ancient Greek historians, Xenophon and Thucydides. Strauss, it might be contended, opposed not historically based thinking but the rejection of a permanent human nature and the primacy of Reason. We would likely be told that one could derive moral wisdom from historical narratives without reducing the study of government or human nature to a listing of historical particularities.

A few responses to these objections may be in order before proceeding on to other topics. Generalizations are permitted even if exceptions can be found. Moreover, the exceptions in these cases reflect the Straussian methodology, which is applied to nonpolitical as well as political questions. Zuckert and Cropsey, for example, assume Strauss's method of reading texts when they address traditional philosophical topics. They share Strauss's doubt that Plato believed in eternal forms and they affirm Strauss's contention that Plato believed not in theology but in the teaching value of myths.

Christians may appropriate for themselves bits and pieces of the Straussian method but they would be wrong to imagine that the corresponding belief system is congruent with Christian truths or with any other form of revealed religion. If devout Christians find nothing objectionable about the Straussian hermeneutic, then they should be willing to reconsider their position. They should recognize the fit between the two worldviews is more problematic than they have been willing to admit. This reassessment may be all the more necessary given the still widespread appeal of Strauss's teachings among Catholic traditionalists. Canadian political theorist Grant Havers, who has a book in progress on this subject, observes that Strauss's popularity among Catholics and Evangelicals has never generated the expected curiosity.[7] Havers addresses the question of why his subjects assume a close tie between revealed religion and Straussian doctrines. One prominent intellectual, Willmoore Kendall, converted at approximately the same time to both traditional Catholicism and Straussianism.

One should also distinguish between drawing moral lessons from historical narratives, the way one would from Aesop's Fables, and investigating historical contexts to make sense of human behavior. It

---

[7] This question is at least suggested in Grant N. Havers, "Romanticism and Universalism: The Case of Leo Strauss," *Dialogue and Universalism* 12, 6–7 (2002): 155–67.

is possible to cite historical examples as illustrative narratives, which is what Strauss does, but this practice should not be equated with historical awareness. Teaching moral lessons is not the same as presenting the circumstances in which political thinkers and historical actors have had to operate. Equally vague are the references of the Straussians to the "ancients" and "moderns" or, even more grandiloquently, to the "modern enterprise." Here one assigns such labels as "ancient" and "modern" without getting specific about the ages that one is purporting to discuss.

Athwart the Modern Age?

Against Historicism, Relativism, and Positivism
The most accessible presentation of this Straussian leitmotiv is in the first two chapters of *Natural Right and History*, but related themes are also raised in the concluding chapter, particularly Strauss's withering comments about Edmund Burke and Burke's imitators. In the introduction, Strauss asserts that our "social science may make us wise or clever as regards the means for any objective that we might choose. It admits being unable to help us in discriminating between legitimate and illegitimate, between just and unjust, objectives. Such a science is instrumental und nothing but instrumental: it is born to be the handmaiden of any power or any interests that be."[8]

This indifference to moral truth in the social sciences is ascribed to Machiavelli, who would have been willing "to give advice with equal competence and alacrity to tyrants as well as to free people."[9] Strauss deplores a similar attitude in the Austrian Jewish refugee jurist Hans Kelsen, who in his *Allgemeine Staatslehre* (Berlin, 1925) remarks that even despotism presupposes a legal order (*Rechtsordnungen*). A despotic regime is a particular kind of government that places the ultimate judicial or political decision "in the hands of the autocrat." Strauss also notes in the introduction that the "German historical sense" brought in its train an "unqualified relativism." This view is now spread into "Western thought in general," and "it would not be the first time that a nation, defeated on the battlefield and, as it

[8] Leo Strauss, *Natural Right and History*, 3–4.
[9] Ibid., 4.

were, annihilated as a political being, has deprived its conquerors of the most sublime fruit of victory by imposing on them the yoke of its own thought."[10]

"Natural Right and the Historical Approach," which is the first chapter after the introduction, dwells on the historicism, "which emerged in reaction to the French Revolution and to the natural rights doctrine that had prepared that cataclysm." This ism unleashed a more radical course of change than even the French Revolution (as we are told again with reference to Burke) by explicitly rejecting "universal or abstract principles."[11] Historicists, who rose to prominence in Germany in the nineteenth century, revolted against Reason or any attempt to judge "conventional," inherited institutions from the standpoint of Reason or any universal standard: "The historical school had obscured the fact that particular or historical standards can become authoritative only on the basis of a universal principle which imposes an obligation on the individual to accept or to bow to the standard suggested by the tradition or the situation which molded him."[12] Strauss also presents historicism as a "particular form of positivism" that outgrew its original framework. Although like positivists, historicists once privileged empirical method in constructing a "science" of history, they came to insist that history could only be understood as process rather than by ordinary empirical methods.

Among its inherent difficulties, beyond its moral cynicism and denial of natural rights, is that historicism cannot deal with its eventual obsolescence. "To assert the historicist thesis means to doubt it and thus to transcend it." Although historicism "claims to have brought to light a truth which has come to stay, a truth valid for all time," even its own insight must change as the setting moves from one age to the next. Against this, the historicist implausibly asserts that historical insight has reached its end with the victory of historicism: "[T]he historicist is not impressed by the prospect that historicism may be superseded in due time by the denial of historicism." Indeed, this ideology "thrives on the fact that it inconsistently exempts itself from its own verdict about all human thought."[13]

[10] Ibid., 2.
[11] Ibid., 13.
[12] Ibid., 15.
[13] Ibid., 25.

One finds among these critical observations a statement of disapproval about Marxism, which may be the historical theory that comes closest to Strauss's description of the historicist fallacy. In the lecture on historicism, the critical focus shifts gradually from counterrevolutionary to progressive historicists. The latter group championed the Enlightenment and its picture of history as a punctuated movement out of an unenlightened past. Theorists such as Marx taught that the renunciation of historicist assumptions would produce a "relapse" into less scientific times.

Some historicists have tried to escape this contradiction, Strauss tells us, between their claim to transcendent knowledge and their belief in historical relativity. A figure of towering importance in this group was Hegel. A German philosopher of the early nineteenth century, he developed the idea of an "absolute moment in history," a privileged point from which one could judge the beliefs of the past without having to deal with the possible evanescence of one's own judgmental perspective.

However, this Hegelian path would be closed to historicists who were not metaphysically inclined. For unlike Hegel, such historicists would not be able to locate an absolute moment "in which philosophy, or the quest for wisdom, had been transformed into wisdom, that is, the moment in which the fundamental riddles have been solved." [14] More pedestrian historicists reject the Hegelian assumptions about a providential history with theological underpinnings. They scoff at any teaching about the Absolute as Spirit – that is, an entity that is pouring out its content into human events and the human mind. Strauss depicts the Marxists as a "radical" subgenus of the historicist movement but one whose radicalism is shown in its disavowal of its Hegelian origins. Marxists have traded metaphysics for material history.

The Fact-Value Dichotomy

Although Strauss revisits this (for him) urgent theme in the essays "Relativism" and "The Political Crisis of Our Time," the fact-value dichotomy receives its fullest treatment from Strauss in the third chapter of *Natural Right and History*. In this chapter, one encounters a detailed

---

[14] Ibid., 29.

examination of the "Distinction between Facts and Values." Strauss's long discussion of this distinction points back to his wrestling with the German academic luminary Max Weber and with his continuing assessment of the German intellectual contribution to the Nazi catastrophe.

The unwillingness among social scientists to notice the interrelatedness of facts and values is supposedly further proof of Strauss's arguments in the preceding two lectures-chapters, namely that the defeated German nation and the illusions of historicism and relativism are corrupting the post–Second World War West. The debate over the relation of facts to values and Max Weber's contribution to this discussion overflow any single chapter and are brought up repeatedly in the Lectures. The meticulous reading of both Weber's *Religionssoziologie* and his *Wissenschaftslehre* suggests the extent of Strauss's preoccupation with their author. Like Heidegger and Nietzsche, Weber was someone whom Strauss never got beyond confronting.

With regard to this engagement, Nasser Behnegar maintains that it is impossible to do justice to Weber's notion of value-free social science without considering Strauss's "corrective" analysis. Although Strauss does not prove beyond doubt that Weber's perspective "leads to nihilism," he does stress that Weber's thinking "fosters not so much nihilism as conformism and philistinism." It thereby lets nihilism in through the back door by fostering "an easygoing conformism and philistinism," a concern that Weber himself expressed more than once.[15]

The assault on Weber's judgments about the Protestant ethic and the spirit of capitalism, together with allusions to Calvin's negative view of capital investment, can be traced back to R. H. Tawney (1880–1962), who wrote on the economic views of the Protestant Reformers. While in England in 1935, Strauss met Tawney, a father of the Christian Socialist Movement, and the two formed a long-time friendship. The references to Calvin and his early followers as being inimical to capital accumulation and unjust pricing are derived from Tawney's magnum opus, *Religion and the Rise of Capitalism* (1926).[16] So too is the view of Weber found in the third lecture as someone who avoided mention

---

[15] Nasser Behnegar, *Leo Strauss, Max Weber and the Study of Politics* (Chicago: University of Chicago Press, 2003), 209.

[16] See Simon J. D. Green, "The Tawney-Strauss Connection," *Journal of Modern History* (June 1995): 255–77; and *Natural Right and History*, 58–22.

of the fact that Calvinism was "corrupted" or had "degenerated": "What Weber should have said was that the corruption of Calvinist theology led to the emergence of the capitalist spirit."

Supposedly Weber would not make such damning judgments because he believed in a value-free analysis. But Strauss ignores a critical factor in Tawney's acidic appraisal of Weber's interpretation of the Calvinist roots of capitalism. Tawney was an outspoken opponent of the capitalist economic system and was far from dispassionate in tracing the Calvinist road to economic modernity. As a corrective, one might consult Benjamin Nelson's *The Idea of Usury: From Tribal Brotherhood to Universal Otherhood*, a work dealing with Calvin's break from medieval scholastic and Rabbinic views about commercial investment.[17]

Perhaps more vital to Strauss's brief than his remarks about Calvinism and capitalism is his examination of Weber's attempt to divorce values from scientific facts. He specifies three problems with Weber's formulation of a social scientific investigation that is value-free or value-neutral. One is that such an approach cannot truly understand the past because it assumes that the value judgments up until the advent of value-free science were flawed: "Knowing beforehand that thought was based on fundamental delusion, he [the social scientist] lacks the incentive to understand the past as it understood itself."[18]

Two is that the examination of values that characterizes the social sciences and history presupposes an appreciation of what one is analyzing. Even the researcher who claims to stand above values is repeatedly forced to judge as well as examine social phenomena. This requires that person "to distinguish between the genuine and the spurious, and between the higher and the lower." Strauss properly asks how the *Auswertung* that Weber considers essential for social research is even possible unless value judgments, however concealed, continue to be formed and expressed: "Only on the basis of such acceptance or rejection of values, of 'ultimate values' do the objects of the social sciences come to sight." Strauss observes that Weber carefully

[17] See Benjamin J. Nelson, *The Idea of Usury: From Tribal Brotherhood to Universal Otherhood* (Chicago: University of Chicago Press, 1969), and my essay "The Western Case against Usury," *Thought*, 60, 236 (March 1985): 89–98.
[18] *Natural Right and History*, 62.

distinguishes cults of magic from more fully developed religion. He inserts into what is supposed to be a "value-free" study of world religions such emotionally loaded terms as "priestly formalism," "petrified maxims," "sublime" religious thinking, and "pure sorcery."[19]

Strauss also attributes to Weber a "neo-Kantian" view of reality that "few people today would be satisfied with." Like Kant, who separated moral judgment from the realm in which actual people live, Weber provided an "articulation of reality" that operated as a construct. It was based on ideal types "which are not even meant to correspond to the intrinsic articulation of social reality," whence the ideal as opposed to real Calvinist capitalist in his study of Protestantism. Whence also Weber's labored attempt to reach value-free judgments while pursuing the study of values.[20]

Three is that Strauss interprets Weber's oft-cited comment in the *Wissenschaftslehre* that "the present age is witnessing a titanic struggle being fought over values" by pointing to two conclusions that this observation is meant to make us aware of. First, "the conflict between values was part of the comprehensive view, according to which human life is inescapable conflict; and second, "there is no hierarchy of values: all values are of the same rank."[21] The question that is not answered but which will be engaged in the next chapter is: What exactly are the "values" to which Weber is referring in this passage? Equally important, should the observation about competing values be accepted as a permanent, inescapable fate, perhaps one decreed by the Eumenides? Or, pace Strauss, is value-competition, as described by Weber, a historically conditioned problem that Weber understood as peculiar to the modern West?

Political Philosophy as the Search for Ultimate Truth

As true "political philosophy," Strauss cites Plato's *Republic*, and particularly Socrates' discussions of the best constitution enforced by the best of men who are guided by *logistikon* (the application of

[19] Ibid., 55.

[20] Ibid., 77–78.

[21] *Natural Right and History*, 63–64, 73–77; Max Weber, *Gesanmmelte Aufsätze. Zur Wissenschaftsehre*, ed. Johannes Winckelmann (Tübingen: Mohr Siebeck, 1998), 507–10, 512–18; and Leo Strauss, "The Social Science of Max Weber," *Measure*, II, 2 (Spring): 204–30.

reasoning power); these are the preconditions for designing a truly virtuous society. In this perfect regime, such ethical virtues as justice (*dikaiosunē*) and restraint (*sophrosunē*) would come to prevail, and Plato assigns to such virtues a special importance inasmuch as they correspond to *eidē aitia*, eternal forms. One might gather from Socrates but not from Strauss that these forms have a divine source and are constituent of human knowledge. Another teaching in the *Republic* that strengthens the correspondence between philosophy and politics concerns the content of the individual soul. Justice in the soul is seen to relate to justice in the city, as Strauss reminds us in his essay "On Plato's Republic" in *The City and Man*.[22]

Moreover, the social organization of the ideal city must be made to reflect the ascending and descending hierarchy of knowledge, from the epistemic truth accessible to the philosophically inclined rulers, to discursive reasoning (*dianoia*) in the city's guardians, to mere opinion or *eidolē* (images) among those who ply unimaginative trades or perform servile labor. The construction of what is intended to be the ideal city is based on perfect justice. It is also a preeminently philosophical enterprise, but one that is circumscribed by specifically Straussian parameters. Ontological and theological questions receive relatively short shrift, whereas the sections dealing with politically relevant virtues are made to occupy front-stage.[23]

Even more significantly, Strauss stresses that for Socrates, as we learn at the end of Book Nine, the ideal republic "can only exist in Heaven."[24] Further, the search for justice that has occupied an entire night's dialogue is an aporetic exercise that ends in unanswered questions. That, for Strauss, is the nature of philosophical inquiry at

---

[22] See Leo Strauss's essay "On Plato's Republic" in *The City and Man* (Chicago: Rand McNally and Company, 1964), 50–138.

[23] See Strauss's essay "Plato" in *History of Political Philosophy*, ed. Leo Strauss and Joseph Cropsey (Chicago: Rand McNally and Company, 1963), 7–63.

[24] See Plato, *Res Publica*, Oxford Classical Texts, book 9 (Oxford: Oxford University Press, 1965), section 592. *The City and Man*, 137–38; Strauss stresses the incompleteness of Socrates's teaching in *The Republic*, in which the philosopher argues that Justice can be found in "the right order of the soul." Strauss maintains that "the parallel between soul and city, which is the premise of the doctrine of the soul," is "evidently questionable and even untenable." He observes that Socrates "cannot bring to light the nature of the soul" and instead approaches his subject by speaking about the body and joys of *eros*. See ibid., 138.

the end of the day: The Socratic *eristikē* is a process that ends not in metaphysical answers but in the search for "knowledge of the good." "What we call moral virtue," observes Strauss in his essay "Jerusalem and Athens" is "the by-product of that quest [for knowledge]."[25]

Just as the best republic cannot be put into practice, as Socrates' interlocutors point out, without creating wealth and other contaminating conditions, the quest for philosophical truth, as the search for political justice, must end with lowered expectations. Strauss reminds us that Plato's student, Aristotle, had lowered his sights in his quest for political virtue. He presented politics in the *Metaphysics* as a form of "technical knowledge" rather than as a higher mode of knowing. This relegation of politics to an order of knowing below philosophy began the fateful divorce of political thought from the study of permanent truth.[26]

Although Strauss is not entirely consistent in his reading of Aristotle, to whom in a later polemic against the "New Political Science" he ascribes the association of science, including political studies, with philosophy,[27] in this more conventional reading, Aristotle's treatment of politics is presented as technical, not epistemic, knowledge. One should also note that Martin Heidegger, who, for Strauss, raised moral difficulties, downplayed the study of politics as philosophy. It was Heidegger who moved the study of Being away from any focus on ethics. According to Strauss, only a reunion of philosophy and politics in pursuit of Justice could help the modern West reverse its path toward nihilism. The dangerous straying that had taken place was already implicit in the loss of interest in political virtues.

Philosophy and Theology: A Fateful Confrontation

Strauss does not depict the antagonism between philosophy as a rational exercise and religion as a nonrational faith in a necessarily invidious

---

[25] See Leo Strauss, *Studies in Platonic Political Philosophy* (Chicago and London: University of Chicago Press, 1983), 126, 172; and Thomas L. Pangle's introduction to this volume, 1–26.

[26] See *The City and Man*, 24–25; Aristotle, *Metaphysica*; Oxford Classical Texts (Oxford: Oxford University Press, 1957) 981, a–b.

[27] While Strauss acknowledges the philosophically inferior position that Aristotle occupies relative to Plato in the discussion of political activity, he also stresses the importance of Aristotle's teaching of prudence (*phronimon*). This quality of mind and character is seen as essential to sound political life. Strauss thereby finds a linkage between his own political philosophy and Aristotle's concept of moral virtue.

way. In "Jerusalem and Athens," he contrasts the prophet as "the faithful servant of the Lord" to the philosopher, "who dedicates his life to
the quest for the good or the idea of the good." Further, "the prophet
addresses the people, while Socrates engages in conversation with one
man, which means that he can address questions to him."[28] In his early
years, as Steven Smith notes, Strauss was preoccupied with the question of Jewish identity, and although he never took the road back to
Orthodoxy or even to Franz Rosenzweig's neo-Orthodox Jewish religiosity, Strauss always wrote with deep respect about Hebrew Scripture.

There are also generally sympathetic statements in the Lectures to
John Calvin as a Christian theologian.[29] Strauss, like other students of
religion (including this author), must have noticed a similarity between
Calvin's sovereign deity and the God of the Old Testament. In the
young Strauss one also finds a speculative defense of Orthodoxy as a
body of ideas, which he employs against the liberal critique of Spinoza:
"For all assertions of Orthodoxy rest on the irrefutable premise that
the omnipotent God, whose will is unfathomable, whose ways are not
our ways, who has decided to dwell in the thick darkness, may exist.
Given this premise, miracles and revelations in particular, are possible.
Spinoza has not succeeded in showing that this premise is contradicted
by anything we know."[30]

Despite such offsetting statements, Strauss generally viewed revealed
religion, from classical Greece onward, as extraneous and occasionally
harmful to the philosophical enterprise. His treatment of Greek religious beliefs in his commentaries on Plato indicates that these images
relate to a teaching method but do not express the real beliefs of those
who wish to be philosophers. Strauss never feels obliged to ask himself
whether Socrates or Plato believes in the Olympian pantheon or in the
heavenly realm described in the *Phaedrus*, *Republic*, and *Timaeus*. True
philosophers supposedly appealed to *mythologia* as a means of reaching their audience through arresting images and familiar narratives.[31]

---

[28] *Studies in Platonic Political Philosophy*, 170.
[29] See *Natural Right and History*, 58–62.
[30] See the "Preface to Spinoza's Critique of Religion," in *Liberalism Ancient and Modern*, 254.
[31] *The City and Man*, 34–35; Strauss properly notes that the *Republic*, Book Ten, begins
with a fierce denunciation of poetry, and particularly tragedy, for confecting what is
a "mere imitation" of philosophical truth.

The ancient philosopher exemplified what Strauss referred to as "classical political rationalism." Such men applied reason to their inquiries without coming to definitive answers, other than the certainty that the Good existed and that it was rationally knowable. Strauss carries this reading of Plato so far that he famously challenges the idea that Plato believed in eternal forms as the source of knowledge. Strauss fell back on Averroes and the Averroistic reading of the *Phaedrus* and other Platonic dialogues to question whether Plato or Socrates took metaphysical and theological assumptions for anything more than a pedagogic device. Mythical narratives were ways of illustrating points or piquing curiosity, but those who earned the appellation "philosopher" never took theology to be anything more.

Notably, there is nothing novel about this approach to reading Greek philosophy. Although scientific rationalists have credited Aristotle rather than Plato with previewing their worldview, the prominent historian and defender of rationalism John Herman Randall traced scientific Reason back to the ancient Greeks. In all fairness, it must be said that Strauss never thought that he was contributing a chapter to anyone's "making of the modern world." But his rationalist reading of the ancients and his skepticism about their theological frame of reference suggest at least some overlap with the modern celebration of the rational tradition.[32] Strauss was no friend of rationalism in its purely "modern" form, but his thinking about the Greeks indicates (to this reader) a modern rationalist perspective in his understanding of Greek philosophy.

Exoteric and Esoteric Readings

An entire tome devoted to *Persecution and the Art of Writing* appeared only in 1952, but discussions of this topic came up in Strauss's early work as well. In the preface to his study of Spinoza's *Theologico-Political Treatise* (written in its first draft in the mid-1920s) and in his interpretive work on Maimonides' *Guide for the Perplexed* (from the

---

[32] See, for example, Strauss's "The Liberalism of Classical Political Philosophy," *The Review of Metaphysics*, XII, 3 (March 1959): 390–439; and Leo Strauss *The Rebirth of Classical Political Rationalsm*, essays and lectures selected and introduced by Thomas L. Pangle (Chicago: University of Chicago Press, 1989).

early 1930s), Strauss hints at his later distinction between esoteric and exoteric readings. This foreshadowing seems to contradict what is stated by Strauss's student Allan Bloom, namely that the study of esoteric meanings is only characteristic of Strauss's "second phase dominated by the discovery of secret writing." The earlier phase, according to Bloom, was shaped by his "individual political-theological concerns," whence came his studies of Spinoza and Maimonides, when Strauss was still in Germany.[33] In his pre-secret-writings phase, according to Bloom, Strauss produced his treatise on Hobbes, without resorting to all his later interpretive tools: "It is no mere accident that the Hobbes book, the book he liked the least, remains the one most reputed and uncontroversial in the scholarly community."[34]

Bloom mentions, however, that the early Strauss showed some interest in secret writing, before his arrival in the United States. For example, Strauss argues, against Hermann Cohen's claim, that Spinoza was not being disloyal to his people by presenting an "idealized Christianity" against a "carnal and political Judaism."[35] This was part of a consistently applied strategy. "The purpose of the *Treatise* – is to show the way toward a liberal society." Its establishment "required in his opinion the abrogation of the Mosaic Law insofar as it is particularistic and political law, and especially the ceremonial law." If Jews are to be allowed to enter a liberal society, they "cannot be at the same time members of two nations and subject to two comprehensive codes."[36]

Strauss also underscores in his writing on Spinoza the fear of the Spanish Inquisition that haunted the Jewish community in Holland, to which Spinoza's family belonged.[37] Even in the relatively tolerant Dutch Protestant society of his day, Spinoza may have felt compelled to adopt protective coloration by defending the New Testament against the Old. At the same time, Spinoza spoke favorably at some points in his tract about the "universalism" of the Jewish Prophets, a hint that indicates his awareness of an Old Testament foundation for universal ethics.

---

[33] Allan Bloom, *Giants and Dwarfs: Essays 1960–1996* (New York: Simon And Schuster, 1990), 244–45.

[34] Ibid., 246.

[35] *Liberalism Ancient and Modern*, 244.

[36] Ibid., 245.

[37] Ibid., 250–51.

According to Strauss, the *Treatise* provides an assimilationist solution for Jews in a liberal society. Jews could become equal citizens of a modern commonwealth if they were willing to give up their particularistic way of life. The *Treatise* teaches a further lesson for those who are able to read between the lines: "Freedom of philosophy requires or seems to require, a liberal state, and a liberal state is a state which is not as such either Christian or Jewish."[38]

In his commentary on the twelfth-century Rabbinic commentator and Aristotelian, Maimonides, Strauss brings to light other esoteric meanings. These supposedly could be discerned if one peered beneath the orthodox Jewish veneer of Maimonides' work: "The *Guide* contains a public teaching and a secret teaching. The public teaching is addressed to every Jew, including the vulgar; the secret teaching is addressed to the elite. The secret teaching is of no use to the vulgar, and the elite does not need the *Guide* for being apprised of the public teaching."[39] The *Guide* is dedicated to the author's disciple, Joseph, who, it is assumed, would be able to grasp the true meaning of the Jewish Law. Strauss also examines closely what seem to be contradictions in the *Guide* and arrives at the conclusion that its author is only affirming on a conventional level "the Law as seen through traditional Jewish interpretation."[40]

This conventional view of the Law is not predicated on philosophical demonstration, nor does the acceptance of the Law result from religious experience, as opposed to the continuity of tradition. Indeed, there is no certainty outside of the acceptance of tradition that revealed truths, including the Decalogue, are anything more than "human speculations." According to Strauss, however, the *Guide* – which is not addressed to the Jewish masses – is concerned with philosophy, not with a vindication of tradition. Faith is seen as only one of other

[38] Ibid., 246. Despite his high praise for Cohen "as the one who surpassed in spiritual power all other German professors of philosophy of his generation," Strauss explicitly rejects Cohen's treatment of Spinoza as a Jewish renegade. He notes the hypocrisy of Cohen's attack on Spinoza for "not rejecting war," considering that Cohen upheld a right to violent revolution as consistent with his Kantian ethic. Strauss also states with impatience that Cohen paid no attention to "revolutionary victims," 246–47.

[39] See the introductory essay to Moses Maimonides, *The Guide of the Perplexed* "How to Begin to Study the Guide of the Perplexed" in *Liberalism Ancient and Modern*, 148.

[40] Ibid., 165.

moral virtues, and it "does not belong to man's ultimate perfection, the perfection of his intellect."[41] Here, we are told, are the beginnings of a Jewish tradition of separating philosophical speculation from the Mosaic Law and its authoritative Rabbinic glosses.

Strauss's treatment of Spinoza, Maimonides, and later Plato as esoteric writers encouraged among his disciples a search for secret meanings in texts addressed to more than one readership. This practice was derived from the belief that past writers hesitated to express their real views, which featured philosophical rationalism and/or political liberalism. Great past thinkers are depicted as having been more skeptical in approaching established authority and revealed religion than others of their generation.

Strauss's defenders insist that their master did not investigate "the art of secret writing" in the way in which he has been charged with doing. Strauss's distinction between exoteric and esoteric readings was not designed to justify undemocratic rule. His examination of political rationalism and liberal attitudes helped him see that political philosophers until recently were forced to hide what they really thought. In *Persecution and the Art of Writing*, Strauss clarified why "writing between the lines" was necessary when investigating thinkers "in an era of persecution, that is, at a time when some political or other orthodoxy was enforced by law or custom."[42] Strauss was only making allowances for the awkward situation in which thinkers found themselves in the predemocratic past. As the Zuckerts explain in *The Truth about Leo Strauss*, those whom Strauss interpreted were not devious individuals trying to mislead others. They were acting in a socially responsible manner in the face of intolerant rulers.[43]

[41] Ibid., 166. Most of the arguments for this reading of Maimonides are present in the Urtext first published in France as "Maimunis Lehre von der Prophetie und ihre Quellen" in *Le Monde Oriental* XXXVIII (1934): 99–139. In the following year, the Maimonides study came out in its book form as *Philosophie und Gesetz: Beiträge zum Verständnis Maimunis und seiner Vorläufer* (Berlin: Schocken, 1935).

[42] Leo Strauss, *Persecution and the Art of Writing*, reprint (Chicago: University of Chicago Press, 1980), 32; Stanley Rosen, *Hermeneutics as Politics* (New York: Oxford University Press, 1987), 112–14; and Michael S. Kochin, "Morality, Nature and Esotericism in Leo Strauss's *Persecution and the Art of Writing*," *Review of Politics* 64, 2 (Spring 2002): 261–83.

[43] Catherine and Michael Zuckert, *The Truth about Leo Strauss: Political Philosophy and American Democracy* (Chicago: University of Chicago Press, 2006), 136–54.

Good vs. Bad Modernity

Contrary to the assertions of their critics, neither Strauss nor his disciples have expressed any desire to restore an ancient political society. One of their major quarrels has been with the New Zealand historian J. G. A. Pocock, who contended that American republicanism was shaped by the classical revival that came out of the Renaissance and especially the works of Machiavelli. Straussians have retorted that there was nothing but the most superficial connection between Roman republicanism and the American founding. According to Thomas L. Pangle, the American constitutional republic was conceived as a Lockean social contract, and the attempt to associate its construction with ancient models is simply misguided. A thousand-page work, *Republics: Ancient and Modern*, by the Straussian Paul Rahe quotes from the American founders and other eighteenth-century figures to prove that the framers of the constitution felt contempt for ancient governments. They were convinced they were fashioning a more open society than any that had existed in the ancient world.[44]

Perhaps the best-known Straussian author to have insisted on the strictly modernist, exclusively Lockean origins of the American republic is Thomas L. Pangle. In *The Spirit of Modern Republicanism: The Moral Vision of the American Founders and the Philosophy of Locke*, Pangle minimizes the effect of classical republican ideas on the achievements of Madison and other American framers. He also maintains that even the complimentary references among the founders to non-Lockean sources should not be assigned excessive importance.[45] The seedbed of the American federal framework was Locke's concept of natural rights and his contractarian view of the formation of civil society. With persistent care, Pangle plays down any Protestant or Christian influence on the constitutional formation of the American Republic.

In only one way would it be proper to say that Strauss and his disciples considered classical antiquity to be superior to their own time

44 Paul A. Rahe, *Republics Ancient and Modern*, Volume III; *Inventions of Prudence: Constituting the American Regime* (Chapel Hill: University of North Carolina Press, 1994).
45 See Thomas L. Pangle, *The Spirit of Modern Republicanism: The Moral Vision of the American Founders and the Philosophy of John Locke* (Chicago: University of Chicago Press, 1988), 28–37, 49–53.

and society. The ancients gave us Plato, who in the Straussian hierarchy was elevated to the paradigmatic political philosopher. When
properly read, Plato could be credited with fathering the intellectual
quest that the Straussians claim to be embarked on. But later thinkers
in antiquity and certainly in the Christian Middle Ages had declined
from Plato's high standard of inquiry, and that decline was perceptible
even before the arrival of Machiavelli, Hobbes, Spinoza, and Locke.
Some Straussian interpreters, and perhaps most notably Mary P.
Nichols, have read into Aristotle and other ancient Greek thinkers ethical views that are compatible with the present age. Nichols has given
a recognizably progressive gloss to Aristotle's comments about slavery and the subordination of women to their husbands in the *Politics*
and *Nicomachean Ethics*. She contends that such comments have been
largely misinterpreted. Aristotle spoke about the natural slave (*doulos
kata phusin*) as a reproach directed against conventional Greek servi-
tude, whereas his assertion that women, as incomplete beings (*ateleis*),
should be under their husbands' care was based on recognition that
in ancient Athens, wives were much younger than their spouses.[46]
However one may read such attempts at reconciling the social positions of Greek philosophers with modern ideas of social equality, such
interpretations should not be imagined to elevate in dignity classical
Greek institutions above our own political arrangements. Rather they
indicate a strenuous effort to make ancient Greek thinkers look like
forerunners of the present age.

Modern Polarities

The critical distinction for Straussians in understanding political life is
not between antiquity and modernity. Rather it is between contrasting

[46] See Mary P. Nichols, *Citizens and Statesmen: A Study of Aristotle's Politics*
(Savage, MD: Rowman and Littlefield, 1992), especially 184, and Aristotle's *Ethica
Nicomachea*, 1161a, 35, 1162, 1–10; *Politica*, 1252a, 31–32; 1277b, 24–25. Contrary
to this view, Aristotle in the *Nicomachean Ethics* considers it a mark of aristocracy
that women should be subordinate to men (*kath akzian*), according to natural rank.
Oligarchy, which is thought to be a morally inferior polity, allows women to control
wealth and to influence political power by virtue of their right to inherit (*epiklēroi*).
1160b, 31–35, 1160a, 1–2. One should also consult M. I. Finley's unsurpassed struc-
turalist examination of slavery in Greco-Roman antiquity in *The Ancient Economy*
(Berkeley and Los Angeles: University of California Press, 1973), especially 62–94.

types of modern societies. The Anglosphere in its liberal democratic phase embodies for Straussians the best of modernity, whereas the German political and cultural heritage illustrates for them its shadow side. Despite the unsavory role assigned to Burke as a father of historicism, the Straussian version of a rogues' gallery includes for the most part Germans.

In contrast to the Anglosphere, pre-Nazi Germany, as evoked in the preface to the English edition of Strauss's Spinoza study, is grim and forbidding. Up until the Weimar Republic, Germany withheld full political rights from Strauss's fellow German Jews, and the election of Field Marshal von Hindenburg as president of the Reich in 1925 "showed everyone who had eyes to see that the Weimar Republic had only a short time to live: the old Germany was stronger – stronger in will – than the new Germany."[47] Although Strauss wrote in bitter disappointment, it is hard to ignore the implications of these emotive statements: "All profound German longings – all those longings for the origins or, negatively expressed, all German dissatisfactions with modernity pointed the way toward a third Reich, for Germany was to be the core of even Nietzsche's Europe ruling the planet." Furthermore, "The Weimar Republic was succeed by the only German regime – by the only regime that ever was anywhere – which had no other clear principle except murderous hatred of the Jews."[48]

Such passages point to a major concern among Strauss's students, namely that the specifically German path toward a viciously anti-Semitic form of fascism must never again be taken in Germany or anywhere else. This concern is already present in Strauss's lecture, titled "German Nihilism," delivered at the New School for Social Research in New York City on February 26, 1941. Indeed, it is hard to find any more definitive statement by Strauss concerning the German cultural danger than this call to arms in 1941. Here Strauss makes clear that "German nihilism is not absolute nihilism, desire for the destruction of everything including oneself, but a desire for the destruction of something specific, of modern civilization."[49] This "negation of

[47] *Liberalism Ancient and Modern*, 224.
[48] Ibid., 226.
[49] Leo Strauss, "German Nihilism," ed. David Janssens and Daniel Tanguay, *Interpretation* 26.3 (Spring 1999): 358.

modern civilization, the No, is not guided, or accompanied, by any moral conception"; nonetheless it is "a moral protest." It favors the "closed society" over the open one and stands "against modern civilization, against the spirit of the West, and in particular the Anglo-Saxon West."[50] In a tribute to his teacher, produced shortly after his death, Bloom reminds the reader that Strauss's prolonged campaign against the social sciences in the United States was really aimed at "German philosophy."[51]

The cult of Churchill among Straussians points back to the ever-present German danger and to the need to guard against this incubus in thought as well as in politics. The Churchill cult also affirms Anglo-American democracy and its exceptional goodness, a judgment that is already present in Strauss's lecture on German nihilism. Finally, the cult of Churchill and its tribute to Anglo-American democracy serve as what Quentin Skinner refers to as "illocutionary" political rhetoric – that is, utterances or gestures that point us toward a particular political practice or context. One intended effect of the Straussian cultic celebrations during the Cold War was generating opposition to the Soviets for their antidemocratic and anti-Israeli positions. Another purpose was to make the receptive reader more vigilant against anti- or undemocratic thought in the academy.

The same political concerns led Strauss's disciple Harry V. Jaffa to set up the Claremont Institute in Pomona as a center for honoring Churchill the model democrat. Straussians would then establish a second center for this cult and its accompanying politics at Hillsdale College in Michigan, where Jaffa's student, Larry P. Arnn, became president. On Hillsdale's grounds one can find a perpetual exhibit to commemorate Churchill's "democratic" achievements.[52] At Claremont

---

[50] Ibid; 358 and 362–64.
[51] *Giants and Dwarfs*, 248.
[52] See the review by Larry Arnn of Paul Johnson's encomiastic biography *Churchill* (New York: Viking, 2010) in *Commentary* (April 2010): 61–62; and Arnn's frequent contributions to the *Claremont Review*. A professionally successful devotee of Jaffa, Arnn was president of the Caremont Institute before he moved on to the presidency at Hillsdale. See the official Larry P. Arnn fan club/facebook, celebrating his contributions to the Churchill cult: www.facebook.com/group.php.gld=2202808862. As a biting corrective, see R. J. Stove's essay on Thomas Babington Macaulay, which also touches on Churchill as a historian and on Strauss as an unqualified admirer of Churchill's oeuvre, "Compulsively Readable," *Annals Australasia* (August 24, 2010): 24–27.

and Hillsdale and on the pages of *National Review*, particularly in the contributions of the Jaffaite Charles Kesler, the cult of democratic heroes has been expanded to include Abraham Lincoln and, occasionally, Woodrow Wilson, or at least the Wilson who was the enemy of German autocracy in the First World War. Whereas Churchill is extolled for battling the German threat to democracy in two world wars, Lincoln is credited with redeeming the promise of the Declaration of Independence by promoting the ideal of democratic equality.

In this now authoritative Straussian view, twentieth-century modernity has brought forth two aberrations the results of which continue to plague us: German political deeds and philosophical transgressions; and the repeated attempts to escape from liberal democratic modernity in its present American incarnation. Political revulsion for the Germans is graphically exemplified by an essay in *The Public Interest* (Spring 1983), published by Strauss's student, David Lewis Schaefer. The target here is the economist John Maynard Keynes, who criticized the Allied demand at Versailles in 1919 that the German pay unspecified reparations.[53] Apparently Keynes, who stressed the possible harmful effects of a "Carthaginian peace" for the postwar European economy, was engaging in moral relativism. Behind his apparent economic analysis was an equation of "German autocracy" with "Anglo-American democracy." Keynes was guilty of what the neoconservative later condemned as the sin of "moral equivalence."

Equally harmful from the Straussian perspective is the attempt to retreat into a premodern political culture, a transgression attributed to participants in the Nietzschean-Heideggerian wave of modernity. Thomas L. Pangle has tweaked the German Jewish scholar Hannah Arendt for her favorable remarks about some premodern political forms. Arendt's praise for Aristotle's polis, and her hope that it could be revived in some modified form, is thought to betray antidemocratic thinking. And this came from a bearer of the German connection, who had been Heidegger's lover as well as disciple. From Pangle's perspective, it would be best to abandon such harmful diversions and to affirm Locke's natural-right concepts.[54]

---

[53] David Lewis Schaefer, "The Political Philosophy of Keynes," *The Public Interest*, 71 (Spring 1983), 45–61.
[54] *The Spirit of Modern Republicanism*, 49–61.

Given their idealization of America as the embodiment of universal democratic values, one can easily understand why Straussians are considered intensely patriotic. They defend their ideal conception of their country, in which the past is praised to whatever extent it leads to the present. We are warned against being too harsh on our shining liberal democratic model lest we do harm to what Strauss's followers view as a contemporary success story.

Afterthoughts

A few qualifying statements may be required to clarify the purpose of this chapter. The focus here has been on texts and passages that illustrate the Straussian hermeneutic. Not everything that Strauss wrote, which runs to thousands of printed pages, is equally suitable for our study. Indeed, long stretches of his writing feature conventional and in some cases not particularly original examinations of political theoretical works. Strauss drew on Paul Friedländer, Werner Jäger, and other classicists in his interpretations of Plato's dialogues, and his brief against Machiavelli as "a teacher of evil" incorporates earlier polemics directed against the Renaissance's father of political realism. One does not find everywhere in Strauss's published work the kind of hermeneutic this study is highlighting.

The interpretive perspective we are dealing with is also the one that Strauss bequeathed to his disciples. From our perspective, *Natural Right and History* is more relevant than Strauss's "Notes on Lucretius," "Marsilius of Padua,"[55] or his work on Thomas Hobbes. Some of Strauss's works exemplify better than others the methodology being explored. This is especially true for those texts that reveal a relation between how Strauss interpreted texts and his stated political positions.

Strauss himself insisted on judging political thinkers by the fruits of their ideas. By this stringent standard, we are urged to admire Locke as a teacher of democratic freedom, however flat his morality may seem to us. Likewise, Strauss provides reasons to shun, or even to keep in a locked drawer, Nietzsche and Heidegger, who in some ways, it is

---

[55] One can find examples of these essays in *Liberalism Ancient and Modern*, 71–139, 185–202.

alleged, greased the skids for Hitler. We are supposed to treat political theorists as at least partly responsible for the effects of their ideas on others. It is therefore fitting that the approach to political philosophy taught by Strauss and his disciples be interpreted not as a value-free method but as one fraught with political values.

Fairness, however, dictates that we mention that unlike his followers, Strauss in the 1960s foresaw the true lines of division between "liberals" and "conservatives." In his preface to *Liberalism Ancient and Modern*, he abandons his customary distinction between "liberal democracy" and its enemies to observe the tension between "modern liberals" and "conservatives." Strauss tries to narrow this difference by stating that most people are "moderate" in their identification with either of the two ideological poles; therefore, the distinction between them might not amount to much in the end. Strauss then muddies the water by telling us that "the conservatism of our age is identical with what was originally liberalism." Indeed, "much of what goes now by the name of conservatism has in the last analysis a common root with present-day liberalism and even with Communism."[56]

All of this repeats what are merely truisms. No one but a historical illiterate or a hardened, time-bound ideologue would deny that the current Right looks like some form of the archaic Left, whether it is celebrating a crusade for human rights or preaching some variation on eighteenth-century anarchism, with appropriate attributions to Tom Paine. What is more interesting, however, than these references is Strauss's pinpointing of two diametrically opposed worldviews. Partisans of the Left, according to his interpretation, look toward a "universal homogeneous state," a creation that Strauss's correspondent Kojève defended in his writings. Any "approximation to the universal and homogeneous state" is for liberals a move in the proper direction, although they may conceal their enthusiasm by pretending to be advocates of "hardheaded politics," who believe that "that state has been rendered necessary by economic and technological progress," "the necessity of making nuclear war impossible for all the future and by the "increasing wealth of the advanced countries."[57]

[56] Ibid., V.
[57] Ibid., VI.

Against this liberal vision Strauss opposes an essentialist conservative one. Its advocates "regard the universal and homogeneous state as either undesirable, though possible, or as both undesirable and impossible." Conservatives may have to accept in the short run a United Free Europe, as an alliance against the Soviet communist threat, but:

[T]hey are likely to understand such units differently from liberals. An outstanding European conservative has spoken of *l'Europe des patries*. Conservatives look with greater sympathy than liberals on the particular or particularist and the heterogeneous; at least they are more willing than liberals to respect and perpetuate a more fundamental diversity than the one ordinarily respected or taken for granted by liberals and even by Communists, which is the diversity regarding language, folksongs, pottery and the like.[58]

Furthermore, "[i]nasmuch as the universalism in politics is founded on the universalism proceeding from reason, conservatism is frequently characterized by distrust of reason or by trust in a tradition which is necessarily this or that tradition and hence particular."[59] Finally, "[c]onservatism is therefore exposed to criticism that is guided by the notion of the unity of truth," whereas liberals, "especially those who know that their aspirations have their roots in the Western tradition, are not sufficiently concerned with the fact that that tradition is ever more eroded by the changes in the direction of the One World which they demand or applaud."[60]

It would be hard to find a more perceptive analysis than this one for addressing the distinction between Left and Right. The underlying insight goes back to Carl Schmitt and his criticism of the "universal, homogeneous state." Strauss is repeating here Schmitt's critical observations for the benefit of Anglo-American readers. He assumes Schmitt's famous equation of the universal state with universal tyranny, and he incorporates this distinctive perspective into his delineation of the

---

[58] Ibid.
[59] Ibid., VII.
[60] Ibid: the same argument about the nature of conservatism is presented more fully in Karl Mannheim's *Konservatismus: Ein Beitrag zur Soziologie des Wissens* (Frankfurt: Suhrkamp Verlag, 1984), particularly 136–84. See also Paul Edward Gottfried, *Conservatism in America: Making Sense of the American Right* (New York: Palgrave Macmillan, 2007), 1–31; and John Kekes, *A Case for Conservatism* (Ithaca, NY: Cornell University Press, 2001).

conservative worldview.[61] Strauss also cites Charles de Gaulle, who as French president in the 1960s argued against an overly close union of European states in favor of a continued national consciousness among European peoples. Strauss presents this conservative type as the exact opposite of the liberal, with his unrealistic and utopian expectations. This conservative antithesis is nothing, however, that he finds disagreeable or which he feels threatens "liberal democracy."

Still and all, it would be a mistake to associate Strauss with his conservative pole too closely. The "conservative" side in his analysis bears a certain resemblance to his targets in *Natural Right and History*, particularly to Burke and the German romantic conservatives, whom Strauss considered to be more revolutionary than even the Jacobins. One must also keep in mind Strauss's descriptions of "conventionalism" as an obstacle to philosophy and his insistence that the true search for virtue and justice necessarily encompasses the universal.

Strauss's implied criticism that conservatives believe excessively in the "unity of truth" goes back to his brief against relativism. He long complained against those who paid homage to Tradition as Truth and he was now reviving this animadversion in a less incriminatory fashion. The unwillingness to apply a universal standard of Reason, we are told in *Natural Right and History*, has led to destructive wars and has precipitated the demoralization of liberal education. Like his students, Strauss saw this failure to apply rational judgment because of an infatuation with particularities as a conservative flaw. But the Left also occasionally appealed to particularity, albeit more disingenuously, to win acceptance for its "one world" idea. In the short run, it stressed the diversity that it would ultimately have to remove to fashion a universal homogeneous state based on uniform human rights.

No one is claiming that Strauss was a conservative by default. What is suggested is that he could write lucidly and intelligently about a "conservative" worldview; in the preface to *Liberalism Ancient and*

---

[61] Schmitt's most devastating remarks about the struggle over competing values can be found in "Die Tyrannei der Werte" in *Die Tyrannei der Werte*, ed. Carl Schmitt, Eberhard Jüngel, and Sepp Schelz (Hamburg: Lutherisches Verlagshaus, 1979), 31–40; Leo Strauss, *On Tyranny: Including the Strauss-Kojève Correspondence*, ed. Victor Gourevitch and Michael Roth (Chicago: University of Chicago Press, 2000), 172–239; and Alexandre Kojève, *Introduction to the Reading of Hegel*, trans. Torres H. Nichols, Jr., ed. Allan Bloom (New York: Basic Books, 1968), 39–52, 192–93.

Modern, he proves that he fully understood that view. Although in other ways his disciples struggled to be like him, in this respect most of them did not. They were too driven by their "liberal" universalist commitments to notice what Strauss more than once treated respectfully as conservative thinking. Unlike their teacher, most of his devotees would find nothing in this conservative worldview that deserved their sympathy.

In another way, Strauss showed a wider cultural understanding than his disciples. Despite his contrasting of German antimodern modernism with a more admirable Anglo-American modernity, Strauss displayed a surprising appreciation for German counterrevolutionaries. He recognized the "noble protest" and moral seriousness in thinkers whom he otherwise castigated as antiliberals and antidemocrats.

His lecture on German nihilism, which he delivered in February 1941, drew a careful distinction between German conservative revolutionaries, like Arthur Moeller van den Bruck, Ernst Jünger, Carl Schmitt, and even Heidegger and those Nazis who "vulgarized" their ideas.[62] By the standards of other refugee scholars who had fled from the Nazis, Strauss did not stand out as an especially vengeful exile. Indeed in his preface to the English edition of his work on Spinoza, he deplores the Treaty of Versailles as an unwise act of vengeance inflicted by the Allies on a "liberal democratic" German republic.[63] Unlike some of his disciples, Strauss exhibited not so much Germanophobia as understandable disappointment over the failure of Jews to find entrance into German society. One can fully appreciate this disappointment even when it took bitter expression.

What bestowed significance on these negative comments, however, was their integration into what his disciples came to teach. Strauss's experience as a German refugee had for his epigones a different meaning from how the followers of the Austrian economist Ludwig von Mises responded to their teacher's flight from Nazi persecution. Although Mises's followers embraced his views about economic cycles and the informational function of pricing, they were never fixed on his diatribes against "the spirit of Prussian militarism."[64] The occasional

[62] "On German Nihilism," 362.
[63] *Liberalism Ancient and Modern*, 225.
[64] See Jörg Guido Hülsmann, *Mises: The Last Knight of Liberalism* (Auburn: LudwigVon Mises Institute, 2007); and Ludwig Von Mises, *Omnipotent Government: The Rise of*

laments about the German heritage in Mises and in another Austrian economist, Friedrich von Hayek, had little impact on their followers, save as negative observations about state planning.

Among Straussians, however, their teacher's experience with German anti-Semitism and his attacks on German illiberalism gained more, not less, importance over time. Behind this were the reactions of his predominantly Jewish following to the Holocaust and their attendant glorification of Anglo-American modernity as a haven from German persecution. This reaction exemplified what Gadamer had in mind when he referred to those "impenetrable prejudices (*undurchschaute Vorurteile*) "the origins of which remain hidden from the bearer and which can no longer be critically examined."

Whereas some "preconceptions (*Vormeinungen*)" may be said to enrich our interpretations, others are so deeply personal that they escape critical assessment.[65] The Straussian hermeneutic, for better or worse, has been shaped by the operation of certain "impenetrable prejudices." An assessment of their cult of "liberal democratic" heroes and their editorializing against the "German connection" would indicate that Strauss's students, even more than their teacher, were continuing to react to Nazi tyranny.

Whether at least part of their interpretive method could be defended absent this reaction is a different question. Interpretive approaches are not rendered entirely useless because of the baggage they may bring. It is possible to read works by Straussians in which their prejudices do not mar their scholarship. One can even read the corpus of Stanley Rosen, and particularly his *Hermeneutics as Politics*, without encountering any of the fixations associated with other Straussians. Rosen identifies Nietzschean judgments as the framework of Strauss's critical

---

the Total State and Total War, 18–78. Unlike the grim references among Strauss's disciples to their teacher's birth land, the Ludwig Von Mises Institute, which honors its Austrian namesake, celebrates Vienna and the Habsburg Empire as the intellectually rich setting of Mises's early life. Mises's flight from the Nazi state is generally viewed by his admirers as an escape from a particularly vicious form of the planned economy. See the web site maintained by Jeffrey Tucker (www.ludwigvonmises.com) for an overview of the history of Austrian Economics, and Eugen Maria Schulak and Herbert Unterköfler, *Die Wiener Schule der Nationalökonomie*, Volume VII of *Enzyclopädie des Wiener Wissens* (Vienna: Bibliothek der Provinz, 2009).

[65] See the essay by Günter Figal, "*Wahreit und Methode* als ontologischer Entwurf" in *Wahrheit und Methode*, ed. Günter Figal (Berlin: Akademie Verlag, 2007), 219–36.

encounter with his age. One does not have to buy this interpretation, however, to notice what is refreshing about its author. He betrays none of those hang-ups that are all too typical of other students of Strauss.[66]

All the same, Rosen may be the exception that proves the rule. One must therefore consider the rule and not just the exception to understand fully the thinking of Strauss's followers. Moreover, what was understandable in the master, given his biographical experience, becomes an irritating quirk in his disciples – and, *a fortiori*, their disciples.[67]

Finally, to note the obvious one more time before ending this chapter. It is possible, as emphasized in Chapter 6, to encounter journeyman-scholarship among Straussians from which the characteristic template is absent. Such heavily footnoted works as Dena Goodman's *Criticism in Action: Enlightenment Experiments in Political Writing* and Zdravko Planinc's *Plato through Homer: Poetry and Philosophy in the Cosmological Dialogues* do not reveal the pattern to which we have tried to call attention. For evidence of this pattern, one has to look to those Straussians who are better established and more influential. There one can see the template fully in operation, mixed with certain "impenetrable prejudices."

---

[66] Stanley Rosen, *Hermeneutics as Politics* (New York: Oxford University Press, 1987), 91–140.

[67] We should mention for its balanced treatment of a Teutonic figure usually demonized by leading first-generation Straussians Thomas L. Pangle's essay, "The Roots of Contemporary Nihilism and Its Political Consequences According to Nietzsche," *Review of Politics* 45, 1 (1983): 45–70. A perhaps more censorious treatment of the same themes by Pangle is "Nihilism and Modern Democracy in the Thought of Nietzsche" in *The Crisis of Modern Democracy*, 180–211.

4

The Method under Assault

A Variety of Critics

The critics of Strauss and his followers can be easily divided into three groups. The first consists of those whom Strauss's devotees are more than willing to address and who would seem to be their most formidable opponents. Shadia Drury, Anne Norton, Alan Wolfe, Nick Xenos, and John McCormick are all anti-Straussians we are meant to respect. It is they who arouse the combative energy of Michael and Catherine Zuckert, Peter Minowitz, David Lewis Schaefer, and other movement adepts. Although Strauss's apologists do not coddle these critics, they consider some of them to be pesky but "brilliant" adversaries.[1]

It is also the case that Straussians can counter most of these foes without working up a sweat. They have effectively taken on Drury, Xenos, and Wolfe for closely linking Strauss to Carl Schmitt and other right-wing thinkers without adequate proof. They have had no trouble disproving the charge that Strauss cultivated fascist friends because of his long-standing friendship with Kojève, who visited Carl Schmitt at his home in Plettenberg.

---

[1] See Scott Horton's interview with Minowitz on Harpers Online http://www.harpers. org/archive/2009/09.90005789; and Peter Minowitz, *Straussophobia: Defending Leo Strauss and Straussians against Shadia Drury and Other Accusers* (Lanham, MD: Lexington Books, 2009).

Counter to an implied assumption, Kojève was never on the right, and Drury admits that he was a long-time Soviet sympathizer.[2] Xenos makes the mistake of quoting out of context Strauss's letter to Karl Löwith from May 19, 1933, which includes a slighting reference to the "rights of man" and which praises Roman-style authoritarianism. Xenos's observation does not prove that Strauss was a bona fide "fascist," but rather that he was looking toward Mussolini's Italy to protect European Jewry against Nazi Germany.[3] Up until the late 1930s, Mussolini was widely seen as Hitler's major continental adversary. Even more outlandishly, Alan Wolfe has tried to link Strauss to my scholarship as proof of his immoderate right-wing views. But the most Wolfe can come up with to prove this linkage is that Strauss and I have both published works on Carl Schmitt (sixty years apart).[4]

Another line of attack has consisted of treating Strauss and his disciples as quasi-fascists because of their praise of military virtue. These disciples are said to advocate wars as a test of virility and because they hope to place themselves in charge of the American people. Supposedly this elitist vision can be discerned in Strauss's efforts to tease esoteric readings out of political texts. Drury, Xenos, and Wolfe all argue that Strauss's method of interpreting Plato, Maimonides, and Spinoza contain a justification for the rule of Straussian philosopher-kings.[5]

Strauss's followers have done a good job exposing the flimsiness of most of these accusations. The relevant fact here may be that neither Strauss nor his disciples, contrary to what their critics on the left and their adulators on the right may choose to believe, belong to the "right," except in two qualified senses. First, in discussions of Israel or Jewish nationalism, Straussians often sound like members of the

[2] Shadia B. Drury, *Alexandre Kojève: The Roots of Postmodern Politics* (New York: St. Martin's Press, 1994), 36, 37, 180–82.

[3] See Nicholas Xenos, "Leo Strauss and the Rhetoric of the War on Terror," *Logos* 32 (Spring 2008): 8. An even more dubious attempt to link Strauss to Nazism, Imperial Germany, and Nietzsche is John Mearsheimer's "On the Germanic Formation of Leo Strauss," in *Democratic Individualist*, http://democratic-individuality.blogspot.com/2010/02/john-mearsheimer-on-germanic-for

[4] Alan Wolfe, "A Fascist Philosopher Helps Us Understand Contemporary Politics," *Harpers*, April 2, 2004, http://chroniclecom/article/a-fascist-philosopher-helps-us/20483

[5] Michael Zuckert treats this charge in *The Truth about Leo Strauss*, 155–94, and Minowitz in *Straussophobia* examines it in his endnotes, 168–78.

Israeli Right or far Right, and this has been taken as evidence that they lean right on everything else. However, the Straussian defense of Israel is pursued within the context of defending Anglo-American liberal democracy. Israel is presented as an outpost of democratic enlightenment, and its defenses by Straussians are no different from those that emanate from such Jewish liberal Democrats as Alan Dershowitz, Abe Foxman, and Rahm Emanuel.

Critics of the current Israeli government may disagree with this interpretation of Israeli politics or with the Israelis' treatment of the Palestinians, but there is no way that one could mistake the Straussian defense of Israel (however disingenuous it may seem) for fascist ideology. It is even hard to mistake these defenses for the fascist-tinged language of the Zionist Revisionists of the interwar period. Although Strauss himself fell into such romantic nationalist speech when he was discussing Israel's virtues, it would be hard to locate such tropes among his disciples, and even among such fervent advocates of Israel as Allan Bloom and Harry Jaffa.

Second, most of the Straussians in their political statements are what used to be called Cold War liberals. They are admirers of the American welfare state that developed under Wilson, FDR, Truman, and possibly Lyndon Johnson. Unlike other intellectuals, however, they were equally outspoken opponents of communist tyranny. They took their anti-Soviet position as supporters of suppressed labor unions and Jewish refuseniks in the communist bloc. Save for a few of their Catholic fellow travelers, Straussians were never McCarthyites or those identifiably right-wing anticommunists who were a force to be reckoned with in the 1950s.

Before the Democrats' shift to the left in foreign policy in the late 1960s, Straussians were happy as clams in the Democratic Party, and none of their prominent representatives, with the exception of Harry Jaffa, who broke ranks to back Barry Goldwater in 1964, stood as far to the right as the Republican Party until the 1970s. As far as one can ascertain, Straussians still view themselves as defenders of good welfare-state democracy against its later derailments.

Such facts need to be stressed to discredit the sometimes grotesque charges that have been hurled at Strauss and his disciples as a far right fifth column. Equally bizarre is the very loose chain of association that John McCormick claims to trace in a book allegedly about Carl Schmitt, going from Carl Schmitt and various German Nazi sympathizers through Strauss and his disciples down to former GOP Speaker of the House Newt Gingrich.[6] McCormick's links are so gossamer-like that it would not take rocket science to refute them. Clearly some intellectuals are unhappy that Straussians are not far enough on the left to please them. They therefore depict them as right-wing extremists. Pace Shadia Drury, the "abhorrence of modernity" attributed to Strauss and his followers remains for the most part an unproved charge.[7]

Straussians do not shrink back from answering such intemperate attacks. They shine in these confrontations, as they step forth as practitioners of moderation in combat against immoderate foes. There are, however, other lines of criticism that they find less to their liking. The first is the proliferating mass of methodological criticisms that has arisen in the Academy. Fortunately for the Straussians, these reactions are written by and for scholars and are not likely to cause a stir in learned circles.

It is therefore safe for a movement with national and even international resonance to ignore what much of its fan base would never notice. If the Straussians treat the negative commentary of famous literati, it is done by subalterns for their guild journal, *Interpretation*. Here one notices remarks by Gadamer made during interviews or an occasional sympathetic reading of Weber.[8] In *Interpretation* it is possible to acknowledge some critics or theoretical deviationists but not to attract undue attention while doing so.

The least appealing source of opposition to Strauss and his textual readings, however, has come from a third body of critics, linked to the intellectual Right. It comprises thinkers whom the Straussians view as abusive reactionaries, and because they have no significant media presence, it makes perfectly good sense to disregard them – or to treat them as unfit for civil discourse. Such opposition has also been largely excluded from those conservative movement publications that the Straussians have been able to guide.

---

[6] John P. McCormick, *Carl Schmitt's Critique of Liberalism: Against Politics as Technology*, (Cambridge: Cambridge University Press, 1999), 293–314.

[7] See *Alexandre Kojève*, 154, and Minowitz, *Straussophobia*, 148–67.

[8] See *Interpretation*, 12.1 (January 1984), and 21.11 (Fall 1999).

Responding to these critics would be an intellectually honest act, but it would not be necessary to hold on to those resources that Straussians have at their disposal. There is no practical reason to answer inconsequential critics who are not likely to get their day in the court of public opinion. Nonetheless, this chapter will examine these apparent losers for two compelling reasons. One, their critical commentaries are often cogent; and two, I myself am sympathetic to the outcast group in question and shall admit to having a professional interest in their critical assessments.

The more mainstream group of critics (which is the second one discussed) has produced some of the same observations about Strauss that one meets among his critics on the right. These pertinent observations are found in among other places the essays on meaning and historical contexts by Quentin Skinner and the works of John Gunnell, Hans-Georg Gadamer, and Tzvetan Todorov.

The overlapping critiques of the second and third groups go against a mindset that is present among public intellectuals. They fly in the face of the widespread tendency in our media and educational system to turn "human rights" into a god term, to the point of demanding that the American regime fight for these rights throughout the world. Although not all the critics about to be cited would categorically reject such notions or the accompanying mission, they would insist on the need to relate political values to the historical contexts in which they arose. They have also warned against the error of looking too hard into the past for what intellectuals today would hold as preferred values.

Factual and Interpretive Critiques

A massive body of critical literature abounds that challenges Strauss's interpretations of certain thinkers who are deemed "political philosophers." Because it would take entire volumes to reproduce all these criticisms, we restrict ourselves in this section to certain recurrent objections and to those who have advanced them. Significantly, Spinoza expert Brayton Polka, American religious historian Barry Allan Shain, and linguistic philosopher David Gordon have all devoted many pages of criticism to the defects of the Straussian interpretive grid, without eliciting appropriate responses. Basic to these criticisms is the contention that the Straussians misrepresent the historical past either by ignoring it or by refusing to notice the religious aspects of what they style "modernity."

Shain in a voluminous study, *The Myth of American Individualism*, examines the pervasive Calvinism of early American society and suggests that it is impossible to dissociate the American founding from the ingrained Protestant convictions of the overwhelming majority of its population. To whatever extent early American political thinkers were drawn to Locke, according to Shain, this influence usually coexisted with other theoretical nourishment.[9] There was a Protestant reason that American Protestants read Locke. This English pamphleteer recycled the contractarian view of civil society that Presbyterians had introduced into Protestant Europe in the sixteenth century. Protestant political activists such as the Scottish Covenanters foreshadowed Locke's view of the origins of civil society. Like Polka, Shain finds no contradiction between modern compact theories of government and the power of biblical tradition.

Polka and Shain both also insist that republicanism has Christian roots and that there is no compelling reason to associate it in its American incarnation with scientific materialism or the rejection of Christian concepts of political life. Note that even after his conversion to Straussian hermeneutics, Willmoore Kendall and his disciple George Carey furnished a similar picture of American Protestant continuity on the basis of the "basic symbols" of the American founding, going from the Mayflower Compact to early American state constitutions.[10]

---

[9] See Barry A. Shain, *Myth of American individualism: The Protestant Origins of American Political Thought* (Princeton, NJ: Princeton University Press, 1994), especially the preface. Shain is currently at work on a documentary history, *The Declaration in Historical Context* (New Haven, CT: Yale University Press, 2012). In 2007, he brought out with the University of Virginia Press a thematically related anthology with his own introductory essay, *The Nature of Rights at the American Founding and Beyond: Constitutionalism and Democracy*. Both works argue that the American revolutionaries were not heavily influenced by Locke and were only incidentally touched by natural-rights thinking. The colonists submitted their grievances to the king, after the Parliament had passed the Stamp Act in 1765, by appealing to the traditions of British constitutionalism. A work that develops this argument and on which Shain draws heavily is J. P. Reid, *Constitutional History of the American Revolution: The Authority to Legislate*, four volumes (Madison: University of Wisconsin Press, 1995).

[10] See Willmoore Kendall and George W. Carey, *The Basic Symbols of the American Political Tradition* (Washington, DC: Catholic University of America, 1995).

The critics of Strauss have presented a counternarrative to his picture and to that of his followers about the secular origins of the American Republic.

Shain observes about a leading Straussian writer explaining the political thinking of the American colonies in the 1770s:

> [H]is rarefied account of eighteenth-century American history is even more unacceptable because of its failure to consider the most immediate stuff of history, that is recent past and immediate present. In his account, one would be hard pressed to learn that the political actors in his drama were all British and, in some form or other, nominally Protestant. Neither feature, quite probably the two most informative elements of America's political culture, is given any weight in his description of Americans as a universal and largely secular people.[11]

Shain contends that the references to "Nature" that are inserted into the Declaration came as a result of a last-minute decision by the Colonial Congress. This decision was reached after the first meeting of the Continental Congress, in September 1774, had seen violent opposition expressed against the inclusion of natural-rights concepts in the case of colonial self-government. Representatives at the Congress, most notably those from New York, saw no reason to ground their rights as Englishmen in what they thought were invented universal principles.[12]

Some of the same questioning can be found, at least by implication, in scholars who were not assailing the Lockean interpretation of the American founding, which is the narrative issuing from Strauss, Pangle, Mansfield, Rahe, Bloom, and Zuckert. In *Novus Ordo Seclorum*, the constitutional historian Forrest McDonald has interpreted the "intellectual origins of the constitution" as an extremely eclectic process. According to McDonald, Hume, Montesquieu, Polybius, and many other thinkers beside Locke shaped the thinking of the constitutional convention that drafted the design for the American federal government.

---

[11] Barry A. Shain, "Harry Jaffa and the Demise of the Old Republic," *Modern Age* 45.4 (Fall 2007), 481; and Barry A. Shain, "Fighting Words: The American Nation of Conservatism," *Modern Age* 43 (Winter 2000), 118–27.

[12] See Barry A. Shain, "Rights Natural and Civil in the Declaration of Independence," in *The Nature of Rights at the American Founding and Beyond* (Charlottesville: University of Virginia Press, 2007), 116–62.

McDonald points out that although Locke's "theory of the origin and nature of rights" "served the goals of the Patriots in 1776," and therefore shaped the rhetoric of the Declaration, this Lockean theory about origins gradually dwindled in importance. By the time the constitution was being considered, some of its drafters felt deep suspicions about Locke's view of property. They realized that Locke had been concerned with property as land that had to be worked; the *Second Treatise on Government* indicates that "charity gives every man a title to so much out of another's plenty as will keep him from extreme want."[13]

McDonald suggests, without quoting him directly, related comments from the historian Richard Ashcraft. Long before the American Patriots turned to Locke on the eve of the Revolution, the English philosopher's main readership, according to Ashcraft, had been reform-minded English Protestants, particularly the antimonarchical Levellers. Locke's core readers in Europe were therefore zealous Christians and mostly small landowners, who had extracted their social-contract idea from the Covenanters of the sixteenth century. Ashcraft questioned the attempt to link the salability of Locke to secular, material interests. If Locke's followers were "modernists," it would be impossible, according to Ashcraft, to divorce their understanding of Locke from Protestant political theology: "To consider Locke's position on the relationship of labor to property divorced from its theological underpinnings is not only a serious interpretive mistake in terms of the intentional structure of Locke's intellectual commitment in the *Two Treatises*, it also misrepresents through omission a crucial dimension of the political radicalism that work expresses."[14]

Ashcraft proceeds to read the *Treatises* – the first a response to Robert Filmer, a defender of divine right monarchy, and the second a presentation of a social-contract theory of civil society – as texts that appeal to, among other things, religious beliefs. Locke's depiction of God as "sole Lord and Proprietor of the whole world" is an implicit challenge to the established church and to the absolute power of the

[13] Richard Ashcraft, *Revolutionary Politics and Locke's Two Treatises of Government* (Princeton, NJ: Princeton University Press, 1986), 262; this is a restatement of the lines found in John Locke, *Second Treatise of Government*, second edition (Cambridge: Cambridge University Press, 1967), par. 35.

[14] Richard Ashcraft, *Revolutionary Politics and Locke's Two Treatises of Government*, 258.

monarchy but certainly not to the authority of the Bible. Moreover, Locke's Deity "by commanding to subdue [in Genesis], gave authority to appropriate. And the condition of human life, which requires labor and materials to work on, necessarily introduces private possession."[15] Ashcraft relate such statements to the view of creationism found in the Levellers and in other Protestants outside the Anglican Church, one that stressed the equal right of all human creatures to appropriate property by mixing their labor with it. Although it can be argued, as the Straussians do, that Locke left behind a profusion of hints that he was not a true Christian, this may have nothing to do with his appeal during and after his life. The question is not what resided in Locke's heart but how his readers understood him.[16]

Brayton Polka's two-volume work, *Between Philosophy and Religion: Spinoza, the Bible and Modernity*, contain an explicit criticism of Strauss for distorting the relation between modernity and biblical religion. Polka's investigation is partly designed to refute Strauss's contention that "fundamentally, Spinoza's procedure is that of modern science according to its original conception – to make the universe completely clear and distinct, a completely mathematizable unit." Polka further challenges Strauss's assertion that "there was one man who tried to force the issue [of an incomprehensible Deity] by denying the incomprehensibility of God's essence."[17]

In an exploration of the *Theologico-Political Treatise* and the *Ethics*, Polka presents a dramatically different reading of Spinoza from Strauss's. Spinoza is depicted as having been what the German poet Novalis believed he was – "ein gottbetrunkener Denker." Spinoza's affirmation of the ontological argument for God's existence, which bases the truth of God's existence on His presence in the human mind, suggests that Spinoza's theological and biblical convictions were real. Arguments about God's necessary existence and His presence in our consciousness are a staple in the works of modern philosophers, going from Descartes through Spinoza to Hegel. According to Polka, these arguments are not an attempt to trivialize biblical religion or to identify

---

[15] See Ashcraft's response to C.B. Macpherson, ibid., 150–59.
[16] Brayton Polka, *Between Philosophy and Religion: Spinoza, the Bible, and Modernity*, I, *Hermeneutics and Ontology* (Lanham, MD: Lexington Books, 2007), 252.
[17] Ibid., 258–59.

faith with the physical and mathematical sciences. Nor is there reason to believe, like Strauss, that Spinoza posited an unbridgeable divide between faith and science. A tendency that was present in some "lesser thinkers," it was not the one that, according to Polka, can be justifiably ascribed to Spinoza.[18]

Being fair to both sides, it would be proper to note that Strauss could have challenged some elements of Polka's depiction of Spinoza. For example, Strauss questioned, with some justification, whether Spinoza's notion of God as Substance that is present in our minds and in Nature is compatible with biblical Creation. Strauss insists that the idea of a Deity creating the world ex nihilo is foundational for Hebraic religion. Later Christians took over this Jewish God of Creation and integrated Him into Christian dogmatic theology. Strauss maintains with good reason that what Spinoza describes as Natura Naturans is not such a Deity.

Polka moves on to firmer ground, however, when he seeks to defend two other positions in his work: first, the biblical religious concerns of "modern" thinkers, and then the idea that Spinoza was not dissembling when he expressed biblically based religious convictions. Polka's view of modernity, like that of Shain, finds specifically biblical roots for republicanism. Equally important, Polka finds a pervasive quest for the hidden God in modern philosophical speculation, and what Strauss and his followers consider to be the skepticism of modern science becomes in this alternative reading an earnest wrestling with theological problems.[19]

Polka denies that Spinoza was being devious when he expressed preference for the "spiritual" and "incorporeal" teachings of Jesus over the legalism and search for earthly power in the Mosaic revelation. And it is certainly not necessary to assume that Spinoza was being mean-spirited or duplicitous by comparing an ideal Christianity to an earthly Judaism, a form of Judaism that, unlike ideal Christianity, carried with it the signs of human imperfections. Spinoza is comparing

---

[18] Ibid., 254–56.

[19] Ibid., 2–40; Brayton Polka, *The Dialectic of Biblical Critique* (New York: St. Martin's Press, 1986); and Grant N. Havers, "Was Spinoza a Liberal?" *Political Science Reviewer* 36 (2007): 143–74. See also Leo Strauss's "Preface to "Spinoza's "Critique of Religion" in *Liberalism: Ancient and Modern*, 241–45. For an attempt to explain, without defending in any unqualified way Spinoza's view of God as eternal, unchanging Substance, see Victor Delbos, *Le Spinozisme* (Paris: J. Vrin, 2005), 23–77.

two ideals and picking one ideal over the other. Polka and, even more explicitly, his student Grant Havers stress the privileged status of "Christian universalism" in Spinoza's commentary on the Bible. They challenge Strauss's idea that Spinoza was disguising his real thoughts as a marginalized Dutch Jew to attract Christian readers.[20]

Strauss may have offered this view of Spinoza's religious predilection at least partly to assuage Hermann Cohen and Cohen's predominantly Jewish disciples. He may have been trying to render Spinoza less alien to the Jewish community of which Strauss himself was a part. Thus he indicates that Spinoza's stress on religion as ethics prepared the way for the Kantian form of Judaism that Cohen would later teach; and so, if properly read, Spinoza, like Cohen, was advocating an ethical form of Jewish religion. But Polka and Havers offer a simpler explanation for Spinoza's preference for Jesus over Moses: The philosopher actually believed what he said.[21] Spinoza was presenting the position that Kant would later articulate about the moral universalism of the Gospels; as an (excommunicated) Jew, Spinoza might well have agreed with this view.

Spinoza found the primordially Christian concepts of universalism and charity essential for his political task, namely to justify and inspirit popular government. Whatever merits Spinoza may have attributed to Jewish particularity as a community bound by ritual and hereditary ties, this legacy did not advance his political project. Spinoza, as suggested by Strauss and Polka, viewed Jewish Rabbinic practice as extraneous to the political society that he wished to see established.

According to Havers, the Straussians cannot accept the fact that the "universality" that they invoke is not a classical Greek but a Christian concept.[22] The Hellenic world was sharply and rigidly defined by ethnicities and subethnicities. Socrates teaches in the *Republic*, Book Five,

[20] Ibid; and Grant Havers, "Romanticism and Universalism: The Case of Leo Strauss," *Dialogue and Universalism*, 12, 6–7 (2002): 155–67.

[21] Havers, "The Meaning of Neo-Paganism: Rethinking the Relation between Nature and Freedom," in *Humanity at the Turning Point: Rethinking Nature, Culture and Freedom* (Helsinki: Renvall Institute of Publications, 2006), 159–69.

[22] See Grant N. Havers, *Lincoln and the Politics of Christian Love* (Columbia: University of Missouri Press, 2009), 43–53; and Paul Gottfried, "Thoughts on Our Protestant Legacy," *Political Science Reviewer* 39.1 (Fall 2010): 129–42. For a study of the Protestant moral divisions in the struggle between the Union and the Confederacy, see Harry S. Stout, *Upon the Altar of the Nation: A Moral History of the American Civil War* (New York: Penguin, 2007).

that whereas Greeks and barbarians are natural enemies, no matter how much Greeks may quarrel, some form of "reconciliation" is their natural state and proper end. The philosopher Aristotle was enraged when his student Alexander encouraged racial mingling between Greeks and Persians, and he wrote his tract, *Peri Epigamias*, against the presumed evil of intermarriage.

Havers unloads even more ammunition against his targets. He quotes the Danish theologian Kierkegaard to the effect that Plato's *Republic* illustrates the "tragic Greek irony" that opposition to tyranny in a pre-Christian philosophical world required the subordination of the many to the few. His attempt to escape unjust rule led Plato to recommend a dictatorship run by philosopher-kings as the best of all worlds. Such a pre-Christian attitude, Havers maintains, may cause some Straussians to identify a "democratic" society with one that is safely under their control.

It was the Hellenized Jew Paul who announced in Galatians that "Jews and Greeks, men and women, all are one in Christ." It was also Christian or Judeo-Christian civilization that, unlike the Graeco-Roman world, condemned slavery, as an expression of religious principle. Havers contends that slavery had not become economically useless at the time it was abolished. Its existence caused moral outrage even when slavery was materially profitable. Despite his outraged tone, Havers does raise a reasonable question that Straussians would prefer not to answer. He wants to know why they ascribe to ancient Greeks but not to Bible-reading Christians those moral positions they claim to value. Why do they attribute to pagans positions that they can more easily discover in nineteenth-century Christianity?[23]

The Polka-Havers counterinterpretation of Spinoza may occasion two critical comments about Strauss's "art of secret writing." First, while nobody would question that up until the end of the eighteenth century, political thinkers may well have felt inhibited about expressing "liberal" views, it is also possible, says Tzvetan Todorov, that some political authors have tried to make us experience their contradictions "by placing us in contact with two or even three voices that reveal, each in a way coherent with itself, a partial truth."[24]

---

[23] Ibid., 116–37.
[24] Tzvetan Todorov, *The Morals of History*, trans. Alyson Waters (Minneapolis: University of Minnesota Press, 1995), 124.

One might further observe that "the condition of modern man is itself contradictory." Some of those authors whom Strauss examined may have been themselves deeply ambivalent about certain theological and political questions.[25] They were not hiding what they really thought but exposing internal conflicts. For example, in Strauss's book on Hobbes, following a pattern that one finds in other interpreters, there are references to its subject's materialist theory of knowledge and ethics. Strauss traces this reference point back to ancient naturalist authors, particularly Epicurus and Lucretius. Supposedly one could locate the sources of Hobbes's thinking in certain ancient authors without having to show that he was philosophically dependent on seventeenth-century physical sciences. Strauss treats the affirmative references to Christian doctrine and Christian natural law in *Leviathan* as protective coloration. The author was presumably throwing in such language to lull the naïve or to keep Christian censors off his back.

It is also entirely possible, however, as Francis Hood and Howard Warrender have both maintained, to present Hobbes as a Christian thinker, albeit one who may have held contradictory views about revealed religion and the nature of God. Such an argument is worth pondering, even if the conventional view generally accords with Strauss's reading of Hobbes as a materialist.[26]

One may even perceive contradictory loyalties in Hobbes's case: Having been raised in a strictly Protestant Christian home, his favorable references in *Leviathan* to "Christ as the savior" and his essentially Augustinian picture of a cowardly or bullying human nature indicate a nonmaterialist basis for his ideas. There is a Christian aspect, however blurred, in his work and this element should occasion no surprise. Hobbes was partly molded by and spent his life in a seventeenth-century Christian society. The conventional view that he was a materialist shaped by naturalist thought does not rule out the hypothesis that he was simultaneously marked by other cultural

---

[25] Ibid., 125.

[26] This alternative reading of Hobbes as a recognizable Christian thinker can be found among other interpreters, in F.C. Hood, *The Divine Politics of Thomas Hobbes: An Interpretation of "Leviathan"* (London: Oxford University Press, 1964); and Howard Warrender, *The Political Philosophy of Thomas Hobbes: His Theory of Obligation* (Oxford: Clarendon Press, 1957).

forces. The contradiction in his work reflects to some degree the unresolved contradictions in his life.

Demystifying the Ancients?

An oft-noted problem about Strauss's interpretations of secret writing is that it is underdetermined. A telling illustration of this problem is Strauss's interpretation of Socrates in the context of his discussion of Plato's dialogues. According to Strauss, who draws heavily here on medieval Arab philosophers, it is unnecessary to assume that Plato or his teacher believed in eternal forms – or in their divine source. To whatever extent theological subjects entered the dialogues, it is appropriate to view them mostly as teaching tools.[27]

Now it is possible to read much of Strauss's work on Platonic dialogues, which are careful accounts of these conversations, without noticing their defining hermeneutic characteristic. One can marvel at how Strauss digested classical Greek texts without having to consider his unsettling idea that Plato did not believe in eternal forms. One can also appreciate the fact that unlike Christian Platonists and even such pagan neo-Platonists as Plotinus, Proclus, and Porphyry, Strauss does not belabor the allusions in Plato's text to the "soul returning to its divine origin." By the time the emperor Justinian banned the teaching of pagan philosophy in Athens in 525 AD, philosophy had become identified with neo-Platonism, and that form of philosophy long operated as a mystical alternative to Christianity.[28] Strauss may have done the scholarly world a service by reading Plato in a sharply contrasting way. He puts into relief the *zētēma*, the form of inquiry that he finds at the heart of the Socratic search for virtue and truth.

Unfortunately, Strauss and his disciples never show that what Plato seems to accept is not what he in fact believes. Their evidence for this denial is so exiguous that it may be possible to speak here of a Straussian leap of faith. One brief example may suffice. A favorite text for the Averroistic reading of Plato is the dialogue, *Phaedrus*, in which

---

[27] For a discussion of this aspect of Strauss's hermeneutic, see Allan Bloom, *Giants and Dwarfs* (New York: Simon and Schuster, 1990), 105–23; and Steven B. Smith, *Reading Leo Strauss*, 87–93.

[28] See *Historia Philosophiae Graecae*, ed. H. Ritter and L. Preller (Gotha: F. A. Perthes Verlag, 1888), 566–68.

Socrates converses with a young Athenian by that name, who has just heard the rhetorician Lysius offer a discourse on Eros. Phaedrus cannot quite recall Lysius's exact wording but he does remember that the speech was "not for the sake of the one who is loved but contains a certain subtlety [*alla auto dē touto kekompseutai.*] He [Lysias] says that it is necessary to bestow the prize on the one who does not love rather than on the one who does."[29] This leads into a series of speeches: two by Phaedrus trying to reconstruct Lysius's drift in favor of the nonlover (*mē eronti*); and one memorable final discourse by Socrates, on Eros as the ascent of the Soul.[30]

Although considerably more than half the dialogue is a hymn to the ascent of the soul, the *anabasis tēs psuxēs* – a theme encountered elsewhere in Plato – the Averroistic-Straussian interpretation emphasizes the improvised nature of the speeches. Socrates is devising the rhetorical means to turn Phaedrus away from the mere subtlety (*kompseia*) of Lysius's cynical descriptions of love. He hopes to draw his interlocutor into a philosophical discussion, as opposed to a mere forensic exercise.

Moreover, at the beginning of the dialogue, Phaedrus shows Socrates an altar to Boreas, the god of the wind, and refers to the legend in which this god was frolicking with a demigoddess, Pharmakeia. After her death as the result of a fall, "it is said that Boreas carried her away." Socrates is asked whether he accepts "such myths as being true," to which he rejoins that "if I were skeptical, like the wise, this would not be unreasonable."[31] At this point, Socrates proceeds to reason in the conventional manner (*sophismenos*) about the fateful meeting of Boreas and Pharmakeia. He then recounts other dubious legends about Centaurs, Gorgons, and the Chimera "which require a great deal of leisure to discuss," especially "if one approaches such ideas distrustfully as a form of rural wisdom [*atē agroika sophia tini sophia xromenos*]."[32]

Presumably the skepticism about these mythological creatures encapsulates Socrates's or Plato's partly hidden views about theology.

---

[29] Plato, *Phaedrus*, Oxford Classical Texts (Oxford: Oxford University Press, 1965), 277 c.
[30] Ibid., 227 d.
[31] Ibid., 229 d.
[32] Ibid., 229 e.

We may now fast-forward to the later discourse in the same dialogue, about the soul beholding the beatific vision as it wings above the corporeal world. Should we assume that this vision is nothing more than a manner of transmitting a rational concept or whetting someone's appetite for philosophical inquiry? Not so fast! There is no intrinsic reason to believe that Plato viewed all references to the soul or to the divine source of being as he did "the rustic wisdom" associated with Boreas and the Gorgons. Plato is repeatedly drawing distinctions between conventional Greek religion and what a truly good person must believe about Zeus as the source of justice. We may therefore not assume that both types of references to the Divine or to something that transcends mortal life are to be treated in the same fashion. Clearly the mystical vision in Plato's or Socrates' mind was accorded more credibility than mere "rustic wisdom."

Plato also devotes considerable space in the *Republic* and in other dialogues to telling us how human perceptions and forms of knowing can be traced back to eternal forms. Is this idle speculation or an attempt to mislead his listeners?[33] Were the members of Plato's Academy who believed in the eidetic nature of reality the victims of a deception or of a misapprehension, one that was allowed to continue for more than a thousand years until a medieval Arab discovered what Plato meant to say? Such a rationalist reading of Plato may be defensible, but it hardly qualifies as an axiom that is beyond the need for proof.

The Conceptual Challenge

Another form of criticism that has been aimed at Straussian methodology is conceptual; here the criticism that has come from the Old Right may be particularly pertinent. An economic libertarian and linguistic philosopher David Gordon has argued that in *Natural Right and History*, Strauss set up false or exaggerated polarities by means

---

[33] For a meticulous reading of *The Republic* that avoids unwarranted metaphysical conclusions, see N. R. Murphy, *The Interpretation of Plato's Republic* (Oxford: Clarendon Press, 1951); and for an unmistakably neo-Platonic reading of the text, see Eric Voegelin's *Plato* (Columbia: University of Missouri Press, 2000). The now standard Straussian interpretation of the work is Allan Bloom's *The Republic of Plato*, second edition (New York: Basic Books, 1991).

of which he hoped to prevail in the court of public opinion. Strauss's crusade against historicism, relativism, and nihilism misrepresent the alternatives to his own positions. For example, Strauss never proves that Hans Kelsen makes no moral distinctions between dictatorial and liberal democratic authorities. He simply lets us know that Kelsen in his *Allgemeine Staatslehre* believes that despotic forms of government include "legal orders." The author may not have fancied with equal relish all the orders he talks about, given his known social democratic opinions. But it was incumbent on him as a legal scholar to enumerate dispassionately those forms of government that he was placing on a comprehensive list.[34]

Gordon also notes that there is no proof that those who try to explain systems of ideas by looking at historical contexts are without moral convictions. Some scholars who exhibit historicist leanings, like Leopold Ranke and Herbert Butterfield, were devout Christians. Strauss's historical relativism was an attempt to be fair to the past or, in Butterfield's case, a reaction to the "Whig theory of history." Gordon also imputes to the Straussians a flawed understanding of the past, which is predicated on their hidden assumptions about Progress. These theorists raise "liberal democratic values" to the level of inviolate truth, while playing hanging judge over other ages and peoples from the standpoint of their age and culture. Like the Whig historians whom Butterfield criticized, Straussians refuse to face their own presentist conceit.[35]

Finally Gordon suggests that a distinction may be in order between method and conviction. A historian or legal scholar may adopt for purposes of examining and organizing data a Marxist reading or some other approach that offended Strauss. But he may also hold beliefs about the world and his own spiritual destiny, which go beyond his approach to historical facts. A historian's methodology may be selected for scientific or heuristic purposes rather than for expressing religious convictions.

---

[34] In correspondence with the author, March 25, 2010; see also the relevant remarks in Paul Gottfried, "Morgenthau and Strauss as an Instructive Polarity," in *One Hundred Year Commemoration to the Life of Hans Morgenthau*, ed. G.O. Mazur (New York: Semenenko Foundation, 2004), 115–18.

[35] See Herbert Butterfield, *The Whig Interpretation of History* (London: G. Bell and Sons, Ltd. 1968), especially 64–89, dealing with value judgments in history.

Gordon also maintains that those moralistic polarities that we find in Straussians have justified their rhetorical bullying. Those who question their values or cult of democratic heroes are demonized as nihilists and relativists. Once the Straussians establish their dualisms as self-evident, they then feel free to attack those who controvert them as enemies of the Good or American survival.[36]

Gordon himself has tried in vain to argue with Harry Jaffa, Charles Kesler, and other disciples of Strauss, who insist that their reading of the Declaration of Independence provides a necessary moral perspective for interpreting the Constitution. Because some Straussians (although not all of them) think that the American Republic instantiates their ideas about equality and natural right, they have presented these ideas, and their accompanying glosses, as integral to the constitutional document. According to Gordon, Jaffa and his disciples have been especially hypocritical when they go after the Left for speaking about a "living constitution."[37] This is precisely what the Jaffaites have tried to impose on the unsuspecting by pushing their values as eternal verities.

Gordon finds Strauss to be at fault for his emphatic rejection of the fact-value dichotomy, and he contrasts his views here to those of Ludwig von Mises. Although facts and values, as Max Weber and Mises both recognized, are interrelated concepts, it is possible and even necessary to separate the two in scientific and social scientific research.[38] Strauss famously asserted the opposite position and told us that there is no way one could describe shady human activities or make distinctions between "higher and lower religions" without rendering moral judgments. To which Gordon and Mises respond: There may be less loaded terms than those that are presently in use to describe prostitution or theft, or to characterize the distinction between belief in a universal spiritual

---

[36] This is the subject of a long manuscript by Gordon, *Jaffa On Equality, Democracy and Morality*, which analyzes the value preferences and value dualities in the work of one of Strauss's best-known and closest students, Harry V. Jaffa. For an Internet copy of this incisive study, see http://www.Lewrockwell.com/Gordon/gordon5.htm/

[37] See Gordon's review of Thomas L. Krannawitter, *Vindicating Lincoln: Defending the Politics of our Greatest President* in *Mises Review* 14.3 (Fall 2008).

[38] See David Gordon, "The Philosophical Contribution of Ludwig Von Mises," *Journal of Austrian Economics*, 7.1: 95–106; and Ludwig Von Mises, *Epistemological Problems of Economics* (New York: New York University Press, 1981), 46.

Deity and animism. Nonetheless, the now prevalent terms do convey a factual content, so it would be unwise to treat facts and values as indistinguishable concepts because they sometimes overlap.

A particularly relevant discussion of the fact-value distinction and of Strauss's assessment of it, particularly in *Natural Right and History*, is available in Todorov's *The Morals of History*. In chapter 14 of this work, one finds a qualified defense of Weber against Strauss's charge that the famous sociologist disguised the necessary relation between facts and values. Todorov argues that it would be impossible for Weber or for any other social scientist to engage in serious research without making the very distinction Strauss condemns. First of all, Weber never denies that "references to values" are characteristic of social science. Indeed, these references influence our research choices and how we relate to them. What Weber excludes from the research process are "value judgments." But even that exclusion is heavily qualified. Social scientists should not apply value judgments "during the main and specifically cognitive stage of knowledge but they will intervene before and after this stage."[39] Despite such strenuous efforts at separating the phases of social research, Weber was aware that in the end, the researcher may express moral judgments, although he considered them a "deviation from the model and merely a transitional stage in the process of causal explanation."[40]

Although Todorov treats Weber's model construction as problematic, he reacts even more strongly to Strauss "who refused to separate fact from value in the field of what is specifically human."[41] Strauss went overboard when he charged Weber with shirking his moral responsibility by pointing to moral alternatives but then refusing to choose between them. Although Weber spoke about

---

[39] Tzvetan Todorov, *The Morals of History*, trans. Alyson Waters (Minneapolis: University of Minnesota Press), 198.

[40] Ibid., 207–08. An implicit critique of Strauss's attempt to escape the demands of "political science" is a work by two Romanian scholars, Elena Puha and George Poede, *Dischideri Spre O Epistemologie A Stiinti Politice* (Bucharest: Editura Dimitrie Cantemir, 2000). A concise survey of political sociology dealing with, among other thinkers, Weber and Alfred Schütz, this book is mostly a defense of "political epistemology." Puha and Poede contend that the social sciences require a special idiom that cannot be derived from the traditional humanities.

[41] Tzvetan Todorov, *The Morals of History*, 198–99.

the "two possible directions in the evolution of humanity, spiritual renewal and moral petrifaction," "he refused to make a value judgment about them."[42]

This was not Weber's job, however, argues Todorov, to whatever extent he was being a social scientist. Such a practitioner cannot help but exhibit a "moral sense like other human beings, but what makes him an expert is not this characteristic but something more, which we call, rightly or wrongly, his science." Strauss (perhaps quite expectedly) invokes the example of someone who is asked to "give a strictly factual description of the overt acts that can be observed in a concentration camp and perhaps an equally factual analysis of the motivation of the actors concerned," but who "would not be permitted to speak of cruelty." Strauss exclaims that "every reader of such a description who is not completely stupid would, of course, see that the actions described are cruel." This too, according to Todorov, misses the mark. In trying to inject his moral concerns directly into the social sciences, Strauss was reducing his method of inquiry to a venting of moral judgments. He thereby created a situation in which we could no longer "distinguish between science and sermon (upon seeing the concentration camp we are satisfied with crying out: cruelty!) or between science and propaganda."[43]

Todorov does not entirely reject Strauss's critique of Weber and believes Strauss finds genuine inconsistencies in Weber's scientific method. Todorov agrees with Strauss that Weber's talk about an "ethic of responsibility" privileges what are purely subjective moral judgments. When Weber defines the ethical choices that are open to modern Western man, he leaves room only for individual stands that are intensely felt and shaped by particular circumstances. Once communities based on tradition no longer exist, and once rationality becomes the principle by which governing takes place, the educated individual, according to Weber, is thrown back on his conscience, or whatever else fills that moral function. According to Todorov, Strauss may have been right to notice the moral vacuum in Weber's reaction to the modern conflict of values.

[42] See *Natural Right and History*, 49–50.
[43] Ibid., 200.

Thunder from the Right

A far-reaching conceptual critique of the Straussian approach to political theory has come from those who consider morality and philosophy inseparable from tradition and historical conditions. These critics (not surprisingly) draw on some of the same arguments that Strauss attributes to Burke and his disciples, who are labeled misguided historicists. They incline toward a worldview that Strauss in *Liberalism: Ancient and Modern* identifies with "conservative" critics of universal institutions and universal rights. This perspective, however, is not necessarily a partisan ideology. Its users are stating the intellectually respectable position that traditions and inherited belief systems are necessary for arriving at a usable conception of the Just and the Good.[44]

Those who embrace this position have reacted against the methodology of Strauss and the Straussians on two grounds: first, for positing a gulf between, on the one hand, the conventional and the traditional and, on the other hand, the pursuit of philosophical inquiry; and second, for denying the significance of particularity in filtering and humanizing what are considered "universal ideals." As opponents of Strauss's reading of Burke in *Natural Right and History*, these anti-Straussians oppose to "abstract universals" what they consider to be historically derived truths. They prefer prescribed and historical liberties to natural rights, communal attachment to American globalism, and concrete identities to the Straussian and neoconservative concept of a propositional, universal America.[45]

These critics are happy with Aristotle's correction of Plato's ideal society, and particularly with Aristotle's attempt to relate Justice to the diverse qualities and skills of those who occupy real social positions. They also favor Aristotle's view that political institutions, properly understood, should be seen as an extension of the family and community. Far from being the mere embodiment of universal ideals or

---

[44] See Claes G. Ryn, *The New Jacobinism: Can Democracy Survive?* (Washington, DC: National Humanities Institute, 1991); *America The Virtuous: The Crisis of Democracy and the Quest for Empire* (New Brunswick, NJ: Transaction Publishers, 2003); "The Ideology of American Empire," *Orbis* 473 (Summer 2003); 388–97; and Peter J. Stanlis, *Edmund Burke and the Natural Law* (Ann Arbor: University of Michigan Press, 1959).

[45] See Barry A. Shain's spirited review of Thomas G. West's *Vindicating the Founders* in *Modern Age* 42.1 (Winter 2000): 63–65.

of a string of propositions about equality and democracy, early America for these anti-Straussians belonged to a specific time and culture.

Although the United States may have evolved beyond or deviated from the way it started out, it is necessary, according to this view, to go back to a situated people to understand America's foundations.[46] The search for the local and concrete is characteristic of those historically minded anti-Straussians who, unlike their opponents, are drenched in the past. They also focus on the experiences of historical nations and doggedly refuse to abandon this frame of reference for value talk and civic patriotism.

Those who take such positions have a hard row to hoe in the present cultural climate. Here we are speaking about such anti-Straussians on the right as Shain, the Southern cultural historian M. E. Bradford, the Burke-scholar Peter Stanlis, the critic of liberalism James Kalb, the Swedish-American philosopher Claes Ryn, and the traditionalist man of letters Russell Kirk. All these theorists have anchored their hermeneutics in a conservative vision of the good society.[47] It is this vision as much as anything else that separates them from Strauss and his disciples.

Typical of the broad conceptual differences between the two camps is Shain's observation that Straussians

flirt with modern political rationalism, while seeking, they claim, to recover the pre-modern meanings of key political and moral concepts that have been deformed by modern rationalism. However, by promoting individualism, abstract rationalism, natural rights, and national centralization of power, no matter how they attempt to control the definitions of these concepts, they do nothing to support a conservative and decentralist understanding of America and to the degree anyone other than misguided conservatives are paying attention, do much to undermine it.[48]

---

[46] For a sympathetic but critical assessment of this reading about the origins of the American Republic, see my *Conservatism in America: Making Sense of the American Right* (New York: Palgrave Macmillan, 2007), 1–30; and Russell Kirk, *The Roots of American Order* (LaSalle, IL: Open Court Press, 1974).

[47] Russell Kirk, *The Conservative Mind: From Burke to Eliot*, seventh revised edition (Washington, DC: Regency Books, 1987), especially 3–12, 457–91; Robert Nisbet, *Conservatism: Dream and Reality* (Minneapolis: University of Minnesota Press, 1986); and W. Wesley McDonald, *Russell Kirk and the Age of Ideology* (Columbia: University of Missouri Press, 2004), especially 42–55, 139–69.

[48] Barry L. Shain, "Harry Jaffa, and the Demise of the Old Republic," *Modern Age* 49.4 (Fall 2007): 486. Patrick Allitt's observation about Michael Novak – a neoconservative

Shain comments on what Ryn has described as "the new Jacobinism," and he piles high those sins he attributes to the Straussians, including an attempt to exaggerate the radicalism of the American Revolution while denying the religious-cultural character of early America. Moreover, Shain, George Carey, Willmoore Kendall, Forrest McDonald, and Bradford all insist that we interpret the Declaration "contextually."

Such authors deny any importance of the "All men are created equal" passage in the founding of the American republic. Bradford lists prominent Federalists and even Virginia governor – and the cousin of Thomas Jefferson – Edmund Randolph as figures who deplored the Declaration's straying into universal-rights language. These early American leaders complained that Jefferson cribbed lines from Locke about natural rights, which he inserted into what should have been a pure bill of grievances against the British government. Prominent early Americans, including his fellow Virginians, believed that Jefferson had placed "a bomb perpetually ticking in the basement of the citadel of republican liberty." Such notables found the charge that British government had incited "domestic insurrections" against the colonists to be more revealing than appeals to universal rights.[49]

Bradford and Kendall maintain that it was Lincoln who changed the nature of the republic by making the passage in question fit his plan for an American re-founding. Significantly, Straussians, anti-Straussian conservatives, and maverick leftist Gary Wills have all made this point, albeit from different value positions. McDonald adds his own wrinkle by noting that the natural-rights appeal in the Declaration was largely ignored after the Revolution. At most, it furnished boilerplate phraseology for post-Revolutionary state constitutions. The operative passage gained significance only once the Civil War broke out. This happened first when the state of South Carolina appealed to natural rights during its secession from the federal Union. The next appeal to "all men are created equal" came when Lincoln

---

author who claims to be defending traditional Catholic beliefs – that a conservative seems to mean a "celebrant of the present" might apply equally well to the targets of Shain's diatribe. See Patrick Allitt, *Catholic Intellectuals and Conservative Politics in America*, 276.

[49] M. E. Bradford: *The Reactionary Imperative: Essays Literary and Political* (Peru, IL: Sherwood Snyder, 1990), 122–23.

invoked the same passages to justify his re-founding of a country then embroiled in civil war.[50]

The anti-Straussian Right also presents an integralist interpretation of the thinking of the American founders. Bradford interprets them with reference to the cultures in which Jefferson, John Taylor, George Mason, Patrick Henry, Washington, and other members of the Southern planter class lived and worked. He tries to show the problem of presenting these figures primarily as representatives of Lockean social-contract theory or of an Enlightenment-based natural-rights theory. Although interpreted by a later generation as religiously free-thinking, most of the founders spent their lives as active members of Christian churches, and in privileged social positions. Moreover, with very few exceptions, they saw no glaring inconsistency between their occasional use of Lockean rhetoric and their public social positions. (Bradford is particularly fond of noting that Locke himself drew up a constitution for the Carolina colonies, making provision for slavery.)[51]

Such depictions are intended to remind us that actual people did not embody abstract ideals but existed in particular societies, the leaders of which treated political theories as tools for dealing with time-specific concerns. Contrary to the Straussian scheme of the world, actual historical actors are something other than the temporal means for carrying out what later political theorists would consider desirable reforms.

Critics of the Straussians on the right often treat their opponents as arrogant and dogmatic. Bradford contends the Straussians have created a false legality based on historical and methodological distortions. What should be decisive for the U.S. government today is its

---

[50] The same problems about the implications of the "All men are created equal" passage of the Declaration are brought up in Forrest McDonald's *Novus Ordo Seclorum*, 58–60. McDonald treats the Declaration's appeal to natural right as a "can of worms" that implicitly challenged the "legitimacy of existing relations," including property relations, by returning the American colonists to a Lockean state of nature. See likewise Willmoore Kendall, *Conservative Affirmation*, reprint (Washington, DC: Regnery, 1985), 17–18, 249–52; and the work by Kendall and George Carey, *The Basic Symbols of the American Political Tradition* (Baton Rouge: University of Louisiana Press, 1970), chapters 5–6.

[51] See Paul Gottfried, *The Search for Historical Meaning: Hegel and the postwar American Right*, second edition, especially 104–34; and Robert A. Nisbet's review of the first edition, "A Farewell to History," *National Review* (May 22, 1987): 44–46.

founding document, its civil law, and other forms of legality. What should count for far less are the political precepts that Straussians see fit to impose on us. Neither their cult of heroes nor their privileged values should be viewed as having legal or intellectual status, according to Bradford.

An Uncompleted Dialogue

The presentation of this anti-Straussian view from the right has rarely taken place as a pure academic exercise. It has been mostly a debate in which one side refuses to show up. Because of this, any critical discussion of Strauss from the intellectual Right reveals a fragmentary character. This incompleteness is certainly evident in my book, *The Search for Historical Meaning*, a study that examines the Straussian "rejection of the lived historical past" in the context of a larger problem of American self-identity. My book is at least partly a response to the Straussian presence in universities and political journalism, and it seeks to set the stage for a dialectical encounter that never occurs.[52]

There is an inherent problem with trying to frame arguments in this way. Unanswered polemics do not lead to fruitful discussions in which the two conflicting sides have to consider each other's arguments. But such a dialogue did take place, however inchoately, between Shain and Pangle in 1987 and 1988. Unfortunately, this correspondence resembles the arrested dialogue between Strauss and Schmitt in 1932 and 1933, revealing far more eagerness on one side than on the other to continue the initiated conversation. The impetus here came entirely from Shain, who on March 23, 1987, sent Pangle at the University of Toronto an outline for a dissertation then being prepared at Yale, which eventually turned into *The Myth of American Individualism*. The outline arrived with an accompanying note, mentioning Pangle's recent piece on the Lockean origins of the American regime in the neoconservative periodical *The Public Interest*.[53]

---

[52] This correspondence was made available to the author courtesy of Professor Shain. See also Thomas L. Pangle, "The Constitution's Human Vision," *The Public Interest* 86 (Winter 1987): 77–90.

[53] Pangle's response to Shain, June 25, 1987; this refers to remarks made by Shain in a letter dated March 23, 1987.

Pangle's response sums up his rejection of the idea that Christianity had any critical bearing on the American political founding. He cites Ben Franklin's *Poor Richard's Almanac* and the eighteenth-century Massachusetts revolutionary documents collected by Oscar and Mary Handlin to support his Straussian view of early America. Pangle also dismisses the notion that the "Biblical covenant" or "traditional Christianity" influenced the revolutionary era in any significant way, and he stresses the incompatibility between "democratic thought" and "traditional Christianity," which is based on "hierarchical principles" and in the case of the Calvinists includes clearly "antidemocratic implications."

Pangle launches a moral attack on Christian theology and its social effects and berates Shain for refusing to understand that "the cause of democracy and the cause of the liberal Enlightenment are inextricably joined." Pangle warns Shain that he is playing with fire by "unearthing" Protestant Christian sources for the American republic. He is especially annoyed that Shain refers to the "founding elite" in talking about the Constitution, thereby implying that a robbery had taken place and that our founding document lacked "democratic legitimacy."

Pangle accuses Shain of being "extraordinarily imprudent." "The language [presumably in Shain's earlier note mentioning a 'bourgeois elite'] recalls the language of Carl Schmitt in 1934." "Granted this is not what you meant to evoke, my question would still be, what do you intend? To delegitimate political theory underlying the Constitution is to undermine decent republicanism as we know it." Unless the two debated these questions in a manner that Pangle considered reflective of "respect and even reverence" for "the moral and even intellectual greatness" of the Founders, the discussants would expose themselves to certain unspecified "dangers."

Shain responds in a "dilatory" fashion on March 23, 1988, in which he makes it appear that he and the respondent barely know each other, except for this exchange of letters and for a brief meeting at a professional conference the preceding summer. Shain vows to "phrase every disagreement in the appropriately deferential language," and he begs Pangle "to ignore any disrespectful comments, as no disrespect is intended."[54]

---

[54] Shain's letter to Pangle, dated March 23, 1988.

Much of this recalls Strauss trying to solicit a response from Schmitt in 1933, after Schmitt had opportunistically joined the Nazi Party. Nonetheless, Shain is far less "deferential" than the young Strauss had been in addressing Schmitt. In his (unanswered) letter, he becomes pugnacious when he mocks Pangle's moral defense of Lockean skepticism and materialism as the basis of the American regime. Shain indicates his apparent "difficulty" in grasping certain concepts such as "Enlightenments, varieties of liberalism (for example, rationalistic and romantic) and even Lockeanism." He also asks about a situation in which "a radical Christian commonwealth, a proto-liberal (whatever you take that to mean), a radical Whig all affirmed their belief in popular sovereignty." Should we assume all these advocates meant the same thing when they spoke about sovereignty? Was their understanding of that concept the same as the one that Pangle puts forth in his interpretation of Locke?

Shain then raises the question of how could it be that "large numbers of Americans, especially in the Southern and Middle colonies became more pious and embraced a very traditional form of Christianity at the same time that elites were abandoning many of the dogmas of traditional Christianity." He then asks whether a "traditional outlook," especially in early America, could not coexist with "traditional peasant communalism." Why is it necessary to identify all traditionalism or its defense with "19th century reactionary Catholic conservatism"? Perhaps there is an American exception here, which in the Anglo-American world was especially apparent in "the Reformed tradition" that Perry Miller and other American historians traced back to Puritanism.[55]

Having revisited such Old Right themes as the multifarious sources of American republicanism, the continuities between the European and American traditions, and America's "anomalous" conservatism, Shain tears into Pangle's high seriousness. He explains that he does research as an intellectual exercise and that he has never felt obliged to deliver lectures on liberal democracy. Shain freely admits that he feels "no special attraction to democracy or populism." The subjects that interested him until he began his latest project were "Hinayana Buddhism and Italian fascism."

[55] Ibid., and correspondence with the author on July 11, 2011.

Although Shain expresses respect for "Hamilton's great and preco-cious intelligence, integrity and visionary quality," he also concludes from reading him that Hamilton was "frequently pedestrian" when he turned to philosophy. Shain feels no special regard for Jefferson as a reflective thinker because he thinks that much of what Jefferson said sounds "superficial and inconsistent." Finally as for the "danger to which you advert," states Shain, "I fully accept it as a necessary consequence of living a fully human life." One could not write his-tory while imagining that any stray thought that landed up in print might "undermine" the American republic and create general chaos. Shain was responding, not without a touch of sarcasm, to the right-eous tone that he is not alone in noticing in Straussian discourse. But he was also highlighting a problem inherent in how the other side argues.

William Altman finds this moralizing tendency already present in Strauss when Strauss lectured on the danger of not believing those things that we are supposed to believe to be good Americans. According to Altman, Strauss "is castigating us for neglecting those truths" that he himself may not have inwardly embraced but which, he complains, we are not espousing with enough conviction.[56] Like his students and like Bloom's student Pangle, Strauss was not above manipulating the conscience of others. Pangle's letter reveals the same conscience game when he urged the letter recipient to be "circumspect" and to approach the Founders with "reverence." Shain was being told that he should venerate certain eighteenth-century Americans as an act of responsible citizenship. Implied, if not explicitly stated, in this exhortation is that Shain should venerate great Americans as Pangle and other Straussians chose to interpret them.

Skinner and Gadamer and their Comprehensive Critiques

The critical commentaries about to be discussed were not fashioned in the course of a bitter war. They came out of a more reflective posture than the one discernible in the Old Right adversaries of the Straussians. Indeed, what make these commentaries effective are their generally

---

[56] William H. F. Altman, *The German Stranger*, 43.

measured quality and the fact that they arose among internationally recognized authorities in the history of ideas.

An architect of one such counterhermeneutic is the Cambridge University professor of political theory, Quentin Skinner. In his *Foundations of Modern Political Thought* and in such essays as "Meaning and Understanding in the History of Ideas" and "Social Meaning and the Explanation of Social Action," Skinner expounds a method for reading political texts based on political-historical situations. He makes it plain that it is wrongheaded to speak about long-term trends in the history of political thought, or to draw the distinctions that Straussians are famous for, as between "antiquity" and "modernity" or lowered or raised horizons, without focusing on the specific political problem that past authors were addressing. Skinner is equally impatient with certain overblown generalizations, such as that Machiavelli was "standing at the gateway of the modern world" or that Locke was a "liberal political theorist" looking toward the American founding.[57]

He warns against the "process of historical foreshortening" and "the mythology of prolepsis," which are basic to the Straussian method. He also goes after the "whole repertoire of Einfluss studies" by which, for example, Hobbes is a continuation of Machiavelli or Locke an intended refinement on Hobbes. Skinner argues that it is quite possible to find the ideas of Locke's *Second Treatise* in a "whole range of de facto 1650 political writings – which, indeed, Locke is at least known to have read, while it is not at all clear that he read Hobbes's work."[58] Moreover, although Hobbes may have been guided by Machiavelli, "by whom everyone is said to have been influenced," Hobbes fails to cite Machiavelli anywhere in his political tracts.[59] Skinner does not deny that there have been loosely defined schools of political thought. What he rejects is the typically Straussian idea that all the "moderns" are traceable to Machiavelli. This assumption is usually accompanied by the tendency to portray all political thinkers since the early modern

---

[57] Quentin Skinner and James Tully, *Meaning and Context: Quentin Skinner and His Critics* (Princeton, NJ: Princeton University Press, 1988), 46; and Quentin Skinner, "Meaning and Understanding in the History of Ideas," *History and Theory*, 8 (1969): 3–53.

[58] Ibid., 46–47, 49.

[59] Ibid., 46.

period, often on the basis of nothing more than conjecture, as extensions of or as variations on someone else.

Skinner shifts the focus away from what he sees as "naïve" "teleological" intellectual history toward examinations of the contexts in which notable writers fashioned their political arguments. Without "preconceived paradigms," the historian of political thought should consider the "intention" of an author with reference to the task he was addressing in his own age. Apropos of the medieval critic of papal power, Marsilius of Padua, Skinner notes that presenting an antipapalist pamphleteer as someone who previewed "the doctrine of separation of powers" praised by Montesquieu and then honored by America's founders was "meaningless" in terms of Marsilius's concerns in the fourteenth century. This polemicist did not intend "to contribute to an eighteenth-century French constitutionalist." He was making an argument against the temporal power claimed by the Papacy in the late Middle Ages.[60]

It is equally fallacious, Skinner maintains, to interpret Machiavelli's *The Prince* as some kind of instructional tract that was produced and conventionalized during the Italian Renaissance. One cannot put *The Prince* into context without looking at the "point of Machiavelli's argument in the later chapters of his book." Machiavelli adopted a particular form of discourse to put forth his case for Italian independence and the construction of a government that would be adequate for his goal. Skinner also notes that there are operative terms in Machiavelli like "virtu" for which there may be no modern English equivalents. Contrary to a popular impression that the Renaissance author was probably "confused" about the moral or semantic implications of what he was expressing, Skinner looks for the "confusion" elsewhere. Apparent inconsistencies may reveal our imperfect understanding of what someone in the past was trying to say.[61]

In some cases, authors were "signaling" to their readers to rouse them to particular actions or to warn them against others. These were not secret writings but exhortations or warnings, as one might find

---

[60] Ibid., 42–43; Quentin Skinner, "Motives, Intentions, and the Interpretation of Texts," in *On Literary Intention*, ed. D. Newton de Molina (Edinburgh: Edinburgh University Press, 1976), 210–21.

[61] *Meaning and Context*, 95, 253–59; and Quentin Skinner, *Foundations of Modern Political Thought* (Cambridge: Cambridge University Press, 1978), I, 88–101, 180–86.

in Machiavelli when he wrote about ancient Romans to instruct the conquered Italians of his time. His contemporaries reading this would grasp what the examples cited were meant to suggest. Having added these qualifications, however, Skinner remarks that there are limits to our understanding of past thinkers, and it would be best to acknowledge these limits rather than claim to discern meanings that go beyond our capacity to determine.

He also engages the question about whether someone who examines a past "belief system" is willfully ignoring the search for Truth unless he judges that system by his own standards. Is taking a situational approach to texts, without applying contemporary understandings of moral or factual truth, an escape into relativism? Skinner explains that when he examines what are considered political classics, he sets out to "analyze the conditions which are necessary and perhaps sufficient for an understanding of these texts." Such a task does not require him to come up with modern rationales for past beliefs, for example by explaining as one might do in a science class that Jean Bodin mistook some natural occurrence for the supernatural power of witches.[62]

One should rather point out that Bodin believed in what others of his time accepted, in the Bible as the Word of God and in the Old Testament injunction that we should not suffer a witch to live. Those were prevalent beliefs in sixteenth-century Europe, and it is not the interpreter's job to explain away Bodin's conviction to make him fit a narrative of liberal democratic progress. It is irrelevant whether or not the interpreter accepts the belief of someone living in another age. The intellectual historian should approach that belief by considering the temporal and cultural situation in which it was formed.

As Skinner explains:

[B]y learning his language and by seeing what concepts he uses and how he reasons with them, I can nevertheless hope to identify without much difficulty where he is talking about witches and what he thinks about them. It is above all fatal to introduce the question of truth into social explanation. To do so is to assume that, whenever an historian encounters a belief which he or she judges to be false, the explanatory problem must always be that of accounting for a lapse of rationality. But this is to equate the holding of rational beliefs with the holding of beliefs that the historian judges to be true.[63]

---

[62] *Meaning and Context*, 237–38.
[63] Ibid., 239.

This last point brings us back to a rationalist fallacy present in Strauss's view of secret writing. He and his disciples typically find the esoteric meaning of texts to entail beliefs *they* themselves consider rational and even beneficent. Instead of thinking that their subjects are people, like ourselves, belonging to specific ages and cultures, we are made to assume that they really embraced the values and beliefs of their later interpreters. If this cannot be determined at first glance, then we must look deeper, until we can arrive at the desired coincidence of views.

Needless to say, the "hidden" views never turn out to be Christian heresies or any belief that would not accord with the prescribed rationalist worldview. A frequently heard joke about this "foreshortening" hermeneutic is that a properly read text for a Straussian would reveal that its author is probably a Jewish intellectual who resides in New York or Chicago. Being a person of moderation, the author, like his interpreter, would have attended synagogue services twice a year, on the High Holy Days – and then probably not in an Orthodox synagogue.

Another architect of a counterhermeneutic is Gadamer, who commended precisely those Teutonic poisons that Strauss warned against. Gadamer was the opposite philosophically of everything Strauss and his disciples offered as sources of American civic virtue. He referred to his teacher Heidegger with gratitude, and his writings are full of favorable allusions to Nietzsche and to historicists whom Strauss denounced in *Natural Right and History.* Contrary to a now hoary legend, it is doubtful that he and Strauss developed much of a friendship, although the two scholars grew up a few miles apart in the German province of Brunswick, where they had met as contemporaries at an early age. In the 1950s, Strauss continued to address his childhood acquaintance in letters as "Mr. Gadamer." Although Gadamer had visited the exiled Strauss in Paris in the 1930s, it is clear their relation never went very far.

Gadamer seems to have been more impressed by Jacob Klein, the expert on Plato's mathematical theories and Strauss's alter ego, than he was by Klein's apparent intellectual superior. The self-effacing Klein was for Gadamer the more interesting of the two figures.[64] It is equally

---

[64] Gadamer attributes to Klein the discovery of the relation between numbers and the structure of being in Plato's work in Klein's treatise "Platos ungeschriebene Dialektik" (1968) in *Griechische Philosophie II, Gesammelte Schriften,* 6 (Tübingen: J.C.B. Mohr, 1985), 129–54.

noteworthy that when pressed by Strauss on whether he was proposing a "general hermeneutic theory," Gadamer responded that he was
writing as the descendant of a German Protestant tradition.[65] Whereas
Strauss produced his textual interpretations in response to political
crises, more specifically his Jewishness in an insufficiently liberal
German society, the rise and triumph of Nazism, and the unwillingness
of American professors to affirm their loyalty to "liberal democracy,"
Gadamer offered less dramatic reasons for his intellectual odyssey. In
a "philosophical self-observation" published in 1976, he dwells on his
"learning experience," starting with the "provincialization of Europe
after the First World War." His learning was a form of self-discovery,
which led from the pre-Socratics all the way down to Heidegger,
through Kant, Hegel, Husserl, Dilthey, and the Bible.[66]

Strauss's correspondent was not negating the possibility that others
of different backgrounds could interpret texts intelligently and even
insightfully. He was simply declaring his own tradition, which he considered to be an intrinsic part of his learning experience. Although it is
possible to infer a critique of Strauss and his disciples from other studies by Gadamer, his most explicit and detailed critique is in his best-
known tract, *Wahrheit und Methode*. In this work, Gadamer proves to
be more radically traditionalist and more open to new ideas than were
Strauss and his school.

Gadamer's response to Strauss's attack on historicism constitutes
the appendix to his magnum opus, and here one has to look hard
for his differences with his subject because of the compliments that
are generously mixed in with them. After a discussion of the revolt
against an intense historical-mindedness in Nietzsche and Karl Löwith,
Gadamer points to Strauss as "a still more radical opponent of the
historical beliefs of modernity, who has stated his ideas in a series of
outstanding books. It is one of the heartening signs of our increasingly
narrow world in terms of the space for free thought that this professor of political philosophy at the University of Chicago can function
as such a radical critic of the political thinking of the modern age."[67]

---

[65] See the Strauss-Gadamer correspondence concerning *Wahrheit und Methode* in *The Independent Journal of Philosophy*, 2 (1978): 5–6.

[66] See Gadamer's sketch of his intellectual odyssey in *Kleine Schriften* (Tübingen: J.C.B. Mohr, 1977), 4, 257–61.

[67] Hans Gadamer, *Wahrheit und Methode: Grundzüge einer Philosophischen Hermeneutik*, third edition (Tübingen: J.C.B. Mohr, 1972), 503.

Throughout the key commentary, Gadamer wishes us to believe that "essentially [*der Sache nach*]" he and Strauss are in agreement. Earlier references in the book, to the studies on Hobbes and Spinoza, suggest that Gadamer approves of Strauss's work, especially his achievement in awakening an interest in classical studies.

What is explicitly critical in Gadamer is directed specifically at *Natural Right and History*, and particularly at those sections dealing with historicism. Gadamer charges Strauss with reductionism for associating all historicism with a "naïve" subgenus that Gadamer already criticized in addressing the father of intellectual history, Wilhelm Dilthey. This thinker had wrongly imagined that there was a vantage point in the present that allowed the observer to judge all past "worldviews" in a definitive manner.[68] Because of Dilthey's transcendent moment, we could supposedly classify the "irrational" and dogmatic thinking that had clung to earlier thinkers. Gadamer denies that he was defending this Diltheyan assumption in the preceding 500 pages of his work. Rather he was saying that an interpretation is inseparable from a historical and biographical moment. Contrary to what Strauss asserts, there is no contradiction to believing that "all knowledge is historically conditioned" and that "my knowledge is not conditioned." The two statements do "not operate at the same level." A form of "historicism that takes itself seriously must deal with the probability that one day what we now believe, may be shown to be wrong or inadequate," and this possibility exists at the interpretive as well as factual level.[69]

Nor is Gadamer defending another position that Strauss indiscriminately ascribes to all historicists: insisting that people at the present time can achieve an "unsurpassed understanding of what ancient thinkers were teaching," indeed a better understanding than what the ancient authors understood about their own work, because of philological or scientific advances. Gadamer is underlining the self-evident point that we do not think like ancient authors because our historical experiences are not the same.[70]

[68] Ibid., 505, 218–29.
[69] Ibid., 504–05
[70] This point is clearly stated in the section of *Wahrheit und Methode* dealing with "Historicism and Hermeneutics," ibid., 477–503; see also the earlier explication of the historicity of understanding in the same work, 329–44.

In fact, Strauss may be returning to "the standpoint of a perfected historical Enlightenment" when he affirms that he can understand "objectively" what an ancient author was saying, "providing it is not confused." "Leaping over the hermeneutic problem," Strauss "considers it possible to understand not what one understands about oneself, but what someone else understands himself to be saying. He also maintains that he can understand the teaching of someone else at another time and that he can understand a source in the same sense in which its author did."[71]

Strauss confidently states that "authors understand themselves necessarily and adequately."[72] He thereby backs into a naive Enlightenment standpoint by claiming to find total consistency in a text or else by attributing its inconsistency to "hidden writing" that foreshadows modern ideas. Omitted from this approach is the likelihood that inconsistent authors may be trying out "extreme possibilities" as an intellectual exercise: Particularly in the case of playful authors, "Contradictoriness may in some respects be a criterion of truth," but then again it may be what it looks like. It is altogether possible that even great authors produce contradictory statements because of oversights or because of mental exhaustion.

Gadamer assumes a more modest role for an interpreter than the one Strauss claims for himself: as someone who can achieve "objective knowledge" of what an author meant. Gadamer cites the case of a modern who might read Aristotle by applying his own form of understanding (*Verstehensweise*). The result would not be an improvement over Aristotle's call for prudential judgment (*phronēsis*), but rather an effort to relate ancient teachings to the present. That, insists Gadamer, is different from presuming to offer an improved interpretation of Aristotle's ethics. Rather we are trying to understand Aristotle's teaching in terms of our life and time, and at least partly as a "critique of abstract generality." Gadamer suggests that Strauss turns his back on this modest task because he is morally driven. Like others who have ascribed what they dislike about the present age to the heightening of historical consciousness, Strauss may be elevating "his philosophical opposition to history" to nothing more promising than "a new dogmatism."[73]

---

[71] Ibid., 506.
[72] Ibid., 512.
[73] Ibid., 284–89.

Equally relevant for this discussion are Gadamer's extended observations about "prejudice." In contrast to the Enlightenment and Strauss's political rationalism, Gadamer treats prejudice as an inescapable part of our judgment about the surrounding world. Cultural and historical prejudgment is not only the heritage that we bring to our study of the past and its authors; it is an "authority" and "tradition" that is necessary for understanding and without which our knowledge would be deficient.[74] Gadamer invokes Heidegger and his notion of "facticity." As individuals, Heidegger says, we can only grasp our relation to the ground of our existence (*Sein*) by becoming aware of our historically concrete mortal beings (*Dasein and Sein zum Tode*). We cannot transcend what we are simply by positing an objective world and then by imagining ourselves to be detached spectators. Our historicity, Heidegger taught us, permeates our self-understanding, and the culture and biographies we carry around with us contribute to what we know or seek to know.[75] To Bloom's objection that German historicists corrupted the modern West by harping on Plato's and Aristotle's Hellenic identities, Gadamer might have retorted that it is not necessary to consult German classicists about an obvious fact. Ancient philosophers were conscious of their cultural and political background, just as Strauss knew, and did not let us forget, that he was a German Jewish refugee.

There are two additional points that should be raised about Gadamer's defense of prejudice as foundational for learning. First, as Gadamer's student Günter Figal stresses, his teacher carefully distinguished between a personal peeve (such as compulsively disliking some individual or ethnic group) and a true cultural prejudice (such as thinking like a German Protestant or an ancient Athenian). Whereas the former may be a cognitive nonstarter, the latter can be historically effective (*wirkungsgeschichtlich*) in directing our understanding and enriching our knowledge.[76] Second, the value of prejudice depends

---

[74] Ibid., 250–83.
[75] *Hans-George Gadamer: Wahrheit und Methode*, ed. Günter Figal (Berlin: Akademie Verlag, 2007), 1–8, 219–36. On the existential, time-specific aspect of Heidegger's concepts of Auslegung (interpretation) and Verstehen, see Martin Heidegger, *Sein und Zeit*, seventeenth printing (Tubingen: Max Niemeyer Verlag, 1993), 150–53.
[76] See *Wahrheit und Methode*, 504; and Aristotle, *Ethica Nicomachea*, Book V (Oxford: Oxford University Press, 1965), section 134, VII, 25–30. Here Aristotle famously observes that "much of what is assumed to be natural exists by law (*nomikon*) or convention (*sunthēkē*) and both [of these norms] are necessarily mutable (*kinēta*)."

on our ability to think about it critically, even while recognizing its authority as a starting point for our hermeneutic enterprise. A diligent scholar will review his inherited and historically conditioned attitudes because, like all knowledge, these attitudes must be subject to rethinking in light of new facts.

Recognizing prejudice as integral to knowledge but subject to review may be a way of understanding the fact-value relation. Instead of a rejection of the fact-value distinction, Gadamer starts with the cultural and historical context in which our interpretations are produced, while stressing the need for critical assessment. It is not Gadamer but Strauss, the self-described antirelativist, who relativizes facts by loading values on them. By insisting that facts must serve value-ends, Strauss ends up thrusting *his* values into the center of his interpretive work. By contrast, Gadamer embraces a more judicious course. In his theory of knowledge, there is room for the weight of moral and cultural tradition but equally for critical Reason. Prejudice and critical thinking, although separate, operate together to broaden our knowledge about what is being examined.

Despite his generally penetrating response to Strauss, Gadamer makes two mistakes in his judgments about Strauss. First, he wrongly attributes to him the view that medieval natural law came out of Aristotle's comments in the *Nicomachean Ethics* about "universal laws" – for example, the constancy of wind and rain or the tendency of most people's right hand to be stronger than their left. Supposedly Strauss's return to the classics was based on the attempt to "rise above the catastrophe of modernity" by "finding a constant standard of the Just and the Unjust."[77] Thus Strauss, who was at war with historicism, "tested all arguments in light of classical philosophy." There is no evidence, however, in *Natural Right and History*, with due respect to Gadamer and to Strauss's Catholic devotees, that Strauss mistook Aristotle for a medieval scholastic. Strauss's student Harry Jaffa wrote his first book pointing out the critical differences between

---

[77] *Wahrheit und Methode*, 505; see also *Kleine Schriften*, 4,262, for Gadamer's notable observation about how "only the experienced world that is constantly presented to us as an unending task" is one in which "lack of familiarity can be overcome, and where illumination, insight and appropriation can occur and where the hermeneutic process of bringing (our percentions) into language and consciousness can complete itself."

the Aristotelian and later medieval understandings of a natural law. Certainly there is nothing in Strauss that would suggest that he held different opinion on this subject.[78]

Second, Gadamer groups Strauss with Karl Löwith among critics of historicism who were reacting against "the catastrophes of the modern era." Despite the epistolary friendship between the two exiles, their views about historicism and its alternatives were not the same. Löwith was an introspective Protestant, albeit of Jewish ancestry, and his rejection of historicism reflected a deeply religious sensibility. It involved an emphatic turning away from modern thinking characterized by the belief in Progress. So passionately opposed was Löwith to any melioristic concept of time that he was mildly critical of St. Augustine for launching linear history in the West.[79] Löwith's work, *Heilsgeschichte und Weltgeschehen*, ends with the hope that the Western world would return to a pre-Christian vision of a constant nature, or that Christianity could be cleansed of the dangerous idea that human history was moving toward a final godly age.

Although Strauss rejected historicism and studied Plato intensively, he did not seek a metaphysical solution to the problems of modernity. What Strauss privileged were "liberal democratic" values, and he scolded his fellow academics for not rallying to this political cause with suitable enthusiasm. The other loyalty that Strauss passionately expressed throughout his life was to Jewishness and the Jewish state. This loyalty came through with unmistakable force in his conversations and social judgments, even if Strauss spent only a single year of his life in Israel and even if he observed on more than one occasion that Zionism would not suffice to hold Jews together.

[78] See Harry V. Jaffa, *Thomism and Aristotelianism: A Study of the Commentary of Thomas Aquinas on the Nicomachean Ethics*, new edition (Westport and London: Greenwood Press, 1979). For yet another depiction of Strauss as someone driven by nostalgia for antiquity, see Conal Condren, *The Status and Appraisal of Ancient Texts: An Essay in Political Theory, Its Inheritance, and the History of Ideas* (Princeton, NJ: Princeton University Press, 1985), 59.

[79] A contemplative, otherworldly quality is especially evident in Löwith's post–Second World War essay, "Die Dynamik der Geschichte und des Historismus," *Eranos* 21 (1952).

5

From Political Theory to Political Practice

Defending Liberal Democracy

The study of political theory among Strauss and his disciples does not begin and end with reflections on dead white thinkers. Their studies have mandated political commitments, and it would be hard to ignore the transition from theory to practice already evident in the movement's founder. In the 1960s, Strauss engaged in a prolonged, bitter battle with the American Political Science Association and his colleagues in the political science profession. He accused them of shirking their responsibility to defend the United States during the Cold War. In a controversial epilogue to *Essays on the Scientific Studies of Politics* (1962), edited by his student Herbert J. Storing, Strauss excoriates his profession for eschewing the struggle against Soviet totalitarianism: "The crisis of liberal democracy has become concealed by a ritual which calls itself methodology or logic. This almost willful blindness to the crisis of liberal democracy is part of that crisis. No wonder that the new political science has nothing to say against those who unhesitatingly prefer surrender, that is, the abandonment of liberal democracy, to war."[1]

In his epilogue, Strauss famously distinguishes the "new political science," which refuses to take sides against Soviet tyranny, from the "old political science" that had preceded it. The old political science

[1] See *Essays on the Scientific Study of Politics*, ed. Herbert J. Storing (New York: Holt, Rinehart, and Winston, 1962), 327.

recognized a "common good" and "what is required for the good society," but it was supplanted by a new one, as it succumbed to certain moral acids, particularly the fact-value distinction. "The denial of the common good presents itself today as a direct consequence of the distinction between facts and values according to which only factual judgments, not value judgments, can be true and objective."[2] This rapidly spreading relativism swept away even the minimal "public reason" that was present in modernists like Hobbes and which allowed them to see a common interest beyond that of the isolated individual. In the new political science, not even this limited, material standard of the good could prevail. The most political scientists could now offer an individual was to show how his or her "preferences" could be satisfied by paying attention to certain objective facts.

It is the "abstinence" from moral judgment that drove the new political science into moral confusion. It led "science" into sanctioning equally all whims and appetites, on the basis of the belief that "all desires are of equal dignity." Together with this "permissive egalitarianism," political science has brought into play a "value-free analysis" that denies the premises of its own functioning. For "democracy is the tacit presupposition of the data," and without a democratic context, political science would not be able to thrive. The "laws of human behavior" it observes are only relevant where elections, political parties, and other characteristics of democracy are possible.[3]

Unfortunately, according to Strauss, the new political science undermines its own existence "by teaching the equality of all values." Instead of "teaching that there are things that are intrinsically high and others that are intrinsically low," it pretends that all values and desires are of equal worth and that social scientists must focus exclusively on observable phenomena.

Strauss ends his critical remarks with a graphic and now famous passage about those he is scolding: "Only a great fool would call the new political science diabolical: it has no attributes peculiar to fallen angels. It is not even Machiavellian, for Machiavelli's teaching is graceful, subtle and colorful. Nor is it Neronian. Nonetheless, one may say

---

[2] Ibid., 324.
[3] Ibid., 326.

of it that it fiddles while Rome burns. It is excused by two facts: it does not know that it fiddles, and it does not know that Rome burns."[4]

One can easily read into Strauss's epilogue, which certainly evoked strong reactions from his fellow academicians, shades of Carl Schmitt, and particularly Schmitt's *The Concept of the Political*. Like Schmitt, Strauss is stressing the critical situation, which defines "the political," as a friend-enemy confrontation. Like Schmitt, he is distinguishing the *Ernstfall* from existentially inferior activities, such as the gathering of data for a "value-free" study of American elections or the accumulation of statistical information concerning voting turnouts. Like Schmitt, Strauss is equating what is "political" with what is morally serious, namely the struggle between self-identified communities, in which the losing side will pay a high price for its defeat. Whether or not all the losers will forfeit their lives, they will be forced to abandon their way of life, indeed what characterizes them as a polis. Those who refuse to notice what is going on are moral fools or worse.

A second way of interpreting Strauss's brief is as a defense of the freedom of a free society against one that is not and has aggressive designs. Strauss is warning his fellow intellectuals against staying neutral in a struggle in which their very raison d'être is at stake. How could they occupy themselves with trifles when the conditions for a scholarly life had been called into question? If the other side won, there would be neither "objective" independent scholars nor parliamentary processes around which to organize one's political scientific inquiry. Everyone would be the slave of a state that despises freedom. Instead of preparing their students to face such a threat, however, the new political scientists were justifying moral self-indulgence. They were blinding the younger generation to what should truly count for them, namely the preservation of free institutions.

Without excluding other readings, there is an argument here that, for Strauss, may have been the most critical. He is writing in defense of "liberal democracy" as the highest American value, a value to which other values should be subordinated. The "qualitative difference" between liberal democracy and its enemies is at the heart of Strauss's case against the new science of politics, which allegedly believes that "no value judgment, including those supporting liberal democracy,

---

[4] Ibid., 327; and Nasser Behnegar, *Leo Strauss, Max Weber, and the Scientific Study of Politics*, 149–66.

are rational." Although Strauss does not produce the "iron-clad argument" that the other side fails to make, he does try to nudge it toward his position by suggesting that even "the rational society" or the "non-ideological regime" expresses an implied "preference for liberal democracy."[5] That regime is the presupposition for what political science does, although those who depend on this regime have not been honest enough to recognize their dependence on it. They harp on the false distinction between facts and values, going back to Weber, and this allows academic beneficiaries to shirk their obligation to uphold liberal democracy in its hour of peril.

Strauss's attacks on political scientists for their "value-free analysis" and for their implicit moral relativism and indifference to liberal democracy are based on a fallacy that Strauss and his students could never quite abandon. Contrary to what he states, there is no necessary connection between accepting the fact-value distinction and preaching the equality of all moral positions. It is entirely possible to draw a distinction between facts and values while believing no less firmly in objective ethical principles. It is equally possible for someone who accepts the inseparability of values and facts to be an ethical relativist. Why does the acceptance of a certain methodological perspective for investigating political phenomena signify the rejection of moral absolutes? This affirmation of unwarranted conclusions is not an isolated mistake, driven by the rush to battle. It is a fundamental flaw in the understanding of the social sciences that Straussians commit over and over •again.

In an introduction to an anthology of Strauss's essays, titled *The Rebirth of Political Rationalism*, Thomas L. Pangle reinforces the view of liberal democracy as a "vital form of republicanism." Unlike "such philhellenic critics of liberal democracy" as Hannah Arendt, but also unlike Machiavelli, Rousseau, and Nietzsche, Strauss felt "no nostalgic longing for the polis and its vita activa." He rejoiced at living in a liberal democratic regime, although he "saw perhaps more clearly than anyone the disharmony in the American tradition between an older, nobler, but less influential classical and civic ideal and a new, even more triumphant, permissive and individualistic order."[6]

[5] See *Essays on the Scientific Study of Politics*, 324–25.
[6] Thomas L. Pangle, *The Rebirth of Political Rationalism: An Introduction to the Thought of Leo Strauss* (Chicago: University of Chicago, 1989), xxiv.

Strauss also understood, however, the need to mix the "tolerance and respect for personal liberty that are the hallmarks of liberalism" with other older traditions. He recognized the "the tendency of democratic tolerance to degenerate first into the easygoing belief that all points of view are equal and then into the strident belief that anyone who argues for the superiority of a distinctive moral insight, way of life, or human type is somehow elitist or antidemocratic – and hence immoral."[7]

Pangle suggests the manner in which Strauss tried to battle an excess of democracy. He favored a revival of "the Graeco-Roman ideal of an active, proud citizenry imbued with knowledgeable respect for outstanding statesmanship." In what is an obvious reference to the cults of Lincoln and Churchill, Pangle expresses Strauss's disdain for "those thoughtlessly egalitarian historians who debunk rather than make more intelligible the greatness of statesmen."[8]

Pangle appeals to Strauss's legacy when he complains about how "scholarly and teaching fashions" have "undermined the already precarious respect for political debate." Pangle goes on to lament the fact that any deviation from nonjudgmental egalitarianism is now viewed as "elitist or antidemocratic." Strangely enough, he pairs this lament with a concern already voiced by Tocqueville that modern democracy leads to a "soft tyranny of the majority" and to the "chastened and intimidated individual's incapacity to resist the moral authority of mass 'public opinion.'"

It might be asked how liberal democracy has given rise at the same time, according to Pangle, to unqualified relativism and the widespread acceptance of a monolithic "public opinion." Pangle tries to cover both bases when he speaks about a "leveling moralism that disguises itself as relativism" and about a "contemporary democratic moralism" that "overstresses the virtues of a rather soft or flaccid sociability."[9]

The answer to this degenerate democracy seems to be a more virile and more warlike liberal democracy, combined with muscular discourse. Perhaps the closest Straussian academics can come to this desideratum is by lecturing on democratic statesmanship, as embodied by their

[7] Ibid., xxv.
[8] Ibid., xxiv.
[9] Ibid., xxv.

heroes, and by encouraging no-holds-barred debates. Unfortunately, the Straussians have never had any inclination to engage in vigorous debate with the opposition, as the previous chapters indicate. They have preferred occupying and transforming political science departments, and they have happily ignored locking horns with their most spirited critics, particularly those on the right. Although this observation is not a put-down, it does raise questions about how Straussians conceive of "debate" in the liberal democracy that they are trying to salvage.

One effect of their rallying to a liberal democratic regime has been to give new direction to the American conservative movement. Up until the 1970s, conservative thinkers and activists held to the distinction between "constitutional republicanism" and "liberal democracy." Self-described conservatives as diverse as Russell Kirk, Frank Meyer, William F. Buckley, and Murray N. Rothbard insisted that the United States had been founded as a nonegalitarian republic that assigned limited power to the federal union. Over time, this regime had drifted into a highly centralized managerial state that superseded the original design of the Constitution, with its intricate system of divided sovereignty.[10]

From the standpoint of this older republicanism, Lincoln, FDR, and other Straussian heroes were dangerous centralizers and levelers, certainly not paradigms of great statesmanship. In the last thirty years, it is the Straussian concept of liberal democracy, with its succession of world-historical warrior-leaders, that has come to reshape the establishment Right. Such recognized "conservative" authors as Allan Bloom, Harry Jaffa, Charles Kesler, Victor Davis Hanson, and Robert Kagan have glorified liberal democratic statesmanship, and works by "democracy"-boosting Straussians and those who have been

---

[10] See George H. Nash, *The Conservative Intellectual Movement in America since 1945*, 67–78; and the debate over centralized government and equality between Harry Jaffa and M. E. Bradford in "Equality, Justice and the American Revolution," *Modern Age*, 21.2 (Spring 1977): 114–26, and "The Heresy of Equality," *Modern Age* 20.1 (Winter 1976): 627–37. Also relevant to this debate are Robert Nisbet, *The Present Age: Progress and Anarchy in Modern America*, reprint (Indianapolis, IN: Liberty Fund, 2003); and Murray N. Rothbard, *Egalitarianism as a Revolt against Nature*, reprint, ed. David Gordon (Auburn, AL: Mises Institute, 2000). For a plea to return to an older conservative conception of the American Republic, see Pat Buchanan's syndicated column (May 11, 2011) "After the Revolution."

converted to their ideas have found their way on to *National Review*'s list of "conservative classics."[11]

Straussians contributed to the process by which the conservative movement came to redefine itself during the Cold War as the defender of "democratic values" – rather than as what that movement had viewed itself as upholding before its transformation in the 1970s and 1980s. In the 1950s, "conservatives" stood for Christian civilization engaged in mortal combat with godless communism, or else they viewed themselves as fighting socialism, in all its insidious forms, as apostles of the free market. The Straussian reconfiguration of the conservative worldview started in earnest in the late 1960s, as Straussians began writing for movement conservative publications. These contributors emphasized the war against student radicalism, which Bloom, Walter Berns, Werner Dannhauser, and other Straussians had experienced at Cornell when that university was taken over by New Leftist students in 1968.

There were earlier associations, however. *National Review, Modern Age*, and *Intercollegiate Review* all threw open their doors to Strauss and his student Harry Jaffa before the influx of the late 1960s occurred. By the 1970s, the momentum had begun to change irreversibly, in the direction of the newcomers. William F. Buckley, the founder of *National Review*, revealed by 1971 that his older worldview had been jolted by Jaffa's defense of equality as a "conservative value." This led to, among other practical results, Buckley's increasingly favorable view of the civil rights movement and eventually his praise for Lincoln and Martin Luther King, Jr.[12] It would be wrong to imagine that this process of change originated mostly with the newcomers. The movement itself yielded to the force of what seemed irresistible ideas.

This sequence of events was in no way hampered by the competition between two rival schools of Straussians: one organized around Jaffa and his acolytes at Claremont and then extended (in its Catholic

---

[11] For a particularly animated response to this change in the conservative movement, see Bruce Frohnen, "Has Conservatism Lost Its Mind?" in *Policy Review*, 67 (Winter 1994): 62–66; and Paul Gottfried, *Conservatism in America*, 152–67.

[12] See Margot Hentoff's review of Buckley's *The Governor Listeth*, "Unbuckled," in *New York Review of Books* (December 10, 1970): 19. In the anthology *Did You Ever See a Dream Walking?* (Indianapolis, IN and New York: Bobbs and Merrill, 1970), Buckley devotes almost thirty pages (399–427) to reprinting, with obvious reverence, Strauss's defense of liberal democracy in his critique of the "new political science."

embodiment) to the University of Dallas and, finally, Hillsdale College; and the other group claiming to be founded at the University of Chicago and taking its direction from Bloom, Mansfield, and Pangle. This schism may have less relevance for American political and cultural life than the dispute in the early Church over the nature of the Trinity. Whereas Christian authorities were arguing over serious theological questions, it is hard to discern any long-range significance in those issues dividing the two Straussian schools of opinion.

Whether or not Jaffaites claim to find "democratic equality" already prefigured in the middle books of Aristotle's *Politics* or in Judeo-Christian religiosity, and whether or not the Chicago Straussians have stressed the secularist Lockean origin of liberal democracy, the two schools do not reveal sharp ideological differences. They represent only minor variations on shared political and moral positions. A pronounced attitude in favor of wars understood as democratic crusades, sympathy for a "moderate" welfare state and for the civil rights movement, up until the point that it became identified with the awarding of minority quotas and a negative attitude toward Israel, are the shared tenets of both persuasions.[13] *National Review* celebrates simultaneously without any sense of contradiction Bloom's magnum opus *Closing of the American Mind* and Jaffa's *Crisis of the House Divided*, a glowing study of Lincoln and his re-founding of America as a nation dedicated to the universal proposition of equality. Whatever separates the partisans of these authors does not in any way affect the iconic status of either in the conservative movement.[14]

A telling reminder of this is a long review essay in the *Claremont Review of Books* by one of Allan Bloom's stellar students and a professor of political science at the University of Toronto, Clifford Orwin. This essay, which is an attack on Anne Norton's monograph, is done by an "East Coast Straussian" but published in the Jaffaite flagship

---

[13] Although Jaffaites are unfavorable to Woodrow Wilson, their negative attitude is for the most part unrelated to Wilson's decision to enter the First World War on the side of England. The Jaffaites attack Wilson for his "German connection" – that is, for the fact that his constitutional writings "have roots in "German idealism and historicism." Wilson treated rights as products of History rather than as a universal legacy. See Ronald J. Pestritto's comments on this subject in the *Claremont Review of Books* (Winter 2002): 29, and (Summer 2004): 25–26.

[14] See "Books, Arts, and Manners," *National Review* (December 19, 2005): 102–11.

journal. What makes this writing of special interest is not so much its predictable complaints about Norton breaking a trust with those who taught and befriended her at Chicago as what it indicates about Orwin, his teacher, and other Straussian luminaries. In response to Norton's charge that *The Closing of the American Mind* prefigured "the conservative position in the emergent cultural wars," Orwin offers these revealing statements:

But Bloom was never a conservative, and he wrote that book as a liberal addressing liberals. The initial reviews in the liberal press were favorable, and conservatives championed the book only when liberals recommended it by turning against it. Bloom was a lifelong Democrat who revered Roosevelt's New Deal as the peak of American liberal politics. (One thing he shared with Strauss is that both voted for Adlai Stevenson.) Shortly before his death in the fall of 1992, Bloom exhorted me to support Bill Clinton. He insisted that only the Democratic Party had consistently met the challenges of the 20th century.[15]

Orwin lets it be known that, like Bloom and Paul Wolfowitz, he stands in the tradition of "fighting liberal Democrats," and he is sure that if Strauss were around, he would be seconding the war of choice in Iraq: "Would Strauss have supported the bold gambit of extending liberal democracy by draining the Augean stables of Islamic tyranny and theocracy? Yes – if he had accepted the long-term necessity of so doing in order to defend the existing liberal democracies in this age of terrorism and weapons of mass destruction."[16] Here too a bellicose missionary spirit is very much in evidence, but it is doubtful that one could link it to anything identifiably right-wing, including the American conservative movement of twenty years earlier.[17]

---

[15] See Clifford Orwin, "The Straussians Are Coming," *Claremont Review of Books* (Spring 2005): 15.

[16] Ibid., 16; and Thomas West's essay "Leo Strauss and American Foreign Policy," (Summer 2004): 13–16.

[17] A particularly useful commentary for understanding the nonrightist nature of Straussian as well as neoconservative foreign policy is Steven M. Walt, "What intervention in Libya tells us about neocon-liberal alliances," on the *Foreign Policy* Web site, *http://walt.foreignpolicy.com/?sms_ss=email&at_xt=4d87a2d937a4c31b%2Co.* Except for the greater reliance on international institutions to carry out their goals, liberal interventionists, according to Walt, resemble neoconservatives in their understanding of America as an especially democratic society with a universal conversionary mission. This may be a nouvum (on March 21, 2011) that a major academic figure in international relations has published such an observation. More typically,

The Improvised Right

Strauss and the Straussians have succeeded in doing the opposite of what German historian Ernst Nolte and, before him, Marxists credited the fascists with having produced in interwar Europe: "a counter-revolutionary imitation of the Left."[18] The Straussians have pulled off an equally enterprising feat by assuming a certain right-wing style without expressing a right-wing worldview. They have developed and popularized their own hybrid form of political rhetoric, to the consternation of both libertarians and much of the Left. Two libertarian disciples of Ayn Rand, C. Bradley Thompson and Yaron Brook, view the Straussians as fascist-like theorists who have won over neoconservative journalists bent on military adventures. According to Thompson and Brook,

Strauss's philosophical method and ideas shaped the neocons' diagnosis and prognosis of Western society, their condemnation of Enlightenment liberalism, their ironic defense of America and the principles of its revolutionary founding, their call for a new form of statesmanship grounded in Machiavellian prudence, their call for a new political morality that promotes self-sacrifice and service as the highest virtues, their insistence that America devote themselves to religion and nationalism, their demand that government regulate both man's material and spiritual needs, and finally, their call for a reconsideration of classical natural right and Platonic political philosophy.[19]

While there is no need to recapitulate the counterarguments heretofore made, it should be noted that not all of Thompson's and Brook's complaints would displease the Straussians. A generally, if not uniformly, favorable assessment of their book *Neoconservatism: An Obituary for an Idea* was produced by Michael Zuckert, who recently argued in a book undertaken with his wife that neoconservatism and

the neoconservatives are shown by friends and foes alike to be on the flag-waving far right, in contrast to Obama and his supporters, who are thought not to share their fondness for military solutions and American exceptionalist rhetoric. Walt sees the differences between neoconservatives and Obamaites as being one of degree rather than of kind.

[18] François Furet and Ernst Nolte, *Fascisme et Communisme* (Paris: Hachette, 1998), 83–85; and Ernst Nolte, *Der Faschismus in seiner Epoche* (Munich: Piper, 2000), particularly the introduction.

[19] C. Bradley Thompson and Yaron Brook, *Neoconservatism: Obituary for an Idea* (New York: Paradigm Publishers, 2010), 10.

Straussianism are two very different movements. Yet Zuckert wrote a blurb for the Thompson-Brook work, in which he commented on Thompson's "degree of respect and intellectual care" as an interpreter of "relevant texts." With due respect to Zuckert, Thompson and Brook do not show any particular care in examining evidence. They repeat many of the complaints against Strauss that are present in Shadia Drury without adding much insight of their own. Although their politics may be different from that of this earlier critic (unlike Drury, who is a feminist and social democrat, Thompson and Brook define themselves loosely as laissez-faire capitalists), all these critics rail against the Straussians as right-wing militarists.[20]

There is an aspect of the Thompson-Brook brief, however, that Straussians might consider useful, namely the connection assumed between their side and support for international struggles for "universal values." Notably, there is nothing intrinsically right-wing, let alone fascist, about supporting such struggles or defending America's past crusades for democracy. What the international relations scholar Michael Desch describes as "America's liberal illiberalism," namely continuing mobilization for wars to be fought for liberal democratic values, may not be to everyone's taste.

There is no reason, however, to treat "liberal illiberalism" as a function of the historic Right.[21] Fighting wars for universal, egalitarian propositions was never a priority for authoritarian conservatives like Antonio Salazar or Francisco Franco. Nor is this type of crusade an activity that one might associate with American conservative isolationists like Robert Taft. It is an expression of progressive militarism, a form of principled belligerence that French Jacobinism, Wilsonianism, and wars of communist liberation have all exemplified at different times.[22]

---

[20] Similar to the earlier attacks in their book on their subjects is the discussion of the "Mussolinian" derivation of Strauss's statecraft; ibid., 215–17.

[21] Michael Desch, "America's Illiberal Liberalism," *International Security*, 32:3, 9–43.

[22] Lee Congdon's biography, *George Kennan: A Writing Life* (Wilmington, DE: ISI, 2009), makes clear to what extent the American political thinker George Kennan identified military adventurism with the political Left. Kennan associated aggressive designs not so much with military splendor as with the crusading spirit that he traced to the French and Bolshevik revolutions and to Woodrow Wilson's "war to end all wars." See also Richard M. Gamble, *The War for Righteousness: Progressive Christianity, the Great War, and the Messianic Nation* (Wilmington, DE: ISI, 2003);

A defense of such militarism can be found in the work of Strauss's distinguished student, Walter Berns, who is John M. Olin Professor Emeritus at Georgetown and a long-time resident scholar at American Enterprise Institute. An often penetrating analyst of constitutional and judicial questions, Berns has devoted numerous tracts to explaining how the United States is a creedal nation founded on the "all men are created equal" passage in the Declaration of Independence. Among the implications of this founding, Berns explains in his books *In Defense of Liberal Democracy* and *Making Patriots*, is to be steadily engaged in the cause of democracy and equality: "Ours is not a parochial patriotism; precisely because it comprises our attachment to principles that are universal, we cannot be indifferent to the welfare of others. To be indifferent, especially to the rights of others, would be un-American."[23]

Paul Gottfried, "The Invincible Wilsonian Matrix," *Orbis*, 51.2 (Spring 2007): 239–50, and "Antecedents of Neoconservative Foreign Policy," *Historically Speaking*, 12, 1 (January 2010): 35–39. One of the first and only references to the difference between traditional militarism and its revolutionary democratic manifestation is in Thomas Mann's First World War polemic, *Betrachtungen eines Unpolitischen* in *Politische Schriften und Reden*, 1 (Frankfurt am Main: Fischer Bücherei, 1968), 20–31. If one looks beyond the wartime enthusiasms of this 400-page tract, one may notice its insight into the warlike spirit of the "pacifistic, virtuous republican citizen" imposing human rights and cosmopolitanism on other peoples. Particularly useful is Mann's distinction (made earlier by the philosopher Max Scheler) between the *Gesinnungsmilitarismus* in traditional societies, valuing martial virtues, and the *Zweckmilitarismus* pursued by democratic cosmopolites. Unlike the older form of militarism, in which warriors could still behave "in a chivalric fashion" despite their countries being at war, in its updated form, war is functional and subordinated to a "new feeling" and the "sense of a world civilization" based on human rights (ibid., 25). Mann styles both forms of military organization and military élan "militaristic" but predicts that *Zweckmilitarismus* may become the more dominant expression of military energy if the Allies triumph in the War. Mann also observes that *Zweckmilitaristen* and the *Zivilisationsliteraten* (the men of letters who talk about building a world civilization) are delighted to "shed blood," providing it serves a progressive cause (ibid., 46–47). Note that Mann was commenting here not on Wilson's "crusade for democracy," but on intellectuals in neutral countries who took sides against his country and, above all, on Germany's war with the French Republic (a regime that appealed to Jacobin symbols). Although the *Betrachtungen* were not published until 1918, the early part was probably composed in 1915. See my German essay on these contrasting forms of militarism presented in Mann's tract, "Über die Widersprüche der demokratischen Gesinnungsethik," on the Blaue Narzisse Web site, http://www.blauenarzisse.de/index.php/anstoss/2421-thomas
[23] Walter Berns, *Making Patriots* (Chicago: University of Chicago Press, 2001), 8.

For Berns, as for Allan Bloom, American wars have been "educational experiments" undertaken to force those who stubbornly resist them to embrace our democratic values. The most redemptive of these ordeals was Lincoln's righteous war against the slaveholding American South, a struggle that Berns considers a sacred cause, indeed one that, more than any other war, "should make us patriots." Berns considers Lincoln to be "patriotism's poet," and as "our spokesman and poet," Lincoln is and should be viewed the way Europeans view their great national writers. It should be the duty of our public schools to teach us patriotism by calling attention to Lincoln and his struggle to vindicate the foundational teaching of our government that all men are created equal.[24]

Berns finds an imperfect precursor for this country in the ancient Greek polis; more than once he describes the American regime as a "politeia," by which he means, according to Aristotle's usage, a way of life as well as a form of government. Ancient Greeks understood that "patriotism means love of country and implies a willingness to sacrifice for it, to fight for it, perhaps even to give one's life for it." Moreover, Athenians, like Americans who are committed to their country's moral mission, "were enjoined to be lovers of Athens because they were Athens – in a way, by loving their city, they loved themselves – and because by gaining an empire, Athens provided them with the means by which they gained fame and glory."[25]

But Berns is quick to explain that "America is a republic, but not a republic like Athens and Sparta." We cultivate "industrious and other private habits that distinguish us from the Spartans, Athenians, Corinthians, and the rest; there is also the size and composition of our population." We revel in diversity, and unlike ancient Greece with its restrictive citizenship, "anybody can become an American." This is because of "the principles governing our birth as a nation and then incorporated in the Republic we established and ordained."[26]

It was precisely because of our "first principles," according to Berns, which favor privacy as well as equality, and because of the prevalence of Christianity, which separates things of God and Caesar, that patriotic

---

[24] Ibid., 99.
[25] Ibid., 17.
[26] Ibid., 18.

teachings are all the more necessary for us. Equally important, unlike ancient democracy, our form of government involves representation that removes the citizen even further from civic life. Berns seems to be arguing that wars, and especially those waged for our universal democratic faith, may be essential for creating public-minded citizens. He is also concerned that the country will not be able to defend its creed and way of life unless we are firmly convinced of the truth of its founding idea: "Would Americans have fought for the Union – and 359,528 of them died fighting for it – if they had not been taught in their schools that the Union was founded on nothing more than an *opinion* concerning human nature and the rights affixed to it?"[27]

Straussians side unreservedly with the liberal internationalism that prevailed in the monumental struggles of the twentieth century. Their justification for an American world mission hearkens back to the Kennedy and Truman eras, but the Straussians, and particularly the Jaffaites, have added a certain martial fervor that can be discerned in Berns's tribute to Lincoln, the democratic orator and war leader:

War is surely an evil, but as Hegel said, it is not an "absolute evil." It exacts the supreme sacrifice, but precisely because of that it can call forth such sublime rhetoric as Lincoln's. His words at Gettysburg serve to remind Americans in particular of what Hegel said people in general needed to know, and could be made to know by means of war and the sacrifices demanded of them in wars: namely, that their country is more than a "civil society" and the purpose of which is the protection of individual and selfish interests.[28]

Light might be thrown on this agonistic spirit by looking at a letter that Strauss wrote to Willmoore Kendall on September 23, 1963, about "the idiocy" of Kennedy's proposed test-ban treaty with the Soviets. Strauss mocks Kennedy as someone who acts as he does because of an obsession with "image." Kennedy's "indecent respect" for image, Strauss says, may also "come from sheer fear which is a much more decent motivation than the disgraceful delusionism now rampant in Washington." In enlarging on his key point, Strauss adds this observation: "In 1951 or 52 Walter Lippmann wrote a column demanding that the long rule of the Democratic Party must come to an end lest the

[27] Ibid., 143.
[28] Walter Berns, *Defending Liberal Democracy* (Chicago: Gateway Edition, 1984), 152.

festering dissatisfaction would lead to an outbreak of mad right wing extremism. I believe one could use this argument properly restated against the re-election of Kennedy."[29]

Although it would be hard to depict Strauss as a leftist on the basis of his anti-Kennedy strictures, one should not ignore his concerns about the possible "outbreak of mad right wing extremism." As a refugee from a German movement once identified with the far Right and as someone who never quite lost his sense of Jewish marginality, Strauss was anxious about the "festering dissatisfaction" on the American right. A patriotic, anticommunist conservatism, one that was open to the concerns of Strauss and his followers, could lessen this anxiety about right-wing extremism. Such a contrived Right would not locate itself on the nativist or traditional nationalist right, nor would it be closed to progressive winds in the direction of the civil rights revolution that was then taking off. But it would be anti-Soviet – and emphatically pro-Zionist. In a nutshell, it would be Cold War liberalism, with patriotic fanfare. Moreover, it would justify the progressive measures of the 1960s, whether the Civil Rights Act, the Voting Rights Act, or the Immigration Reform of 1965, as necessary steps to mobilize our liberal democracy against the Soviet threat.

Another text pointing favorably toward a militant, reforming democracy is in the preface to the English edition of *The Critique of Spinoza*. Here Strauss cites the reasons that Jews in Germany could not follow the path of assimilation, and he dwells on "the failure of the liberal solution." Unfortunately, "the liberal solution brought at best legal equality, but not social equality; as a demand of reason it had no effect on the feelings of the non-Jews." Although Strauss here is describing what appears to be an obdurately anti-Jewish population, he is also suggesting that Jews in Europe outside of Germany, where liberal solutions were undertaken, "could not regain their honor by assimilating themselves as individuals to the nations among which they lived or by becoming citizens like other citizens of liberal states." [30]

Whereas the Jewish problem might have posed, for Strauss, a particular barrier, given the persistence of anti-Semitic legacies, he

[29] See *Willmoore Kendall: The Maverick of American Conservatism* (Lanham, MD: Lexington Books, 2002), 247–48.

[30] Leo Strauss, *Liberalism Ancient and Modern*, 228.

is also commenting on liberalism itself. By this he means a political theory and a political practice that draw sharp distinctions between what the state is allowed to do to shape human conduct and what should be left to civil society. Strauss is speaking explicitly about the application of classical liberal legal principles, what the Germans call *Rechtsstaatlichkeit*, to political practice, and he is stressing the ineffectiveness of these principles in rooting out millennial prejudices. Strauss in his remark was not expressing a right-wing or classical conservative view; he was conveying the kind of thinking that fueled the civil rights movement and other related crusades against discrimination in the United States, which were going on toward the end of Strauss's life.

The cure for this problem of discrimination against Jews, Strauss indicates in the preface, was "political Zionism," a solution that he backed in principle. What had to be done at the same time, however, was to make life tolerable for those Jews who, like Strauss, did not embrace the Zionist option. Their alternative was "liberal democracy," by which the writer meant something more fortifying than freedom as that term would be understandable to nineteenth-century European bourgeoisie or contemporary libertarians. Strauss may have favored a strong democracy, of the kind that has appealed to Jaffa, Berns, and Bloom. This democracy would be actively committed to universal principles and would see itself in a tradition of democratic heroes stretching back to Lincoln and the signers of the Declaration of Independence.[31]

This sanitized or virtual Right has found a powerful voice in Harry Jaffa's Claremont Institute, a foundation that combines a generally interventionist approach to dealing with America's undemocratic enemies abroad with generally progressive positions on racial and immigration questions. After thirty years, this foundation is a well-endowed presence in the movement conservative community, and figures who are affiliated with the Institute, like Charles Kesler and William Bennett, appear frequently on network TV, including the *Today* show.

[31] For a statement of Jaffa's worldview, see *The Conditions of Freedom: Essays in Political Philosophy* (Baltimore and London: Johns Hopkins Press, 2000), particularly the tribute to Strauss on the first page of the essay "What Is Equality?" 149–60, and the defense of wars waged in the name of human rights, "The Truth about Wars," 262–65.

The Institute's position on Israel is one of unqualified support for the nationalist coalition now ruling the Jewish state. The *Claremont Review of Books* and the speeches of Jaffa strongly suggest the inseparability of "conservative values" from both the crusade against "Islamofascism" and a categorical endorsement of the Israeli Right. The Jaffaites also emphasize the indispensable role of public education in promoting "democratic values." Far from being advocates of a diminished state presence, Jaffa and his followers happily espouse the kind of strong government that is thought to aid their foreign policy and value instruction.[32]

Although Strauss was close to Jaffa and spent considerable time with him in the 1960s, there is no proof that he would have approved of his student's political plan in all its details. What is being suggested is that Strauss's concern about chastening the Right and his favorable view of the Anglo-American liberal democratic regime, and especially Churchill, animated such projects as the Claremont Institute. Without Strauss's teaching and example, their own mission might have been less inspired, if not entirely unthinkable.

The Neoconservative Connection

A vexed question in recent years concerns the alleged ties between Strauss and the Straussians and the rise on neoconservatism. The received wisdom is stated by long-time *International Herald Tribune* editor William Pfaff in his best-selling critique of George W. Bush's foreign policy, *The Irony of Manifest Destiny*. Pfaff goes over what should be familiar ground when he provides a pedigree for the neoconservatives, going back to Carl Schmitt and from Schmitt to the Nazis. Because of this telltale connection, "their (the Straussians') influence was chiefly in emphasizing the primacy of the state as a national community in opposition to 'others,' in justifying exceptional and extreme

---

[32] See the YouTube on Bill Bennett as Claremont Institute's Washington scholar, http://www.bennettmornings.com/pages/meetourteam/; and Joseph Tartakovsky's "Ungrateful Volcano" in the *Claremont Review of Books* (Winter 2006): 8–9. A look at the *Claremont Review*'s fall 2010 issue should confirm that East Coast Straussians, including Harvey Mansfield and Jeremy Rabkin, are well represented in this publication put out by rival Straussians. This is yet another proof that the rift between the two schools has been vastly overstated.

uses of power to assure state security in times of crisis, and in their identification of American liberalism – especially in its 1968 manifest-ation – as a force of national political and cultural decline."[33]

Pfaff's genealogical assertions are offered without proof. He takes at face value certain allegations that have sprung from the media and academics, particularly during the Bush II administration. He never questions the supposed continuity of thought that goes from the neo-conservatives by way of Strauss to European fascism and, at least indi-rectly, the Nazis. These charges are by now old hat and can be traced back to a number of incriminatory works starting in the 1990s. In these broadsides, Strauss is alleged to have been an unreserved Schmittian, whereas Schmitt is depicted as a Nazi from his earliest youth on. The neoconservatives, it is said, slavishly followed Strauss, insofar as Strauss perpetuated Schmittian teachings, which were related to Nazi ideology. In John McCormick's version, a Schmittian-tinged Nazism conveyed by Strauss came to infect the Republican Party, just as Newt Gingrich was becoming Speaker of the House in 1994. In all these accounts, left-of-center partisanship drives the effort to link Schmitt and Strauss to the neoconservatives and the GOP.[34]

The question remains whether there is something in our subjects' approach to political life that renders what is mostly misrepresenta-tion partly believable. This does not mean accepting in its entirety a misrepresentation that has been devised for partisan reasons. It is rather to investigate the link that is proposed between Straussians and neoconservatives. Are there grounds that might cause one to see them as closely interrelated if not totally identical?

A methodological problem with how the Zuckerts dissociate the two is that their work descends rapidly into biographical trifles. Does it really matter whether Clarence Thomas and Irving Kristol studied

---

[33] See William Pfaff, *The Irony of Manifest Destiny: The Tragedy of American Foreign Policy* (New York: Walker & Company, 2010), 174.

[34] One especially penetrating critique of the attempt to link Strauss through Schmitt to European fascism has received strikingly little attention. That may be because this essay does not fit the needs or interests of any major opinion leaders. See the commentary by Paul Piccone and Gary Ulmen "Uses and Abuses of Carl Schmitt," *Telos*, 122 (Winter 2002): 3–12. An earlier version of this paper was delivered in Italian at a conference in Rome, "Carl Schmitt: Pensatore Politico del XX Secolo," on November 27, 2001.

directly under Strauss to notice certain affinities between the admirers and those they admire? Thomas traces back his worldview to Harry Jaffa, whereas Irving Kristol, however limited his knowledge of political theory, declared himself without qualification to be a Straussian. Two neoconservative policy advisors, Paul Wolfowitz and Richard Perle, say the Zuckerts, may be more difficult to subsume under a Straussian rubric. This does not mean, however, that there is no connection between neoconservative policy advisors and the Straussian thinking that these advisors praise to the skies.

The Zuckerts stress the fact that of the twenty-six authors included in Irving Kristol's *The Essential Neoconservative Reader*, only two contributors, Leon Kass and William Kristol, were "recognizably touched by Strauss."[35] Leaving aside the question of how much influence must be assumed to be "recognizably touched" by something, it is nonetheless the case that *Commentary, Weekly Standard, National Review*, and other neoconservative publications are full of contributions from self-described Straussians. In which camp would the Zuckerts place John Podhoretz, the scion of a neocon founding family and the editor of *Commentary*, who studied with and venerates Allan Bloom? What do we do with Irving's wife and Bill's mother, Gertrude Himmelfarb, who has filled her recent essays with flattering references to Straussian authors? Her son Bill, according to Nina Easton in *The Gang of Five*, was considered to be the most enthusiastic Straussian of his generation during his studies at Harvard.[36] Zuckert is correct that Straussians

---

[35] Catherine and Michael Zuckert, *The Truth About Leo Strauss*, 266. In a strained attempt to dissociate the Straussians from the neoconservatives, Peter Minowitz in *Straussophobia* (page 277) tells us that there were "professed Straussians" who opposed the invasion of Iraq as well as those who pushed it. Presumably the invasion enjoyed overwhelming neoconservative endorsement. However, the only opposition from his camp Minowitz could find was from Nathan Tarcov as well as (two presumed liberal Democrats) George Anastaplo and William Galston. Minowitz confesses that he himself "equivocated" at the time. Undoubtedly if he looked harder, he would be able to identify many more Straussians, including his *Dissertationsvater* Harvey Mansfield, who backed the invasion.

[36] Nina J. Easton, *The Gang of Five: Leaders at the Center of the Conservative Crusade* (New York: Simon and Schuster, 2001), 2–10. Daniel J. Mahoney in *Conservative Foundations of the Liberal Order: Defending Democracy against Its Modern Enemies and Immoderate Friends* (Wilmington, DE: ISI Books, 2011), 107–19, presents a more thought-provoking distinction than the one drawn by the Zuckerts. Mahoney observes the growing theoretical gulf between the "old neoconservatives"

more often than neoconservatives are academics rather than journalists. But that by itself does not prove the two groups are unconnected. It may in fact indicate that they are working for the same ideological goals in different occupational settings. To their credit, the Zuckerts dispute various sloppy attempts at attributing to Straussians and neoconservatives a neo-Nazi mindset. However, having defended Strauss against his defamers, the Zuckerts proceed to deny the obvious: that Strauss's disciples and their disciples and the neoconservatives have intertwining relations, which are personal, ethnic, and ideological. The most one can do to invalidate this connection is to insist that it is not as close as some people have imagined.

Straussians previewed those themes that became essential to the neoconservative view of American politics and international relations. They took these positions in conservative venues, before the neoconservatives' ascent to power; and they thereby laid the ground for a later development, in which they played a preliminary role. Further, the Straussians, and particularly Jaffa and his followers, introduced a certain blustering tone into American *Weltpolitik*, which is especially evident in neoconservative advocates Bill Kristol, Robert Kagan, and Victor Davis Hanson. This bellicose rhetoric is reminiscent of the kind of saber-rattling that characterized Europe on the eve of the Great War.

One may be critical here without indulging in the hyperbole of an impassioned detractor, German émigré historian Fritz Stern. A well-known critic of "illiberalism," Stern is now attacking the neoconservatives as dangerous right-wing radicals.[37] Neither the

---

of the 1970s and their successors or reincarnations since the end of the Cold War. Since the 1990s, according to Mahoney, neoconservatives and Straussians, as typified by Francis Fukuyama and his "end of history" scenario, have celebrated America in its current political and economic form as the culminating point of human history. Mahoney contrasts this vulgar presentism to the pessimistic assessments of their own age that one could find in neoconservative polemics forty years ago. The question is whether these gloomy, critical outpourings were ever the dominant aspect of neoconservatism. Even back in the 1980s, neoconservative hand-wringing was mostly about Western timidity during the Cold War. Although Mahoney points to a real difference in emphasis, it is also possible to perceive considerable continuity as well as disparities between the two phases of neoconservatism.

[37] Helmut Schmidt/Fritz Stern, *Unser Jahrhundert.Ein Gespräch* (Munich: Beck Verlag, 2010), 10–20. Stern considers the neoconservatives to be right-wing extremists on the basis of what seems inconclusive evidence, namely their rejection of most of the

neoconservatives nor the Straussians, however, would answer to this description because there is nothing about their values of which Stern should disapprove. Straussians and neoconservatives have pushed such progressive goals as liberating women from patriarchal societies, extending the example of the American civil rights movement to Third World countries, and implanting everywhere American human rights doctrines the way we did in postwar Germany. It is not the substance of their teachings that recalls the militaristic nationalism of the interwar years. It is the style that does; and it is one that has been cultivated in imitation of an older European militaristic Right and of the ideological mobilization of the United States during the two world wars.

The Straussians and, *a fortiori*, their neoconservative pupils advance a claim to world dominance for a nation that they believe should guide the rest of the world. A Straussian, Carnes Lord, who together with Bill Kristol helped manage Vice-President Dan Quayle during the Bush I administration, points back to Theodore Roosevelt as an appropriate precursor for a new American foreign policy. Lord's policy would feature democratic nationalism and be free of the anti-interventionist qualms that bedeviled Americans in the past. Here too Straussians have constructed a model that neoconservatives are happy to follow.[38]

A purely scholarly attempt to link Straussians through their teacher to a European tradition of cultural pessimism has come from the German Strauss commentator, Harald Bluhm, and it concentrates on the Weimar legacy. Like Eric Voegelin, Hannah Arendt, and many other émigrés of this era, Strauss, according to Bluhm, was impressed by Carl Schmitt's distinction between "liberalism" and "democracy."

standard criticism of Israel in the media and their arguments against affirmative action for minorities. A lot more may be needed to substantiate Stern's damning charge. The problem with this name-calling is that those who engage in it are unwilling to move beyond a frozen "antifascist" paradigm. In a review of my work *After Liberalism* in the *New Republic* (June 7, 1999): 37–38, Alan Wolfe complains that I do not take seriously enough present "fascist" dangers. Contrary to the impression Wolfe may convey, my book does not advocate a fascist corporate state or Mussolini's "national revolution." It merely insists on using the term "fascist" in an accurate historical sense.

[38] See Carnes Lord, *The Modern Prince: What Leaders Need to Know Now* (New Haven, CT: Yale University Press, 2004), 4–15.

Like Schmitt, Strauss identified liberalism with a somnolent or self-indulged bourgeoisie seeking material fortune and treating the state as an instrument for protecting its property. Liberals, as Strauss understood them, had no ideals to advance beyond those freedoms necessary to increase their wealth and to maintain their physical safety. In contrast to this ethic of self-indulgence, true democrats were united by communal solidarity and made their concept of popular government contingent on the willingness of citizens to be part of a common enterprise.[39]

Voegelin, Arendt, and Strauss all incorporated the Schmittian distinction between liberal and democratic regimes into worldviews that they expounded in exile, with notable success. In the 1970s, all three won the prestigious Benjamin Lippincott Prize for their contributions to political theory. Arendt recycled the Schmittian concept of democracy as a defense of the "vita activa" by a community of equals, pursuing ordered lives for the sake of a predetermined end. Although not an orthodox Christian and by background a Lutheran, Voegelin identified himself intellectually with the Catholic Church and with what he understood as the "American tradition" to arrive at his concept of a "value-oriented and morally founded democracy." Strauss created his own variation on the Schmittian leitmotif when he called for a morally rehabilitated democracy that would be free of the scourges of relativism and historicism.[40]

Two French journalists, Alain Frachon and Daniel Vernet, present in *Le Monde* a commentary that bears some resemblance to Bluhm's. According to these commentators, the neoconservatives built their worldview by combining the foreign policy of mathematician and political strategist Albert Wohlstetter with Strauss's secretly anti-Enlightenment defense of American liberal democracy. Strauss urged his disciples to treat American liberal democracy with reverence as a "defense against the snares of modernity." This democracy worship would insulate them against the danger of "relativizing the Good, which would have the effect of rendering Americans incapable of resisting tyranny."[41]

[39] Harald Bluhm, *Die Ordnung der Ordnung* (Berlin: Akademie Verlag, 2007), 259–60.
[40] Ibid., 260–61, 270–73.
[41] Alain Frachon and Daniel Vernet, "Le Stratège et le Philosophe," *Le Monde* (16 avril 2003): A11.

There is, of course, something bizarre about this "contradiction," which consists of preferring the Ancients to the Enlightenment while calling for mass worship of an Enlightenment project. But this contradiction is explainable in several ways. First, Strauss's interpretation of the "Ancients" was not as starkly antimodern as Bluhm and his French commentators suggest. It was joined to a rationalist hermeneutic, and the possibility of esoteric readings of texts built into the Straussian system allowed Strauss to treat long-dead political authors as philosophic contemporaries.

Second, Straussians do not have to deal with premodern situations in today's Western world: In view of its pluralistic character and human rights ideology, the United States today looks nothing like the *Volksdemokratie* or ancient polis that Schmitt had in mind when he contrasted democracy to liberalism. Nor have Strauss and his disciples really been upset about the passing of older models. Note how Strauss regretted that European liberalism had not done enough to protect Jews against residual medieval prejudices. Given this concern, it is doubtful that he would have welcomed the organic communitarian democracy that Schmitt held up as a counterpoint to liberalism. Outside of Israel, that is not a regime that Strauss would likely have welcomed.

Moreover, Schmitt's view of democracy has no intrinsic connection to what Straussians consider "the American experiment." Like the neoconservatives, Straussians refer to the United States as a "propositional" or "universal" nation, held together by a natural-rights creed applicable everywhere on the planet. Such a notion, which has become widespread in America, breaks with any notion of "democracy" in the premodern or Schmittian sense. In the 1980s and 1990s, Straussians and their neoconservative allies fought with an older American Right, which they accused of being tribalist and antiglobalist in their patriotism. It would be hard to argue in light of this recent history that the Straussians are trying to apply organicist ideas to a hypothetical American volkisch community.[42]

This nonapplicability may be worked around to some degree, however, if one follows Berns and Jaffa, by presenting the United States as a

---

[42] See George H. Nash, *The Conservative Intellectual Movement in America since 1945*, second edition, 329–41; and Paul Gottfried, *Conservatism in America: Making Sense of the American Right*, 59–76.

"moral community." One may appear to be making this point by rais-ing "liberal democratic values" to the ultimate Good. It is this Good that provides the moral vision for armed struggle against "regimes" spurning "our values." Such struggle is the existential proof that the United States and its liberal founding have produced a true commu-nal democracy, which is on display when it fights for Enlightenment values.

Allan Bloom makes this point in *The Closing of the American Mind*, when he praises our "educational experiment" in the form of war.[43] Bloom insists that this American version of *Volksdemokratie* is based on universal egalitarian premises that everyone on Earth can and should affirm. For those who harbor ancestral memories of Central and Eastern European intolerance, this warlike republic preaching human rights may be more desirable than any that European nation-alists might put in its place. What is undeniable, however, is that this heroic republic does not instantiate any conservative or rightist tradi-tion beyond the one that has been invented on these shores and which journalists for their own reasons choose to call "conservative."

This brings us back to the main question in this section. Why can't liberal internationalists be militaristic but not right wing? In America's past crusades for democracy, interventionists who proclaimed human rights doctrines were seen as progressive. The Straussian view that they are the heirs of Wilson, FDR, and Truman may be true after all. Identifying Straussians with a progressive interventionist foreign policy is a defensible position, despite the fact that they exemplify what Andrew Bacevich calls the "new American militarism," namely an adoration of military pomp and a willingness to deploy armies as a sign of national pride.[44]

Our evaluation of Straussian politics should not be read as an endorsement of what they advocate, their feelings about countries they like or dislike, or their reading of early American history. All that is being argued is that their critics have unfairly attributed to the Straussians extreme right-wing positions in international affairs, which the latter do not seem to hold. Their support of Jewish nation-alism may be the exception, but even here the reason given for their

---

[43] Allan Bloom, *The Closing of the American Mind*, 153.
[44] Andrew Bacevich, *The New American Militarism: How Americans Are Seduced by War* (New York: Oxford University Press, 2005).

Zionism is not ethnic nationalism but the fact that Israel is a liberal democracy like the United States.

To say, as some have argued, that Straussians and neoconservatives act as if it is always 1938, when Prime Minister Chamberlain was negotiating the fate of Czechoslovakia with Chancellor Hitler, is to notice a fixation. That, however, is not the same as suggesting that the attitudes that spring from this obsession are fascistic or un-American. In international affairs the Straussians have been able to get their views across, by representing a position that goes back at least as far as Wilson's "crusade for democracy."

Their role as political advisors in Republican and even Democratic administrations proves they are not out of step with the political class. Neither in public life nor in the academic world can they be described as exotica. They or their neoconservative admirers may be taking advantage of their media access to convert others to their intense civic patriotism, but they also speak for a consensus that already existed before they became politically prominent. William Pfaff's contention that Straussian politics is a German import foreign to our political culture is unfounded. The problem may be exactly the opposite, namely that the fit works all too well.

6

Political Theory as Political Philosophy

Is there Political Philosophy?

Political theory in the Academy is often labeled as "political philosophy." The two terms are sometimes used interchangeably. If a political science faculty wants to hire a "theory person," then a self-described "political philosopher" may fit the bill. I myself have corrected colleagues when they tell me that what I am writing is "political philosophy." Despite my objection, the interlocutor will persist in describing what I do by the term I try to avoid.

Whereas it may be hard to undo this semantic practice, there is instructive value in tracing its genealogy. The concept of "political philosophy" is fundamental to the work of Leo Strauss, and it lives on through his well-placed disciples, who treat their studies of political texts as philosophical activities. Thomas L. Pangle introduces his anthology of Strauss's writings on "classical political rationalism" by stating that his subject focused on the philosophical content of political theory. Strauss found in Plato and Aristotle two precursors for his approach to political thought and philosophy, who also saw them as related facets of the examined life.

Strauss went back to Antiquity in response to the "spiritual crisis of modern rationalism." He considered this contemporary form of rationalism, like its equally mischievous partners, relativism and positivism, to be fraught with moral and intellectual perils. Unlike ancient philosophers, modern rationalists seek to avoid ethical questions. They wrap themselves up in "scientific methodologies" while refusing to recognize the interdependence of facts and values. Scientific methodologists dodge moral decisions without recognizing their own cultural foundations or the liberal democratic preconditions for modern scientific reason. Contrary to what modern rationalists believe, "science does not take place in a vacuum." Presumably the "ancients" knew better and anchored their conversations and treatises in discussions of what is best for the common interest. They never backed away from "the distinctly philosophic question: 'What is virtue?'"[1]

In "On Classical Political Philosophy," Strauss spells out the differences between the desiccated, contradictory rationalism, which he finds at the heart of modern social science, and the philosophical ideals of the ancients. Needless to say, the "ancients" are summed up for Strauss metonymically in a few thinkers, whom he contrasts favorably to modern rationalists, positivists, and relativists. We are shown, for example, Socrates, as depicted by Plato, drawing his fellow Athenians into uplifting discourse. "The political philosopher who has reached his goal is the teacher of legislators. The knowledge of the political philosopher is transferable in the highest degree." Furthermore, "[t]he political philosopher first comes into sight as a good citizen who can perform this function of the good citizen in the best way and on the highest level. In order to perform this function he has to raise ulterior questions, questions that are never raised in the political arena; but in doing so he does not abandon his fundamental orientation, which is the orientation inherent in political life." Above all, by "persuasion," he tries to lead his auditors into becoming "good men," that is, those who are "able to discern in each situation what is noble and right and for no ulterior reason."[2]

In dealing with how ethical instruction can be interpreted as "political" teachings, Strauss comes up with three answers. One, the philosopher builds his discourse around themes that are "of political origin" and that arise in political life out of opposed claims and interests. Two, the substance of this philosophical activity is the "knowledge which would enable a man to teach legislators: Plato demonstrated this *ad oculos* in his dialogue on legislation by presenting in the guise of a stranger [the Athenian

---

[1] *The Rebirth of Classical Rationalism*, 59.
[2] Ibid., 55.

Stranger in the *Laws*] the philosopher who is the teacher of legislators." Finally, the political teachings of classical philosophers, which centered on instruction about virtue, prudence, and justice, were "addressed not to all intelligent men but to all decent men."[3] They were not merely theoretical, but applied to all who participated in public affairs.

Although this kind of activity was most fully developed in the Greek polis where "political life was characterized by controversies between groups struggling for power within political communities," there is nothing "intrinsically Greek" about the search for "political excellence." Aristotle never asserted that such excellence "was identical with the quality of being Greek," and he even commended two non-Greek polities in the Second Book of his *Politics*, some of the qualities of which he recommended to his fellow Greeks. Similarly Xenophon (in the Cyropaideia) praises the Persian state builder Cyrus and implies that "the education Cyrus received in Persia was superior even to Spartan education."[4]

Leaving aside the problematic points of whether ancient Greek thinkers thought their political institutions could be reproduced among barbarians and whether the polis was thought to be transferable to a Persian society, it seems that Strauss is providing a somewhat personal view of "philosophy." He does not deem as more than incidental to his inquiry those metaphysical aspects of classical philosophy that mattered to Plato and Aristotle; nor does Strauss attach to his "political philosophy" the epistemic assumptions that mark Plato's discussion of the Good, the Just, and the Prudent. Strauss wishes to have the political philosopher engage ethical topics as an eristic exercise guided by Reason. But did the ancients understand such an agenda as philosophy, which in their minds entailed knowledge of an ontologically differentiated and divinely structured universe?

In *The Metaphysics*, the study of "beginnings and causes" leads gradually upward, toward the recognition of a Divine First Cause, which is responsible for motion and thought in the sublunary sphere.

---

[3] Ibid., 58; and Helmut Kuhn, "Naturrecht und Historismus," *Zeitschrift für Politik*, 3 (1956): 289–304; and for the effect of this appeal to ancient teachings about virtue on a Canadian High Tory, see Grant Havers, "Leo Strauss's Influence on George Grant," in *Athens and Jerusalem: George Grant's Theology, Philosophy, and Politics* (Toronto: University of Toronto Press, 2006), 124–34.

[4] Ibid., 57.

Given that wisdom (Sophia) requires the investigation of the source of being, the ascent of knowledge leads from the mastery of technical skills through the practice of prudence in political affairs toward a theoretical grasp of the relation of the Divine to what is dependent on it. We find in this cognitive hierarchy not the linkage of politics and philosophy, but the view of the political as a particular skill. This *aretê texnikē* may be helpful for the individual and community once united with a suitably disciplined character.[5]

Strauss and his students show more interest in Plato than Aristotle, which is hardly surprising. Plato's theological references can be treated as heuristic or as pure speculation. It is much harder to do the same with a system that integrates physics, metaphysics, epistemology, and theology into a unified way of looking at the world. Already in Book One Aristotle makes clear that he is dissociating philosophy, as an inquiry into causes and beginnings, from what is done out of pure need (*xrēseos tinos heneken*). The reflection (*phronēsis*) that is required for philosophical inquiry leads from "all present necessities (*panton huparxonton anagkaion*)" toward "a form of ease and way of life (*pros rastunēn kai diagogēn*)" that is appropriate for the kind of exalted activity pursued.[6] Aristotle treats philosophy as something that in its contemplative aspect is so different from civic participation that it may be asked whether he would have accepted such a hybrid as "political philosophy."

Strauss nonetheless insists that there is a "Good" that the "good man," once properly instructed, will seek to achieve. It may be asked, however, on what grounds, other than niceness or expedience, is this "Good" to be accepted as a binding obligation. Why should one choose Strauss's version of "classical rationalism," with its warnings against value-relativism, as against other approaches to moral knowledge, such as some form of utilitarianism or Marx's historical dialectic? Strauss may rail against the fact-value dichotomy and against modern totalitarianism, but we are never shown why such invectives, whatever their intention, constitute a telling argument for his position.

This brings us back to the question of why it is necessary to approach political theory as "philosophy." Why should we think that

---

[5] Aristotle, *Metaphysica*, 981a and b, 982b.
[6] Ibid., 982b: 20–25.

holding discussions with a political leader or a court litigant about one's notion of the "Good" is the "beginning of the ascent" toward philosophical knowledge? Such discussion may have edifying consequences in Socratic dialogues, just as Jesus' telling of parables means something special for those who are studying this particular narrative form. But not everyone who debates about the "Good," even under Straussian guidance, is acting like Socrates and Plato, any more than every deviser of parables is like the main figure in the Gospels. Having graduate students imitate Strauss's Socrates may be a mental exercise, but it is not philosophy, unless that term is stretched very hard.

Strauss and his followers are fond of pointing out that "political philosophy broadly understood is the core of philosophy or rather the 'first philosophy.'"[7] What is thereby meant is that the inquiring mind first meets what are appropriate philosophical subjects (this is certainly true for Plato), while discussing the problem of political justice. It would not be proper, however, to leave the definition this way, without noticing that in classical philosophy the ascent of the soul continues to rise from questions about the earthly city to metaphysical and, finally, theological topics. One might say with Eric Voegelin that Platonic man is seen standing in an in-between state (*to metaxu*), leading from his brute physical nature up to the divine source of his existence. Voegelin makes this case particularly well when pointing to the figure of Diotima in the *Symposium*, who is made to represent this in-between state between what is human and divine.[8] Or one might

---

[7] See Leo Strauss, *The City of Man*, 20.

[8] Eric Voegelin, *Plato* (Columbia: University of Missouri Press, 2000). According to *The Search for Historical Meaning*, 114–15, 154–55, the burden of proof is on Strauss and his followers when they deny that Socrates and Plato believed in eternal forms and in the divine source of *eidē aitia*. Mystical schools had already sprung up building on Plato's philosophy during his life, and for the next thousand years, Platonism and theology were inseparable for both Plato's pagan and Christian proponents. Why should Strauss's reading be assigned more credence than what Plato's students and their students believed they had learned from their teacher? Were these figures in need of enlightenment from certain Arab thinkers who came along a thousand years later and who decided to apply a skeptical approach to Plato's theology? It is also hard to believe that what look like anticipations of the beatific vision in medieval Christianity, as seen, for example, in the *Symposium*, are really a deployment of images intended to teach us the method of philosophical inquiry. The references to "beholding the beautiful in its genuine, pure and unmixed form, not by proceeding back (*anaplein*) from the human body and human hues but by being able to perceive divine beauty

cite Socrates's hymn to Eros in the same dialogue, which makes this point even more explicit. Strauss's "first philosophy" in its classical formulation does not end in mere questioning discourse. Rather it ascends in the case of Plato/Socrates from the spoken word upward to an ideal and, finally, godly realm.

In short, Strauss may be offering not a return to classical philosophy but a truncated version of the real article. He defends what is less than or different from the classical understanding of mind and being; he also does not give any indication of how that antique tradition led by stages toward later philosophical schools and eventually toward such modern alternatives to classical modes of thinking as linguistic and analytic philosophy. Strauss offers at most a selective reconstruction of classical thinking, and it is one that, as Gadamer observed, fails to take into account the time-conditioned and autobiographical factors shaping our interpretive choices.

It may be possible, without oversimplifying, to divide the presentation of "political philosophy" among disciples of Strauss into three distinct but occasionally overlapping activities. At its least informative level, as practiced in neoconservative journals, this defense of "political philosophy" comes in the form of prescribed civics lesson. It emphasizes "values" and focuses on the defense of "liberal democracy" as the best of all governments in the modern era. This civics lesson also comes with warnings against American isolationist tendencies and against the danger of listening to relativists and positivists who lack faith in the American democratic experiment. Although not the only ones who produce it, the Jaffaites seem particularly fond of such sermonizing. In the *Claremont Review*, *Weekly Standard*, *National Review*, and other neoconservative publications, one encounters their interventions with some regularity, often disguised as panegyrics to "philosophy."

At the next ascending level, the Straussian approach to "political philosophy" takes the form of painfully close readings of certain texts by Montesquieu, Hobbes, Locke, and other political thinkers.

in its unique form" and "to beholding the beautiful as something visible that begets not the semblances of excellence just as one who pursues mere semblances [*eidolou ephaptomeno*] but truth as one who pursues truth [*tou alēthous ephaptomeno*]" seem to suggest that Plato took seriously the mystical aspects of his philosophy. See *Symposium*, Cambridge Classical Texts, ed. K. J. Dover (Cambridge: Cambridge University Press, 1980), 211e–212b.

Characteristic of these tracts is the combination of thoroughness in citing sources and a predictable Straussian hermeneutic. Also typical of this tendency is what David Gordon has called "the time chart that saves the interpreter the job of interpreting thinkers as individuals."[9] Ancient and medieval thinkers are thought to have expounded classical rationalism of a kind that is similar to what the master prescribed, although once Christianity took hold, it became increasingly necessary for smart people to hide their skepticism through esoteric phrases. Such concealment was already present in the ancients, who did not want those who were not initiates to know everything they believed. This esoteric approach became particularly useful later on, in Christian societies, which corrupted philosophy with dogma and which often confused theology and philosophy.[10]

This device became less necessary, however, as thinkers entered the modern era, when theorists could at last express their real thoughts. Moreover, identifiably modern thoughts turn out to be not very different from the poorly hidden inclinations of the Straussian interpreter. Their proclivity for liberal democracy, the view of religious revelation as a bundle of myths with varying degrees of usability, and in Spinoza's case, proto-Zionism, are all qualities that Straussians find in the "moderns" as they present them to us. The interpreter need not worry about the massive evidence that modernity flows from Protestant Christianity, with its promotion of bourgeois ethics and its propensity for republican government. In a secular age in which democracy and equality have become god terms, why bother to bring up what most intellectuals do not care about?

It is further necessary, according to this Straussian hermeneutic, to deplore the "lowering of the moral horizon" that set in with the advent of modernity. Materialist and hyperindividualist fashions, we are reminded, accompanied the birth and evolution of political modernity, as seen in, among others, Hobbes and Locke. Nonetheless, the same trend is credited with the creation of liberal democracy, a regime that we are urged to protect and whose empire we should help

---

[9] In conversation with the author, November 21, 2010.
[10] See Strauss's essay "Exoteric Teaching" in *The Rebirth of Classical Political Rationalism*, 63–68; and John Gunnell, "Strauss before Straussianism: Reason, Revelation and Nature," *Review of Politics*, 53, 10, 53–74.

expand. This may be the Straussian version of the "felix culpa" in the Good Friday liturgy, celebrating the Fall of Man as the precondition for redemption through Christ and his Church. Let us note once again Anne Norton's observation that for Straussians, American democracy provides modernity with "a second chance to become something better."[11]

The students of Pangle at Toronto and, more recently, at Texas, as well as their teacher, may be said to represent the second of the three applications of the Straussian hermeneutic. They would all likely tell us that the eighteenth-century French nobleman Montesquieu was not advancing the kind of aristocratic reaction to which he is often linked. The author of *De l'esprit des lois* wanted to build a liberal bourgeois society and to base that society on commerce.[12] Moreover, one need not bother to notice that Locke was addressing other Protestant sectarians. His true concern was preparing the way for a modern democratic society, freed of slavery and politically significant gender distinctions. Locke was also the all-determining theoretical influence on the American founding, a founding that we are urged to consider, other scholarship not to the contrary, to be a strictly modernist enterprise.

Quentin Skinner is right to note that by avoiding historical contexts in reading political texts, one opens the door to "naïve teleology" and "Einfluss studies." The researcher can ignore the nitty-gritty by claiming to be absorbed in the big picture, which is the genealogy of ideas. Usually an astute reader of judicial decisions, Walter Berns exercises his Straussian prerogative when he attributes the worldview of the

[11] See the anthology of essays dealing mostly with the American regime edited by K. L. Deutsch and W. Soffer, *The Crisis of Liberal Democracy: A Straussian Perspective* (Albany: State University of New York Press, 1987). These essays equate liberal democratic values with what is foundationally American – that is, with how the contributors understand the foundations of the American polity.

[12] See Thomas L. Pangle, *Montesquieu's Philosophy of Liberalism: A Commentary on the Spirit of the Law* (Chicago: University of Chicago Press, 1973), particularly the section on "liberal republicanism"; the critical commentary of Pangle's reading by Bernard Manin, "Montesquieu et la Politique Moderne," *Cahiers de la Philosophie Politique* (Centre de Philosophie Politique de l'Université de Rheims, 2 and 3, 1985), 157–229; and Richard Ashcraft's devastating dissection of the supposed Lockean template that Pangle claims to find everywhere in the American founding in *Political Theory*, 18.1 (February 1990): 159–62.

American founding to Locke's supposed mentor Hobbes. Although Berns has made this assertion more than once, including in an acrimonious debate with Jaffa, he does not offer evidence for the Hobbesian pedigree assigned to the American regime.[13] In fact, as Skinner points out, it is not even clear that either one of Locke's two treatises on government owes anything to Hobbes.[14]

The highest level of Straussian scholarship nonetheless includes solid intellectual history, which avoids the rigid controls of the usually overpowering hermeneutic. Examples of such scholarship are furnished by students of Strauss and even by students of his students. Works by Stanley Rosen and Steven Smith on Hegel, Smith's meticulously researched study of the Jewish elements in Strauss, Jules Gleicher's gracefully composed reading of the Pentateuch, Catherine Zuckert's voluminous examination of the figure of Socrates in the life and work of Plato, and Eugene Miller's research on David Hume are only a few cases in point. It would be baseless to contend that a limited application of the Straussian method of interpreting texts inevitably brings with it distortion. Closer to the truth may be the following observation: A productive researcher can make judicious use of the method without becoming obsessed. The same is, of course, true for Marxism. What must be insisted on, however, is that intellectual history is not the same as philosophy. Nor does it change its nature by addressing political theoretical questions. Although a Straussian might agree with this formulation, he would then hasten to add that only properly conducted studies of political theory are truly philosophical.

Another qualification should be made about who does or does not fit our taxonomy. There are Straussians who exhibit the characteristic pattern of thought but who also depart from it so sharply in some ways

---

[13] See Walter Berns, *The First Amendment and the Future of Democracy in America* (Chicago: Regnery, 1985), 2, 15, 22, 43, 44. Berns has a tendency to bunch together early modern political thinkers such as Hobbes, Spinoza, Pierre Bayle, and Machiavelli, who, we are led to believe, shaped, directly or indirectly, early American politics. One must wonder, with due respect to Berns, whether the skeptical theological attitudes displayed by these European writers contributed to the disestablishment of state churches in early America as much as the concentration of Protestant sectarians, especially Baptists, in particular places. See also Berns's "Reply to Harry Jaffa," *National Review* (January 22, 1982): 170–71.

[14] See *Meaning and Context: Quentin Skinner and His Critics*, 43–47; and *Hobbes and Republican Liberty* (Cambridge: Cambridge University Press, 2008).

that they may be viewed as exceptions. One such remarkable exception is the Israeli far right politician and journalist Paul Eidelberg, who
studied dutifully with Strauss at the University of Chicago and then in
1976 settled in Israel. Eidelberg was inspired by Strauss's view of the
aristocratic preferences of classical political philosophy; shortly before
his resettlement in Israel and espousal of very nationalistic Israeli politics, he came out with a trilogy on the American founding that deviated
from received Straussian wisdom. In his work, Eidelberg stressed the
"mixed" nature of the original regime, in accordance with Aristotle's
concept of the *politeia mikta*, a government that tries to offset the
popular will by conceding privileged rights to the wealthy (and presumably educated). Eidelberg tries to shift the interpretive focus associated with Pangle and other mainstream Straussians away from the
Lockean-democratic founding to a less modernist one based less firmly
on the concept of equality.[15]

Although Eidelberg has received a very cold shoulder from others in
his school, there are interests that unite Strauss to this Zionist student.
Jewish nationalism and a sometimes critical perspective about modern democracy, albeit one mixed with prudential praise, were certainly
present in Strauss's lectures and writings. It would be hard to view
Eidelberg, any more than Rosen, as an entirely eccentric interpreter
of Strauss's statements. The same would be true of the octogenarian
constitutional theorist George Anastaplo, who remains a devoted disciple of Strauss, with whom he studied at Chicago, but who has gone
his own way on specific political issues. Anastaplo, who is Greek and
not Jewish, broke from the group in defending the constitutional right
of Nazis to peacefully demonstrate on behalf of their views. He also
took the same position for the right of public dissent for communists
during the Cold War.[16]

---

[15] See Paul Eidelberg, *The Philosophy of the American Constitution* (New York: Free
Press, 1968); *Discourse on Statesmanship* (Urbana: University of Illinois Press, 1974);
and *On the Silence of the Declaration of Independence* (Amherst: University of
Massachusetts Press, 1976).

[16] See George Anastaplo, *Leo Strauss, the Straussians, and the American Regime*
(Lanham, MD: Rowman and Littlefield, 1999); and the two-volume Festschrift for
Anastaplo, *Law and Philosophy* (Athens: Ohio University Press, 1992). In *The Truth
about Leo Strauss* (page 229), the Zuckerts assert that Anastaplo did not follow
other Straussians into the Republican Party but remained with William Galston in
the liberal Democratic camp. Although Anastaplo resisted the "aligning effect" that,

A point originally made in Chapter 2 bears repeating here. Although Strauss's disciples are forever declaring their indebtedness to their teacher, they also work to make his teachings accord with their interests and passions. One is further struck by the sameness of these disciples. Unlike the followers of Hegel, who included conservative monarchists, liberal constitutionalists, self-assertive individualists, and social revolutionaries, Strauss's disciples are a relatively uniform lot. Their critics and defenders can easily treat them as a unified whole because most of them hold strikingly similar views on cultural and political topics. They are self-selected in a way that votaries of other schools of thought have not usually been to the same degree. This makes the exceptions stand out all the more sharply.

Strauss and His Philosophical Moments

When once asked how he would define his vocation, Strauss described himself as an "intellectual historian."[17] Despite his presentation of his study of political theory as philosophical activity, Strauss also viewed it more modestly, as a study of the ideas of others. This form of scholarship is not to be sneered at, and Strauss can be credited with multiple learned investigations of political theorists, both ancient and modern. One need not believe that he was explicating "political philosophy" to appreciate his work – and the mastery of multiple languages that is evident in his scholarship.

It is also possible to discern philosophical moments in Strauss's oeuvre that might rightly be called political philosophy. These are not the moments when Strauss is praising the merits of liberal democracy

according to the Zuckerts, other Straussians underwent in the late 1960s, one cannot explain these differences by referring to Anastaplo's continued alignment with the Left. This maverick has been more critical of Zionists than most of the other Straussians, and he has taken strong constitutional positions favoring the freedom to express unpopular political opinions. One may partly understand these deviations in view of the fact that Anastaplo does not share the peculiarly Jewish concerns characteristic of others of his school.

[17] See Strauss's "On Collingwood's Philosophy of History" in *Review of Metaphysics*, 5.4 (June 1952): 559–86. Strauss defines the work of the intellectual historian as being able to present permanent philosophical questions that go beyond the study of contexts. He also identifies himself in a "Comment" in *Church History*, 30.1 (March 1961): 100–01, as a historian trying to understand the foundations of modernity.

or when he is expounding his notions about the ancients versus the moderns. We are also not referring here to his claims about the art of secret writing or to his drawing of exoteric and esoteric distinctions in certain texts. We are looking at his discussions of philosophical thinkers, which reveal the unexpected – that is, when Strauss steps outside his role as a moral instructor to express true wonder (*thauma kai ekstasis*). In his comments on Plato, Strauss seizes on the drunken raving of the philosopher, as described by Socrates, who is carried away by his quest for truth and who seems truly beside himself (*phrenon eksestanai*) when delving into the secrets of the universe. However, this may be a convenient image that Strauss uses to clothe his conventional view of ancient philosophers as engaging in open-ended exercises in speculative reason. The question is whether Strauss's wonder or ecstasy has any basis other than his pleasure at how certain topics unfold.

In his more philosophical moments, however, Strauss celebrates the towering achievements of philosophers without treating them as vehicles for his hermeneutic or occasions for civics lessons. This reveals itself with particular clarity in "Introduction to Heideggerian Existentialism," an essay that was produced in the 1960s. Martin Heidegger was someone whom Strauss deeply respected despite his best efforts to warn against his ideas. In this essay, Strauss tells how Heidegger broke from his teacher, the father of phenomenology Edmund Husserl, to reconstruct the living world as understood by someone who, according to Strauss, may be judged as "the only German philosopher of the time." It was Husserl who went beyond the neo-Kantian school led by Hermann Cohen by noting its mistake in confusing science with our "primary knowledge of the world." Neo-Kantians failed to recognize that "science is derivative from our knowledge of the world of things: science is not the perfection of man's understanding of the world of things, but a specific modification of that prescientific understanding. The meaningful genesis of science out of the prescientific understanding is a problem: the primary theme is the philosophical understanding of the prescientific world, and therefore in the first place, the analysis of the sensibly perceived thing."[18]

---

[18] *The Rebirth of Classical Political Rationalism*, 28.

It was Husserl's shifting of the epistemological focus from an analysis of scientific method to an examination of the Lebenswelt that provided the entry point for Heidegger's work. According to Husserl's most brilliant student:

[O]ur primary understanding of the world is not an understanding of things as objects but of what the Greeks indicated by *pragmata*. The horizon in which Husserl had analyzed the world of prescientific understanding was the pure consciousness as the absolute being. Heidegger questioned that orientation by referring to the fact the inner time belonging to pure consciousness cannot be understood if one abstracts from the fact that this time is necessarily finite and even constituted by man's mortality.

Science, according to Heidegger, is not only derivative from the world of objects, in which our finite being is situated; what "science" means and how it is interpreted cannot be separated from the temporal context in which it is pursued.

Strauss's exposition of the transition in twentieth-century German philosophy from neo-Kantianism through Phenomenology to Heidegger's existentialist ontology may not be entirely original, but it is prepared with obvious wonder at the luminous insights of someone whom Strauss denounced elsewhere for straying into Nazism and "radical historicism." But there is nothing preachy in how he approaches Heidegger in this essay. Strauss explains about how he told Franz Rosenzweig, "whose name will always be remembered when informed people speak about existentialism," about having listened to Heidegger lecture at Freiburg. He admitted to Rosenzweig:

[I]n comparison to Heidegger, Weber appeared to me as an "orphan child" in regard to precision and probing and competence. I had never seen before such seriousness, profundity and concentration in the interpretation of philosophic texts. I had heard Heidegger's interpretation of certain sections of Aristotle, and sometime later I heard Werner Jaeger in Berlin interpret the same texts. Charity requires me to limit my comparison to the remark that there was no comparison. Gradually the breadth of the revolution of thought which Heidegger was preparing dawned on me and my generation. We saw with our own eyes that there had been no such phenomenon in the world since Hegel."

In this passage, Strauss also favorably compared Heidegger to a paradigmatic German republican, Jaeger, with whose politics Strauss would certainly have agreed more than with Heidegger's disdain for democratic man. He also proceeds to draw even less favorable comparisons between Heidegger and Cassirer, the Jewish democrat and disciple of Cohen, with whom Heidegger debated at Davos. According to Strauss, the debate "revealed the emptiness of this remarkable representative of established academic philosophy to anyone who had eyes."[19] At this point, Strauss drops the other shoe by telling us that the ethical philosophy that Cohen propagated, and that he identified with the Jewish (and during the First World War) German spirit, was a doomed enterprise. "Cassirer had transformed Cohen's system into a new system of philosophy in which ethics had completely disappeared. It had been silently dropped: he had not faced the problem. Heidegger did face the problem. He declared that ethics is impossible, and his whole being was permeated by the awareness that this fact opens an abyss."[20]

It is not being claimed that the *true* Strauss was committed to Heidegger any more than that he was a secret Nietzschean. There are simply too many statements that point in the direction of different conclusions. What would seem more likely is that like an anticommunist who finds certain gems of wisdom in Marx's work, Strauss was reacting with wonder to someone whom he generally regarded with deep suspicion. After all, much of his life's work would consist of covering over the "abyss" that Heidegger had discovered. Strauss became a value booster in the United States, this despite the fact that he tells us in the essay on Heidegger that the neo-Kantian ethics of the predominantly Jewish neo-Kantians at Marburg had ended in intellectual failure.

Presumably there were other ways to restore the identification of philosophy with ethical instruction, and this could be achieved by way of critique. Strauss provided this assistance in the value war by fighting the fact-value distinction and by presenting ethical relativism and liberal democracy as being in conflict. There is furthermore a difference between a "public philosophy," whatever one may choose to call it, and what one knows to be true but generally prefers not to reveal. Those who say that Strauss kept his cards close to his vest are telling us what

---

[19] Ibid., 28.
[20] Ibid., 28; 29–31, 46 *passim*.

is self-evident. Even more importantly, Strauss identified his life with defending what he thought were safe beliefs for others to hold.

His exoteric teachings were already on display in his remarks delivered in England in 1935, castigating German thinkers and praising English democracy, pragmatic forms of thought, and Churchill. Whereas there may have been other aspects to Strauss's thinking, it seems unreasonable to treat his public teachings as extraneous to his real persona. The view that he was only playing games with his reader by saying what he did not believe is more far-fetched as well as less flattering. Those who preach the same lessons for decades generally come around to believing what they say, unless they are sociopaths.

What may be the case is less sinister, namely that Strauss grasped the world of thought more deeply than those whom he trained as democracy boosters. His remarks on Heidegger testify to this, as do other observations offered in the same essay about Heidegger, Nietzsche, and the "sham universality" of the modern era. "The case of Heidegger," who was temporarily seduced by Nazism, reminds Strauss of the "case of Nietzsche." Although "Nietzsche naturally would not have sided with Hitler," there was an "undeniable kinship between Nietzsche's thought and fascism." "If one rejects, as passionately as Nietzsche, conservative constitutional monarchy as well as democracy, with a view to a new aristocracy, the passion of the denials will be much more effective than the necessarily more subtle intimations of the character of the new nobility, to say nothing of the blond beast." [21]

Although Strauss expresses here the same concern as Nietzsche did about "the danger of universal philistinism and creeping conformism" and perhaps above all, the "problem of democracy, of mass industrial democracy," he nonetheless laments Nietzsche's lack of subtlety. This is about as far as he goes in this particular essay in rebuking the great anti-egalitarian. Significantly, Strauss does not criticize Nietzsche for not embracing Anglo-American liberal democracy. At most, he complains about his failure to talk up a "conservative constitutional monarchy," perhaps a slightly more liberal version of the government of the German Second Empire.

He then balances this comment by warning that "it would be wholly unworthy of us as thinking beings not to listen to the critics of

[21] Ibid., 31.

democracy – even if they are enemies of democracy – provided they are thinking men (and especially great thinkers) and not blustering fools." In the next paragraph, Strauss says equally uncharacteristic things after having extolled (perhaps in a perfunctory fashion) the Jewish state, the "nobility" of which is "literally beyond praise." Despite this Zionist achievement, Strauss goes on to observe, "Israel does not afford a solution to the Jewish problem. The 'Judeo-Christian tradition'? This means to blur and conceal grave differences. Cultural pluralism can only be had, it seems, at the price of blunting all edges."[22]

Strauss's critics on the academic left have had a field day with statements such as these, whereas his "liberal democratic" disciples have tried to sweep them under the rug. There is, of course, a way of reconciling these comments with the more conventional teachings of Strauss, without blurring the discrepancies. Such reconciliation may be particularly necessary in the case of the present study because it is being argued that Strauss previewed the ideological course that his followers took. There is also more than enough evidence to show that Strauss typically moved in the opposite direction from the daring ideas put forth in his essay on Heidegger.

There is even a difference in tone between this essay and such homiletic discourses as the lectures on Natural Right and History. The ponderous, multilayered prose that one often encounters in Strauss's texts is most definitely absent from his comments on Heidegger. Instead one finds here heady praise of undemocratic greatness, contempt for democratic pluralist experiments, and derision for such made-in-America products as "Judeo-Christian" values. Neither the tone nor the content is characteristic of Strauss's work. If there is a moment in Strauss's work when that tendency that Ted McAllister has called his "revolt against modernity" comes through, it is unmistakably present in his interpretation of Heidegger.[23] With due respect to McAllister, however, this revolt is far less apparent in his assaults on German thought. Such broadsides are reminiscent of the time-bound commentary produced during the Second World War, as exemplified by John Dewey's diatribes against German philosophy as the seedbed of Nazism.

---

[22] Ibid., 31–32.
[23] Ted Mc Allister, *The Revolt Against Modernity*, especially 271–79.

Arguably the essay on Heideggerian existentialism was written in an unguarded moment, when Strauss was saying things that he sometimes thought but almost always refrained from divulging. These atypical thoughts may be compared to the heretical ideas that could creep into the mind of an otherwise dedicated priest, ideas that he would not care to present to his parishioners. It would be wrong, however, to treat such vagaries as what the priest *really* believed, particularly if that priest spent his life preaching exactly the opposite of what occasionally slipped into his mind. Strauss's comments in the essay on Heidegger should be treated in exactly the same manner.

There is even less connection between Strauss's isolated praise of Heidegger and Nietzsche and what his students took from him. Those who passed under his crook did not become Heideggerian critics of democracy, nor did they devote their lives to denouncing contrived universals and mass democracy or assaulting democratic pluralism and the artificiality of "Judeo-Christian" phraseology. In fact, as Peter Minowitz and the Zuckerts ably demonstrate, his students did exactly the opposite. They devoted their professional energies to glorifying precisely those icons that Strauss belittles in his controversial essay. And they spared no venom attacking the "German connection" and that "last wave of modernity" that Strauss judgmentally linked to the historicism of Nietzsche and Heidegger. These disciples have characteristically spilled rivulets of ink saluting democratic pluralism and the state of Israel as a Middle Eastern outpost of global democratic values.

Moreover, in contrast to Strauss's veiled approval of the German Second Empire, which he criticized Nietzsche for not defending, Allan Bloom's most famous student, Francis Fukuyama, interpreted the German Imperial Army's failure to defeat France in 1914 as one of the great blessings in human history. A German victory, noted Fukuyama in the *Wall Street Journal* (December 31, 1999), "would have left unimpaired the cultural confidence of 19th century European civilization." "A German century may have been peaceful and prosperous but in the social sphere it would also have been stratified, corporatist, ultimately based on racial and ethnic hierarchy – a world made safe for South Africa."

According to Fukuyama, it was the devastation unleashed by the war, and presumably the victory won by the more progressive side, which prepared the way for the glorious American present. "That may have been the price paid for a situation in which 40 percent of the world's population lives in politics that can be reasonably called democratic."[24] What matters here is not so much whether Fukuyama, a fervent admirer of Strauss, is presenting what was really at stake in 1914. It is rather what he imagined was the critical issue at the time.

Fukuyama is praising as the fruits of the Allied victory against the Central Powers the possibility of moving beyond the constitutional, bourgeois world of the early twentieth century into a fully modern democratic regime. He is not extolling bourgeois liberalism – any more than Strauss did when, in his preface to the English edition of the *Critique of Spinoza,* he lamented that European liberalism allowed the *Staatsbürger* to be prejudiced in his private life. Clearly Fukuyama is not looking toward Antiquity for his preferred political model, any more than Strauss was in his critique of liberalism. Both were fixed on American democracy in its present form. In any case, Strauss's positive statements about Anglo-American democracy were fully replicated by the *Wall Street Journal*'s highly prized commentator Francis Fukuyama. Whatever Strauss may have said about Heidegger in other contexts has not influenced most of his followers. These adepts have favored other sentiments and values.

What the Heidegger essay does teach is that Strauss was fascinated by what he considered to be dangerous. He was full of wonder but also fearful about where certain thoughts, once elevated to public teachings, might lead. Political philosophy is the product that he and his students have dispensed to their contemporaries. Still, it is not clear that those who dispense this product have in all cases been aware of the ambivalences of the one who created it. That, however, may count for less than the public teaching. Strauss taught us to revere and fight for our liberal democratic best of all possible worlds. What reservations he may have harbored about this actualized ideal mattered less to him – and even less to his disciples.

---

[24] Francis Fukuyama, "It Could Have Been the German Century," *Wall Street Journal* (December 31, 1999): A10.

7

Conclusion

In an interview with *Le Monde* (April 16, 2003), director at l'Ecole des Hautes Etudes, Pierre Manent states that prominent Straussians went into government service under George W. Bush because they had been "ostracized in the academic profession."[1] Presumably Straussian policy advisors embraced government posts out of professional desperation, according to Manent, a one-time student of Raymond Aron, whom his mentor sent to Chicago to study under that "brilliant" critic of modernity, Leo Strauss. Peter Minowitz repeats the same complaint in *Straussophobia*, when he describes the disciples of Strauss as a "tiny minority" in the American academy. Having been subjected to "anger and prejudice" and having seen that "Straussians of all stripes confront layers of acute suspicion," Minowitz's subjects are forced to live as outcasts.[2] To whatever extent they remain professionally employed, it would seem they are hanging on by their fingertips, perhaps at community colleges in rural North Dakota.

Apropos of this characterization, John Gunnell observes: "This picture is hard to square with the status of Straussians in many major university departments and their prevalence in many colleges. Although it is possible to find instances in which Straussians have arguably been discriminated against because of their scholarly stance, political science journals

---

[1] Alain Frachon and Daniel Vernet, "Le stratège et le philosophe," *Le Monde* (16 avril 2003): A11.

[2] Peter Minowitz, *Straussophobia*, 88 and 89.

and professional meetings have treated their work as commensal."[3]
A one-time leader of the political science profession, Gunnell has furnished a generally dispassionate account of the Straussians' presence in
American higher education: He points out their reach in academic institutions, from the University of Chicago Committee on Social Thought
through political theory departments at elite universities to often prestigious smaller colleges spread across North America.

Gunnell explains that political theory departments were mostly an
American creation that gained ground in the second half of the twentieth century. Once established, these departments became enclaves
for Straussian "political philosophers." Although not hostile to them,
Gunnell is troubled by their "rhetorical stance." He sees no reason,
writing in the 1970s, why other readings of political texts should not
have comparable importance in political theory instruction.[4] It would
be nice, he suggests, if Straussians responded to critics who raise sub-
stantive objections. Such critics are not driven by ideological rancor
but are only seeking to engage in academic discourse.

Straussians have responded, when pushed hard enough, to such
critical giants in their field as J. G. A. Pocock and Quentin Skinner.
This response, however, has often taken place in an exasperated manner and has often come down to insisting that one's critics are just
plain wrong. After all, these critics are rejecting the Straussian hermeneutic, a gesture that is thought to cast doubt on their arguments and
evidence. One often looks in vain amid such grumbling for detailed
vindications that take serious criticism seriously.

Going after gross misrepresentations of their methods by ideological enemies on the left does not vindicate the favored interpretations,
except for those who are already convinced. It is also ridiculous to
identify any attempt to refute the "Straussian tradition" or "rhetorical
stance" with right-wing kooks or unpatriotic opponents of "liberal
democratic values." Since the 1960s, a growing body of counterarguments has emerged from within the academy, as an exercise in critical

[3] See John G. Gunnell's review of *Straussophobia* in *Perspectives in Politics*, 8 (2000): 944.
[4] This argument was anticipated in Gunnell's essay "Political Theory and Politics: The
Case of Leo Strauss," *Political Theory*, 13.3 (1985): 339–61. On the problems of
holding discussions with Strauss and his disciples, see also Gunnell's "Strauss before
Straussianism: Reason, Revelation, and Nature," *Review of Politics*, 53.1 (1991):
53–74.

thinking. If the Straussians were simply interested in the clarification of political theoretical questions, they would be eager to respond to this cumulative brief.

Their feeble response to scholarly criticism may go back to problems that started with the founder of their school. It is hard to separate Strauss's reading of texts from a moral-cultural critique that came out of his early life, particularly from his status as a Jew in Germany in the first third of the twentieth century. His hermeneutic points back to critical points in his life, including his reactions to the rise and triumph of Nazism, his subsequent flight to England, and his long-time residence in the United States.

Although it is possible to downplay this relation between Strauss's hermeneutics and life's experience, there is no intellectual reason to do so. There are, in fact, compelling reasons to think differently. Most interpreters of Strauss place the cart before the horse by emphasizing his "return to the ancients" and his supposedly condescending view of Anglo-American democracy. This text disagrees because it finds the conventional opinions less than convincing. It prefers to draw on Anne Norton's memory, who, as a student at Chicago, heard her Straussian teachers glorify the American (or Anglo-American) regime as a universally applicable form of modernity.[5]

A very different view is present in Harald Bluhm's portrait of Strauss as someone who agonized over the "problem of decadence." Strauss's antidote to whatever aspects of modernity he associated with moral and cultural vulgarization was "concentrating on the text of great thinkers" and, above all, "seeking a return to antiquity." "Resistance to every form of historical contextualization characterized not only his method but was the strict procedure by which he sought a return to classical problems." Strauss bristled at the idea "that his construction was in any way bound to the modern era."[6]

[5] The Zuckerts note in *The Truth about Leo Strauss* (page 23) that Norton in *Leo Strauss and the Politics of Empire* dissociates "political Straussians" from Strauss and his purely academic disciples. This book offers an opposing position to the extent that it emphasizes the difficulty of separating the hermeneutic from the politics of Strauss and his followers. Although it is recognized that not all Straussians are political activists or political journalists, the book treats the "political Straussians" as normative and increasingly common in the group.
[6] See Harald Bluhm's *Die Ordnung der Ordnung*, 274–75.

Further, his critique of modernity is "limited to a diagnosis of decline and therefore problematic," just as his explanation for this decadence is "underdeveloped." An uncompromising antimodernist, Strauss was fixated on cultural decadence, and he produced, perhaps out of despair, oneiric, intricate discourses that, according to Bluhm, "seem disconnected from any concrete context." We are supposed to believe that Strauss's "return to the ancients" had a profound effect on the neoconservatives, a group that would not strike us as wanting to go back into the distant past physically or culturally. Bluhm's attempted connection may be like Strauss's "diagnosis of decadence," a commentary that begs for elaboration.[7]

Even though Strauss's followers may not like everything in the American past, they extract from the Founding certain principles of governance and a way of life that they wish to bestow on other societies. And although there are undoubtedly carryovers from Strauss's German education and his contact with Carl Schmitt to his American persona, these legacies were so thoroughly transformed by the Nazi experience and the idolization of FDR and Churchill that it seems difficult to maintain that Strauss was a Schmitt disciple transported to the New World.

Schmitt was an emphatically anti-American Europeanist who despised liberal democracy as a threat to European civilization. During the Cold War, Schmitt could not even muster enough anticommunist feeling to root for the United States-led side. Moreover, back in the 1920s, when Strauss wrote his commentary on *The Concept of the Political*, as Steven Smith quite plausibly suggests, he may have been really thinking of the Zionist movement. This was his reference point

---

[7] Ibid., 302–26. The prevalent view of Strauss in Bluhm's work, as someone obsessed with decadence and urging a return to the ancients (*ein Rekurs zur Antike*), does not fit well with Bluhm's explanation of Strauss's impact on the neoconservatives. Although a group that is indebted to Strauss, the neoconservatives, and particularly the second generation of them, do not reveal the culturally pessimistic perspectives attributed to their teacher. A persistent problem with continental European treatments of Strauss is that they to draw all too heavily on American writers. Despite the political differences among them, Bluhm's Strauss looks like the one offered by the Catholic professor Pierre Manent in *Le Regard Politique* (Paris: Flammarion, 2010), and it replicates the portrait that appears as the biographical entry for Strauss in the Austrian conservative *Lexikon des Konservatismus* (Graz: Leopold Stocker Verlag, 1996), 542–45. This European image of Strauss and the descriptive terms applied to him seem all but set in stone.

when he contrasted the gravity of the Political to the diversions of *Kultur*. Without having to swallow Heinrich Meier's entire comparison between a demonized Schmitt and a sanctified Strauss, it is clear that Strauss did not agree with all of Schmitt's assertions. Strauss contends that Schmitt has not "transcended the horizons of liberalism." His reduction of the political to the "*Naturzustand*," which consists of friend-enemy relations, was reminiscent of Thomas Hobbes, who helped pioneer liberal political thinking. Strauss ends by noting that "a radical critique of liberalism can only be carried out on the basis of a suitable understanding of Hobbes." This statement points toward Strauss's major project when he traveled to England, which was his study of the ancient materialist influences on Hobbes's political and ethical concepts.

His Anglo-American experience gave Strauss a vision that he found lacking in Hobbes and Schmitt. He was converted to the view of America as a liberal democratic beacon of hope that could be made even better through his value-instruction as a professor. And whereas Strauss's hymn to American liberal democracy became louder with his disciples, he too sang the same hymn, in a less journalistic fashion. In this case, the fruit did not fall far from the tree, although the two are not entirely the same.

Although Strauss separated "philosophy" from "tradition," his rationalist perspective needs to be qualified to be understood. Straussian hermeneutic brings its own legacy, including an "ancient"-"modern" division, a concept of secret writing, and three increasingly destructive tidal waves of modernity. These defining hermeneutic features become for Straussians, according to Gunnell, the permanent, unbreakable Tradition. While English literary scholar Mark Bevir and German hermeneuticist Hans-Georg Gadamer cannot conceive of how one could interpret texts without authority and tradition, Strauss and his disciples demonstrate this argument, albeit unintentionally.[8] Straussianism has become itself a binding tradition, and it has imprinted its adherents' moral, existential, and methodological positions all at the same time.

---

[8] See Mark Bevir, *The Logic of the History of Ideas* (Cambridge: Cambridge University Press, 1999) 200–02; and Hans-Georg Gadamer, *Wahrheit und Methode. Grundzüge einer philosophischen Hermeneutik*, 473–501.

This explains why attacks on the system seem to the initiated graver than gentlemanly disputes. It may also explain why any resistance to the Straussian domination of politics departments is treated as a war against Goodness itself. Although far from the only body of beliefs in universities, and often confronted by hostile feminist or gay advocates, Straussians are as clannish and defensive as those they attack – and for good reason. They are not engaged in open dialectic as much as they are battling Evil. And Evil takes the form of those who oppose their interpretations and their political loyalties and personal associations; the only way to deal with this putative problem is by fighting back while treating unfriendly outsiders as evildoers. At the same time, Straussians work to protect their acolytes, who will carry on the Tradition.[9] Ironically, it is a tradition that denies the philosophical value of tradition, even while fashioning and consecrating one.

Integral to this tradition is something that seems to jar with it but actually does not. Strauss and his disciples often practice postmodernist free association in how they attach meanings to the objects of their analysis. The postmodernist aspect of their work has attracted frequent comment because it is there for their critics to see. The high degree of subjectivity and the application of the notion of secret writing allow Strauss and his followers to take certain liberties with texts in a manner that one usually identifies with postmodernist readings.

An American political theorist Kenneth McIntyre has compared Strauss to the British defender of the local and the traditional, Michael Oakeshott, as someone who, unlike Oakeshott, works to ignore historical contexts. Strauss, according to McIntyre, believes that he is allowed to omit historical explanations because of his claim to understand authorial intention. Thus Strauss explained to his readers: "Before one can use or criticize a statement, one must understand it as its author meant it." "The originator of the doctrine understood it in only one way, providing he was not confused."[10]

---

[9] See John G. Gunnell, "The Myth of Tradition," *American Political Science Review*, 72.1 (1978): 122–34.

[10] See Leo Strauss, *What Is Political Philosophy and Other Studies* (Chicago: University of Chicago Press, 1959), 67; and Kenneth B. McIntyre, "What's Gone and What's Past Help: Oakeshott and Strauss on Historical Explanation," *Journal of the Philosophy of History*, 4 (2010): 78.

The million-dollar question, for McIntyre, is what Strauss "means by intention." "He is unique in that, despite his insistence that intention is the criterion for any correct interpretation, he offers no real explanation of what he means by intention." McIntyre quotes the ethicist Alasdair MacIntyre on this point, who famously notes in *After Virtue*: "We cannot ... characterize behavior independently of intentions, and we cannot characterize intentions independently of those settings which make those intentions intelligible both to agents themselves and to others." Strauss takes an opposing position, according to McIntyre, because he simplistically believed that "language consists of a stable set of concepts." In Strauss's case, this belief approached the "illusions of real essences" and the notion that "nouns are the names of things that are eternal and immutable, and since we can only have knowledge of unchanging things, our knowledge of the world consists of learning proper definitions of unchanging concepts."[11]

The Straussian claim to understand authorial intention on the basis of the unchanging meaning of words, like Justice and the Good, becomes different in practice. Essentialism here is overshadowed by postmodern subjectivity. Because we cannot know the intention of an author in the way that Strauss says we can, we are therefore required to perform a leap of faith by accepting *his* interpretation of authorial intention. To the weight of a tradition that is philosophically opposed to tradition is now added the weight of authority, or the master's claim to truth.

Often the interpretations we are left with are not as straightforward as McIntyre suggests when he brings up Strauss's preoccupation with certain concepts. Although ideas like Justice may change in meaning over time and should be examined contextually, they are more open to understanding than some of the hidden meanings that Strauss and his followers claim to locate in "great thinkers." Here we are dealing not just with the failure to recognize that ideas and words have historic and communal references. The claim to have access to secret meanings serves to justify what are sometimes very strained readings,

---

[11] Ibid; and Alasdair MacIntyre, *After Virtue*, second edition (Notre Dame, IN: Notre Dame University Press, 1984), 206. See also Ian Ward, "Helping the Dead Speak: Leo Strauss, Quentin Skinner, and the Art of Interpretation in Political Thought," *Polity*, 41 (2009): 235–55.

interpretations that are often unintelligible to everyone but an inner circle. This claim has occasioned a scowling response from Pocock to Strauss's study of Machiavelli: "We enter a world in which nobody ever makes a mistake or says anything which he does not intend to say, in which nobody ever omits to say something he did not intend to omit ... and if there are no anomalies ... then everything that Strauss can impute as an intention is an intention."[12]

Pocock in this famous dig may also have been responding to Strauss's paladin Harvey Mansfield, who has vigorously defended his master's view of authorial intention. Mansfield's work *Machiavelli's Virtue* illustrates some of the same hermeneutic problems that can be discerned in his teacher: often opaque prose and labored attempts to uncover multiple layers of meaning in Machiavelli's *Discourses*.[13] If Mansfield intends to reveal what his Renaissance subject really thought, then his interpretation is unnecessarily tortuous, however much research may have gone into it. Predictably, those who publicly praised his book belong to his persuasion or else work for neoconservative publications. This indicates the sources that Straussians are coming to depend on for recognition. And this is not because their critics hate America or reject humanistic learning. Political theorists who do not buy the Straussian Tradition are tired of arguing with people who will only converse with those who agree with them.

It is also disingenuous for Straussians to assert that all their critics can be found on the left or else are obstinate positivists who reject the humanistic tradition. This book has documented the traditionalist conservative direction from whence some of the opponents of Straussian hermeneutics have launched their briefs. Although critics on the right may not be the only ones whom the Straussians try to ignore, these dissenters pose for the initiates a special difficulty. It should not be necessary to convert "conservatives," given that the disciples of Strauss claim to stand for them.

---

[12] See J. G. A. Pocock, "Prophet and Inquisitor: Or, a Church Built on Bayonets Cannot Stand: A Comment on Mansfield's 'Strauss's Machiavelli,'" *Political Theory*, 3 (1975): 393.

[13] See the reviews of Mansfield's work by Bernard Crick and M. S. Kempshall in the *English Historical Review*, 113: 382–83, and *Wilson Quarterly*, 200: 87–88; and the even more withering comments by J. H. Whitfield in *Renaissance Quarterly*, 350: 606–10.

But there are other critics of the Tradition, and they are not at all hostile to humane learning. They have focused their criticism on what they regard as the peculiarities of the Straussian hermeneutic, from attempts to find coded numerology to the reduction of historical studies to modern heroic epics. Such people often wonder why the Straussians consider themselves more humanistic than their methodological critics. They too have studied the classics and other treasures of the Western heritage and often read the languages in which the political texts under consideration were written, with the same facility as those on the other side.

These critical observations are not meant to deny the limited good that Straussians have achieved. Their emphasis on the history of political theory and on the founding principles of regimes has worked to enrich the academic study of politics. And it is entirely possible that some of those who have opposed this emphasis have resented the Straussians for introducing a humanistic approach to the study of politics.

Equally important, Straussians have challenged the study of politics as an imitation of mathematics. They have argued strenuously that human behavior depends on moral and value choices that cannot be reduced to numerical constructs, and they have properly observed that their colleagues in political science are embracing the illusion of the eighteenth-century rationalists, namely that the study of man can be treated as a branch of the physical sciences.

The Straussians are making distinctions here that recall the methodology of German philosophers and social scientists of the likes of Heinrich Rickert and Max Weber. Such thinkers devoted considerable energy to showing how the social sciences were different in kind from the physical sciences. They also came up with tools for pursuing social research, and these were intended to provide what limited knowledge about the human condition *Sozialwissenschaft* could yield.[14] Lastly,

---

[14] For an interesting overview of the problems in late-nineteenth-century German historical thinking, see Herman J. Paul, "A Collapse of Trust: Reconceptualizing the Crisis of Historicism," *Journal of the Philosophy of History*, 2 (2008): 63–82. A new German edition of Friedrich Meinecke's *Die Entstehung des Historismus*, which was once a standard work on the evolution of historicism, has not been published since 1936, when it came out with Oldenbourg Verlag in Berlin. The view that historicism was at the root of the German catastrophe – a view that Strauss and his disciples have

one must credit Strauss and his students with stimulating interest in classical sources as a key to the study of political behavior. Although not solely responsible for this development, Strauss and his followers have contributed to renewed interest to Plato, Aristotle, Xenophon, and Thucydides in the academic world.[15]

Unfortunately, Straussians have also exhibited less attractive behavioral traits. Such characteristic traits of theirs as group-think, arrogant and standoffish relations with intellectual opponents, and counterfactual complaining about being professionally isolated are related to a moral stance that may be hard to alter. Straussians see themselves as being faithful to Strauss's crusade against relativism, historicism, and positivism in the face of multiple enemies. Indeed, they have transferred to the present moment their master's experience as a Jewish refugee fleeing the Nazis and then reaping the benefits of Anglo-American liberal democracy.

Not only politically but also methodologically the Straussians continue to relive 1938, when "the democracies" failed to stand up

helped popularize in the United States – is by no means exceptional or peripheral any longer. For better or worse, it has become the established view of Meinecke in Germany and elsewhere and can be found in, among other places, George G. Iggers, *The German Conception of History: The National Tradition of Historical Thought from Herder to the Present*, revised edition (Middletown, CT: Middletown University Press, 1983), particularly 124–59.

[15] These points are readily conceded by Strauss's more moderate American critics, for example John Gunnell in "Political Theory and Politics: The Case of Leo Strauss," and in the introductory chapter of Norton's *Leo Strauss and the Politics of Empire*. Gunnell explained in correspondence with me (August 23, 2010) that "I am able to communicate with them [Straussians]" precisely of his restraint as a critic. For an example of the labored praise that Strauss continues to elicit as a redeemer-teacher, see the orotund tribute to him in the foreword of Roger D. Masters, *The Nature of Politics* (New Haven, CT and London: Yale University Press, 1989), xxiii. This panegyric starts with the passage: "Without Strauss's teaching it would have been difficult to recover the understanding of the Western political philosophy needed to approach the perennial issue of human nature in a way consistent with contemporary natural science." Many paeans later, we learn that Masters is dedicating his work "to the teacher who reminded his generation that this ('the wholeness of the enterprise' perceived by great thinkers) was the foremost task confronting our time." The book is, in fact, a study in biopolitics, and the only reference to Strauss outside of the wordy tribute in the foreword is a mention of *Natural Right and History* in the bibliography (287). Presumably the extended dedication was intended to show that Masters, although taking an approach that would have been alien to Strauss, was still attached to the society of his epigones.

to a Europe-wide, anti-Semitic threat in the form of Nazi Germany. Academic discourse and current affairs must be understood in relation to that particular disaster, and therefore while we battle against "Islamofascism" abroad, we must also wrestle with other demons at home, particularly the relativists and historicists in our universities. McIntyre explains a great deal about his subject in the following assertion:

> Strauss's experience of the failure of the Weimar government played a significant role in his exaggeration of the danger to Western (and especially America and Britain) liberal and democratic traditions. He never felt that the Anglophone liberal tradition was sufficiently capable of withstanding the onslaught of historicism, positivism, and moral relativism with a solid philosophical foundation, and he rejected the notion that liberalism could supply such a foundation. Thus for Strauss the question of the relationship of philosophy and history called for the intervention of the prophet-professor.[16]

This need for intervention against the forces of the hour also necessitates two Straussian rituals: the celebration of the Anglosphere and the evocation of democratic heroes. One sees here two sides of the same coin. Precisely because one can glimpse the philosophical shallowness of democratic modernity, while recognizing its manifold practical advantages for oneself and one's companions, one is forced to rise every minute to defend this cause. It is not enough to recommend it by indirection and even less beneficial to take a conventional Old Right position, namely that democracy is simply about procedure and counting heads. One must elevate one's regime into a cult and call on the young to spread the faith on foreign shores. Furthermore, these sacrifices should be demanded for nothing as parochial as a tribe or social class, but to teach the entire human race our universal creed.

Even the postmodernist-looking hermeneutics that the Straussians cultivate reflects a moral-rhetorical stance. It is a peculiar reaction to a historicist enemy, which requires ever more extreme hermeneutic efforts to understand the author without "historicizing" his oeuvre. This is the alternative that we are given to historical, contextual explanations. The existential and personal aspects of this hermeneutic and those who embrace it make it difficult for them to debate

---

[16] See K. B. McIntyre, "What's Gone and What's Past Help," 74.

meaningfully with those who are not on the same wavelength. It is not the Straussian insistence that Jerusalem and Athens must forever be separated as much as the Tradition that renders them incapable of reexamining their premises.

It also explains their gravitation toward the current conservative movement, which seeks out and publicizes their polemics. Straussians have found a home in this sloganeering environment and may even occasionally raise its intellectual horizons. They offer background music for the neoconservative foreign policy that the GOP is trying to put into operation. As long as liberal internationalism remains the only foreign policy acceptable to the conservative movement, the neo-Wilsonian rhetoric of the Straussians qua journalists will continue to be in demand. But is this really the best that those wishing to be schol-ars can achieve for themselves? Alas, it may be at the present time. Straussians will not put up with disagreement, and particularly not from the Right, which is the side they purport to represent. They prefer to wall themselves off in academic enclaves. There they can gather the faithful while putting out political statements or reaffirming their Tradition in political journals under their control.

Some do make an effort to process other views, and it would be a mistake to tar all the acolytes with the same brush. Indeed, some younger Straussians who have risen to defend the Tradition, like Peter Minowitz, are fully capable of rethinking their heritage.[17] Even older ones, like Nathan Tarcov, sometimes acquit themselves well when called on to argue with such worthies as Skinner.[18] In a reply to Skinner's attempt to play down the morally dubious side of Machiavelli's political instructions, Tarcov pulls out multiple quotations that suggest a far more negative picture of the Renaissance humanist than the one offered by Skinner. Such exchanges are needed not only to respond to critics but to rethink what the Straussians believe is no longer in need of reexamination. By defending oneself against serious critics, one comes to see one's own scholarship as part of a dialectical process.

---

[17] In *Straussophobia*, Minowitz manages to be both combative and interesting in his responses to Pocock and other critics of the Straussian interpretation of Machiavelli (2233–61). Like the Zuckerts (115–47), Minowitz also makes a reasonable stab at justifying Strauss's understanding of esoteric writing.

[18] Nathan Tarcov, "Quentin Skinner's Method and Machiavelli's *Prince*," in *Meaning and Context: Quentin Skinner and his Critics*, 194–204.

This becomes even more likely if one reconsiders periodically what one is defending. In short, the Straussians can do what other resourceful members of other movements founded by pioneer thinkers have achieved, partly by noticing the defects in their teachings. Self-critical advocates have held on to the substance of other traditions and authorities while disposing of what no longer seemed sustainable. Thomism, Kantianism, and even some forms of Marxism have taken this path, with notable success. Why must Straussians imitate Marxist-Leninism rather than the Freiburg school of phenomenology, which had room for two intellectual giants who were not always in agreement – Husserl and Heidegger?

Still, the disincentives for self-examination may be determining. Straussians are thriving in their splendid isolation. They control sufficiently large assets, like political theory departments, and have access to enough prestigious academic presses so they do not have to worry about their professional future or lack of access to a sympathetic public. Their assets in the conservative movement, which they and their neoconservative admirers have transformed to their advantage, continue to be considerable.

As new Straussian "masterpieces" climb up alongside the teachings of Jaffa and Bloom onto the "conservative canon of great books" in *National Review* and *Human Events*, younger Straussians will likely profit from their predecessors. Movement conservatives will buy these approved sources of inspiration, whether or not they read them.

There is also recognition lavished on Straussians by the national press, such as references in the *New York Times* to their high intelligence and political clout. One could find exuberant compliments in the *Washington Post* about Harvey Mansfield when he was given the honor of delivering the Jefferson Day Lectureship in 2007. Reading in the *Post* about this "dapper," youthful-looking septuagenarian addressing throngs of enthusiastic celebrities, one had to note the utter disconnection between the Straussians' complaints about languishing among their enemies and their national political prominence.[19] Thanks

---

[19] "A Strauss Primer with Glossy Mansfield," by Philip Kennicott in *Washington Post* (May 9, 2007). The celebration started with a luncheon at the *Weekly Standard* offices, hosted by the magazine's editor Bill Kristol, for whom Mansfield remains the teacher par excellence.

to journalists, Mansfield's clouded picture of Machiavelli has gained the respectful attention it never achieved in scholarly circles. All the same, this may not entirely compensate for other sources of recognition. Criticism against Straussian readings and behavior is pouring in from mainstream scholars such as Pocock, Bernard Crick, and Richard Ashcraft, all of whom complain about the imperviousness of Straussians to any suggestion of methodological error. The increasingly stilted flattery of National Review Online, the Claremont Institute, and even some segments of the national press may not be able to make up for this erosion of scholarly credibility.[20]

At the same time, Straussians have held their ground in the professional guild by organizing their own meetings, often under the auspices of the Claremont Institute. Although these gatherings do not give evidence of the professional strength they enjoyed in the 1970s and 1980s, when Gunnell was describing their transformative effect on American political thought, Straussians continue to be a formidable presence among political theorists – and especially at their own well-attended meetings.

---

[20] Typical of this fulsome praise by nonexperts in the field are Yuval Levin's "Celebrating Harvey Mansfield," NR Online, February 20, 2009, http://nationalreview.com corner/177653/celebrating-harvey-mansfield/yuval-levin. Apropos of Mansfield's being awarded the Jefferson Day Lectureship after being chosen by a politically well-disposed board, K. B. McIntyre raised the question in correspondence with me (February 15, 2011) whether such praise can compensate for the displeasure of so many professionals who dismiss "the Straussian big-names" as "beneath comment and contempt." It may not matter to those being scorned in professional circles, if the journalistic praise is loud enough and accompanied by financial rewards. See also Harvey Mansfield's review essay on *The Executive Unbound* by Eric A. Posner and Adrian Vermeule in the *New York Times Book Review* (March 12, 2011): BR 12. One finds here two characteristic features of the Straussian heavy hitters: first, easy access to the liberal Democratic media, which these *cognoscenti* counterfactually insist are closed to them; and second, the strained attempt to link authors on the contemporary left or left-center to the "German connection." One should not be surprised by Mansfield's efforts to throw together Posner and Vermeule as executive centralizers with the "Weimar-Nazi jurist Carl Schmitt." The authors, after all, do cite Schmitt on executive power. But the association is also misleading. The reasons that Schmitt took his position on executive power, particularly between 1931 and 1933, have nothing to do with why Posner and Vermeule are presenting their case for executive government. See Ellen Kennedy's thorough examination of Schmitt's legal thinking in this period *Constitutional Failure: Carl Schmitt in Weimar* (Durham, NC: Duke University Press, 2004).

A young colleague of mine, who leans heavily toward the Skinnerite side, attended last year's panels on political theory and then the gathering sponsored by the Claremont Institute at the American Political Science Association (APSA). He left the meeting with two principal observations: the non-Straussians political theorists controlled the regular APSA sessions, but the Straussians were better focused and more single-minded.[21] The regular theory sessions that were not dominated by Skinner's work were fashionably leftist and centered on minority causes and/or deconstructionist interpretations. These theory sessions attracted sometimes contentious auditors but not of the kind who stayed around very long. Although the participants and auditors seemed to share the same general opinions, they did not represent anything faintly approximating a unified movement.

Those who went to the Claremont meeting, by contrast, had a definite *esprit de corps*. They were mostly buttoned-down young men (there were few women) who had not come to hunt for jobs or to air social grievances. They had come to draw sustenance for their convictions. My colleague concluded that if one were building a "movement," one would do well to recruit such single-minded people, however minimal their intellectual curiosity. They had come not for the sake of scholarly disputes or professional advancement, but to win wars for their values.

To this impression of continued academic solidarity one must add the political and journalistic vitality that the Straussians continue to exhibit. Reading newspapers, one would have to question whether

[21] I am grateful to Michael C. Pisapia for researching this question and thinking it through with me. See for the panels on political thought at the 2010 APSA gathering http://www.apsanet.org/mtgs/program2010/divisionsindex.cfm. It may be useful to note as a final point that for several decades, the Straussians have withdrawn from national meetings of the APSA and concentrated their efforts on regional meetings, particularly in the Northeast and Midwest. I myself have been invited to participate in several such seminars. Because the Straussians are building independent centers for their activity, there is no need for them any longer to run around inserting their panels into APSA national gatherings. The Claremont Institute, for example, can fly its colors by holding sumptuous, heavily attended meetings as independent events at national political science association meetings. Having attended one such meeting, Michael Pisapia waggishly observed: "You knew you were there because they were all wearing blue blazers." Presumably those who attended the regular APSA sessions were less formally and less uniformly attired.

these self-described victims of persecution are victims at all. Critical attention is better for intellectuals than no attention at all.[22] Nor is it evident that the attention in question from the mainstream press has been uniformly critical. One may thus have to conclude that there is no pressure on Straussians to change course or even to acknowledge perceptive critics. While they may notice these critics, such observations will not likely change their habits or direction.

[22] A conspicuously flattering picture of the Straussians can be found in James Atlas's "Leo-Cons," published in the *New York Times* (May 4, 2003), section 4, page 1. The author has had decades of friendly relations with his subjects, and it speaks volumes that he was asked to produce this feature story. The complaint made by the Zuckerts in *The Truth about Leo Strauss* (11, 12, 16) that Atlas exaggerates the connection between "Leocons" and "neocons" seems piddling in view of the respectful treatment that Atlas bestows on his subjects. Equally revealing is the *New York Times'* choice of Harry Jaffa to review a recent translation of Aristotle's *Nicomachean Ethics*, which was the work of two other Straussians. (See the *Sunday New York Times Book Review* [July 1, 2011]: 16.) Jaffa's review provides little, if anything, of scholarly value but manages to heap praise on both Strauss and Winston Churchill. Although we are told that Churchill had no interest in Aristotle's treatise, this presumably did not matter because "the classical tradition informed more of his upbringing, at home and at school, than he realized." University of Chicago philosophy professor Brian Leiter (http://leiterreports.typepad.com/blog/2011/07/why-would-the-ny-times-invite-an-actual-aristotle-scholar-to-review-a-n) protested the *Times'* decision to allow Jaffa to turn its book review section into a bully pulpit for himself. In his blog, Leiter asks: "Why would the NY Times invite an actual Aristotle scholar to review a new edition of the *Nicomachean Ethics* when it can get a card-carrying member of the Strauss cult to do it?"

Appendix

It is hard to end without including a slightly different interpretation of why non-Straussians have had to struggle in their dealings with my subjects. My second explanation is by no means incompatible with the first and therefore may be treated as supplemental. It began to take form in my mind as the result of a friendship with a social theorist about my age, when the two of us were teaching in a humanities program at Michigan State in the late 1960s. My friend and I were both disturbed by the antiwar protests on campus, and particularly by the degree to which these demonstrations were turning abusively anti-American. We were even more upset by the willingness of our antiwar colleagues to praise communist governments while running down their own country, indeed a country that permitted them to express their dissent. Such protesters seemed to me and my colleague to have gone beyond moral equivalence between us and the communists. They were emotionally and rhetorically on the other side.

But my friend, who was a self-described Straussian, added to these objections a strange analysis of what was occurring. Supposedly those who offended us were relativists and probably nihilists to boot. They were infected with the kinds of ideas that had poisoned the minds of Germans before Hitler came to power. I responded that what I was witnessing was not pleasant but did not seem related to Weber, notions of value-free science, or the supposed triumph of nihilism in interwar Germany. It looked to me as if the red-diaper babies born to radical leftist parents had grown up. They had found jobs in universities and were now busily creating a constituency among young men who did not want to be sent to Vietnam.[1]

My friend then tried to nudge me in his direction by lending me books by Strauss that were lying on his shelf. The first I received, *Persecution and the Art of Writing*, seemed overly speculative and raised in my mind the problem of authorial intention that the last chapter examined. The second book I was urged to read, *Natural Right and History*, struck me as more lucid and more convincing. Unfortunately it also included overgeneralizations and finger-pointing that detracted from its instructional value.

My friend, however, unlike me, felt a deep need for these explanations and was disappointed that I did not share his feeling. Once at supper he told me that he was engaged to a Canadian citizen but was insisting that she apply for American citizenship before they got married. Being American was better than being Canadian, which meant for him supporting the British monarchy. We in America, by contrast, lived in a country founded on the theory of universal individual rights. (Probably my friend accepted this view before having learned that Anglo-American democracy forms a seamless garb.) Although his mother was Polish, I later discovered that his father had been Jewish, and possibly killed by the Nazis. Once in discussion with someone who had lost a family member in the same circumstances, he tried to explain that the Nazis behaved so thuggishly because they had not been taught democratic values. His interlocutor retorted that a lot of other people had not been taught democratic values but had not gone around murdering their neighbors.

---

[1] A wide variety of interpretations for the rise of the student movements in the United States and in Europe in the 1960s is available, without having to privilege the dominant Straussian view later taken over by movement conservatives. See, for example, S. Robert Lichter and Stanley Rothman, *Roots of Radicalism: Jews, Christians, and the Left* (New Brunswick, NJ: Transaction Publishers, 1996); Paul Gottfried, *The Strange Death of Marxism: the European Left in the New Millennium* (Columbia: University of Missouri Press, 2005); and the insightful research of the Italian scholar Danilo Breschi on the convergence of industrialization and an abundance of idle youth fascinated by the utopian writings of the Frankfurt School in his native Italy in the 1960s. See Danilo Breschi, *Sognando la rivoluzione: La sinistra italiana e le origini del '68* (Florence: Mauro Paglia Editore, 2008), and "La contestazione all'ombra die Rousseau," *Rivista di Politica* 1 (January–March 2010), 33–61. In short there is no compelling reason that one would be drawn to the explanation of student radicalism provided by Strauss or his disciples, unless one were already predisposed to accept it.

Even though the person who gave this answer was objectively correct, he did not begin to understand the importance for my friend of the convictions he held. This friend was not worried about whether his highly abstract theory explained with any degree of exactitude an unhappy series of events. He was enunciating a worldview, in which certain things go together in a way that they do not for others, not even for the man who had lost family in the Second World War.

Since that time I have met other Straussians who were starting out on academic careers, and most have exhibited the same intense beliefs as my friend at Michigan State. I have also come to know from conferences some of the more prominent movement members, and I do not perceive any major differences in outlook between them and their followers. I would submit that what may render it hard for outsiders to debate such intellectuals are differing commitments. Pocock, Ashcraft, Skinner, and their associates are scholars who browse around in archives and debate their findings with other archival scholars. Straussians, by contrast, view themselves as playing on a larger stage. They are engaged in a *Kulturkampf* against enemies who must be defeated at every turn and who in their minds have already struck at their family or ethnic group. Although not all Straussians may believe with the same urgency in the need for confrontation, most of them nonetheless seem fixed on an ever-present antidemocratic danger.

Like the neoconservatives, Straussians carry around the memories of 1938 and the need for liberal democratic vigilance against new enemies who look remarkably similar to old ones. But this may seem over the top. It might be objected that not all Straussians share the same memory or template. Indeed one can read such scholars as Herbert Storing, Martin Diamond, and Stanley Rosen, all students of Strauss, who did not share the dominant folk memories and who did not dwell on their love affair with America in its present liberal democratic incarnation. Arguably, however, those who do not fully reflect these concerns are at least sympathetic to those who do. Moreover, among the non-Jews, the correspondence seems sometimes closer than it does among Strauss's Jewish followers. The non-Jewish celebrities Pangle, Mansfield, and Berns cultivate the same heroes and historical narratives, and perhaps with greater zeal, than some of their Jewish colleagues.

I would also note the futility of trying to dissociate Straussian politics from Straussian hermeneutics. The two become closely joined, as soon as one moves beyond isolated interpretations. Let us say that one finds oneself seconding a Straussian on a particular point, for example, that the references in Locke's *Second Treatise* to the Anglican theologian Richard Hooker are simply for show. One might concede, in accordance with the Straussian Authorized Version, that Locke was not a believing Anglican or any kind of believing Christian, but a wily religious skeptic. One might then agree with a second Straussian, that the American founders were less influenced by ancient republicanism than Professor Pocock would lead us to believe. We might also concede merit to the view of Paul Rahe and Thomas L. Pangle, who explain that Jefferson and other early American leaders looked back to the ancient world as a nightmare of repression.

Even with these points yielded, however, the argument is not at an end. All beliefs in the Straussian worldview go together and are related to accompanying ones. One does not become a Straussian simply because one sides with Rahe against Pocock or Zuckert against Ashcraft. It is a question of the complete package, and partial compliance is not an option. This disparity between Straussians and their academic opponents may be compared to the difference that Carl Schmitt observed between the "political" and mere cultural activities. Unlike those who come to a conference to test or debate their findings, the Straussians view themselves as facing the *Ernstfall*. They are fighting the enemies of democracy, Israel, or whatever they understand as first-order things, with their backs to the walls. Moreover, they consider their vocation as "scholars" to be bound up with this cosmic struggle.

This sense of urgency may also help explain the outrage that Straussians feel for their opponents on the right. These adversaries are not viewed as mere academics who are "fiddling while Rome burns." They incorporate an alien worldview that is not rooted in those memories or prejudices that inform the Straussian understanding of the world. These right-wingers do not believe in America as a universal democracy that is supposed to bring enlightenment to the rest of the world.

These obscurantists stress the particularistic, the ethnic, and the historically contingent, and they scorn those heroes who put us on the road to becoming the crusading democratic people we are now.

Although some of their progressive views may be widely shared in the academia, the Straussians have their own grievances against dissenters on the right. Those whom they ostracize do not accept *their* propositional understanding of the "American experiment," and they will not stand up for liberal democracy, as Straussians define that concept.

When the Straussians broke from the leftward-drifting Democrats, they were still politically different from what could be described as the traditionalist American Right. They were not looking to return to an older America. They in fact generally liked the way things were going, until the New Left came on the scene. And while like Strauss, they called for resisting Soviet pressures in international affairs, they had no serious complaints about the direction taken by the welfare state or the nonviolent civil rights movement. The students of Strauss felt driven into new alliances not because they felt the American people had strayed with the New Deal or with the War to End All Wars, but because they believed that a progressive American regime was endangered by what happened in the 1960s. They also lamented the rise of the counterculture; like Norman Podhoretz in the 1970s, they thought that the movement would weaken the national resolve to fight for democratic values. Although Straussians were staking out positions to the right of their colleagues, they were clearly not part of any older American Right.

This older Right has now been defunded and booted out of the visible conservative movement, but opponents on the right could still conceivably come back to plague the Straussians. Their influence on the conservative movement rose at a particularly auspicious time. Catholic intellectuals were looking for a defense against moral relativism and an affirmation of natural law; there was a widespread quest for a coherent explanation for the "crisis of the West" in the 1950s; and a disalignment of some Jewish journalists and academics from the Democratic Party and a subsequent tropism toward the Republicans began in the 1970s, a process that involved Straussians as well as their neoconservative allies. All these developments were moments in the rise to political fortune of Strauss and his disciples.

What started with the ascendancy of someone whom Kenneth McIntyre describes as "the prophet-professor" – that is, someone who in some ways reprised the role that Heidegger played for an earlier generation in Weimar Germany – became more world historical with

his followers. The celebration of Mansfield in 2007, as a national pre-
ceptor in the movement conservative press, was the equal in lavishness
to any celebration that Strauss had enjoyed during his lifetime. And it
was done for a figure whose intellectual accomplishments have been
significantly less. But the honor accorded to the disciple is given to the
teacher as well, and so the manes of Strauss and his generation continue to haunt the politically engaged movement they helped launch.

Further, it is essential to stress the political side of this movement,
not as an extraneous feature but as something belonging to its essence.
Pace Anne Norton, it has always been about politics. Shadia Drury is
right on this point, however much she may exaggerate the fascist, antidemocratic elements of a movement she dislikes. Since the time that
Gunnell first wrote on this subject, the influence of Straussians in universities has not substantially grown. Not all "political philosophy"
courses are in their hands any longer (if they ever were). It is in the
political and journalistic area that they have been achieving their most
notable recent successes, and this may jar with the impression of them
as a strictly academic school of thought.

But given their first-order interest, which is influencing the polity,
why should this shift from the universities to political journalism
(which is only partial in any case) upset the actors? Straussians are
generally committed to preserving and expanding the reach of the political order. Although what occurs in the classroom or at scholarly
conferences has some value for them, it counts less for Straussians
than being able to reshape a national party or being able to design
a prodemocratic foreign policy. Instilling the proper hermeneutic is
vital, but among those who wish to go forward professionally, it is
necessary to look beyond this instructional task. The hermeneutic may
be considered as a kind of propaedeia for those aspiring to politically
more significant activities. All catechumens are expected to complete
the propaedeia, and produce appropriate responses, but not every one
of them will be allowed to advance to the same degree.

This is not to imply that there are no Straussians who deal mostly or
even exclusively with hermeneutic questions. Political theory departments at small colleges abound in such followers, and many of them
continue to read prescribed texts in the Straussian manner and to write
for *Interpretation*, *Review of Politics*, or *Modern Age* in accordance
with the Tradition. Furthermore, there are Catholic Straussians who

believe that Strauss can be enlisted in making the case for a Thomistic understanding of natural law. These Catholics are used to bringing up Strauss to highlight the differences between two worlds, liberal modernity and an older classical tradition of thought.[2]

In any case, there are people who expound Strauss's hermeneutics without thinking beyond the classroom. None of this contradicts what is being argued. Our main points are that the vital center of the Straussian movement has shifted toward direct political involvement and that those who count in that movement are increasingly political players. To whatever extent this has occurred, the shift does not represent a deviation from our subjects' political engagement. Political concerns and the desire to be political players have animated them as a group all along.

Finally, the window of opportunity may close as dramatically as it opened. The good fortune prominent Straussians now enjoy could come to an end, or so they may fear, in a different political climate. And although it is unlikely that the Old Right of forty years ago will make a comeback and reshape the GOP or whatever becomes the conservative movement, libertarians may play a more prominent part in a future American right. This alternative group is not as keen as the Straussians are about human rights crusades, liberal interventionism, and backing up the Israeli government. Libertarians may start assaulting with some success the democratic welfare state in which Straussian intellectuals have found employment and have been able to shine, particularly in the Department of Education and in the National Endowment for Democracy. With regard to even the near term, policy influence may be for more important for those with these concerns than debates about Machiavelli's *Discourses* – or cozying up to the editors of *Renaissance Quarterly*.

[2] Exemplifying the Catholic Straussian who confines himself to theoretical questions is Peter Augustine Lawler (1951–) at Berry College. The coauthor of anthologies with among other Straussians David Lewis Schaefer and James W. Ceasar, Lawler combines traditional Catholic moral teachings with a Straussian reading of political texts. See, for example, *Democracy Reconsidered*, co-edited by Elizabeth Kaufer Busch (Lanham, MD: Lexington Books, 2009); and P. A. Lawler, *Postmodernism Rightly Understood* (Lanham, MD: Rowman and Littlefield, 1999). The 2007 issue of *Political Science Reviewer* (XXXVI) is full of contributions from Catholic Straussians, including a symposium feature, "Strauss, Straussians, and Faith-Based Students of Strauss," organized by Lawler.

This shift toward policy questions and direct advocacy explains a visual shift, namely toward organizations like the Claremont Institute, which aid in the dissemination of policy positions. Claremont gatherings are ideologically driven rallies that attract a predictable crowd of the already convinced. These are not the people that Central European Jewish intellectuals would have drawn into theoretical discussions at the University of Chicago sixty years ago. They are, however, the face of a growing partisan movement.

There is also a new leadership class taking charge of the movement in change. It is typified by a former Marine officer, who was recently appointed editor of *Orbis*, Mackubin T. Owens. A frequent, honored guest at Claremont and a contributor to *Wall Street Journal* and *NationalReviewOnline*, Owens is an effusive follower of the teachings of Harry Jaffa. He readily mixes lectures about universally valid democratic propositions with calls for an interventionist foreign policy. Owens fuses a picture of America's steady march toward equality and civil rights for all citizens through warrior presidents with support for the "Bush doctrine" of democratic emancipation throughout the world.[3]

The same rhetoric resonates from Owens's friend Brian T. Kennedy, the president of Claremont Institute and the publisher of *Claremont Review of Books*. In a speech delivered at Hillsdale on January 7, 2011, the second holiest center of truth in Jaffaite ecclesiology, Kennedy tried to prepare his audience for yet another Munich. China and Russia, the new threats to the democracies, were supposedly in the midst of a massive military buildup, and this may mean that we will soon be in a new global war: "Who is to say there will never come a time when the destruction or nuclear blackmail of the US will be in the interest of the Russians or Chinese? Do we imagine that respect for human life or human rights will stop these brutal tyrannies from acting on such a determination?"[4]

---

[3] See Mackubin T. Owens, "The Bush Doctrine: The Foreign Policy of Republican Empire," *Orbis* 53.1 (January 2009); "Lincoln's Strategy," NRO, http: /old.nationalreview.com/owens/200505090744.asp.; and Owens's inspirational paper published separately by the Foreign Policy Research Institute (January 2009) "Abraham Lincoln: Leadership and Democratic Statesmanship in Wartime," 3–37. For Claremont's sketch of its ally at the FPRI, see http://www.claremont.org/scholar/id.21/scholar.asp

[4] See Kennedy's speech, "It's Never Just the Economy, Stupid" in *Imprimis* 40.1 (January 2011).

If Strauss and Jacob Klein were polyglot humanists in the old German tradition, we are now dealing with epigones with far less humanistic erudition but with a warlike devotion to democracy and human rights. It is likely that there will be a further dwindling of the bookish Straussian types, consisting of those who deal mostly in "ideas." Partisan harangues will likely take the place of discourse, and those who are inclined to deliver them will relocate from universities to neoconservative think tanks. But this is to be expected in a movement that has gone from being partly political to becoming totally absorbed in the Political as an intense friend/enemy relation. We are witnessing a shift in emphasis but not the abandonment of an established worldview for one that is totally different.

Index